R0083112474

04/2015

D1238524

# Law and the Gay Rights Story

# Law and the Gay Rights Story

## The Long Search for Equal Justice in a Divided Democracy

WALTER FRANK

RUTGERS UNIVERSITY PRESS

NEW BRUNSWICK, NEW JERSEY AND LONDON

Second cloth printing, 2014

Library of Congress Cataloging-in-Publication Data

Frank, Walter, 1945– author.

Law and the gay rights story: the long search for equal justice in a divided democracy / Walter Frank.

pages cm

Includes bibliographical references and index.

ISBN 978-0-8135-6871-3 (hardcover: alk. paper) — ISBN 978-0-8135-6872-0 (e-book)

1. Homosexuality—Law and legislation—United States—History. 2. Gay rights—United States—History. 3. Stonewall Riots, New York, N.Y., 1969. 4. Gay rights movement—United States—History. 5. Gay liberation movement—United States—History. I. Title.

KF4754.5.F73 2014

342.7308'7—dc23

2013037752

A British Cataloging-in-Publication record for this book is available from the British Library.

Visit our website: http://rutgerspress.rutgers.edu

Manufactured in the United States of America

For Eva and her parents,
grandparents, great grandparents, aunts and uncles

# CONTENTS

## PART III
# The Right to Marry

# ACKNOWLEDGMENTS

I have received encouragement and support for this project from many people, including a number of scholars and others who graciously answered my e-mail queries. I would like to single out a few people for special thanks: Chris Bram's enthusiasm after reviewing a portion of the manuscript meant a great deal to me. Only a generous soul would undertake such a task for a complete stranger, and getting to know him has been one of the great pleasures of this project. Carlos Ball undertook a review of the manuscript for the Press and provided a set of comments and suggestions, particularly with respect to organization, that have improved the book immensely. As I am an admirer of his law books, his support has been particularly gratifying. I would be remiss if I did not thank Kathryn Gohl for her thoughtful and thorough work in copyediting the manuscript. I could not have been in better hands. Marlie Wasserman and her able staff at Rutgers University Press have been enormously helpful in bringing this project to fruition, and I could not be more appreciative of their support. Finally, I thank Lydia, my wife of thirty-eight years, who shares my love of books but knows that there are still a few things even more important.

# Introduction

In 1958, in a little noticed decision, the Supreme Court of the United States told the United States Postal Service that it could not suppress an obscure publication, *ONE* magazine, aimed at a homosexual audience. The October 1954 issue had been seized on the ground that it was obscene. Without issuing a written opinion, the Court simply determined that the issue did not meet the Court's recently enunciated definition of obscenity. Even by the more prudish standards of the fifties, characterizing this magazine as obscene was patently absurd. The subtext, however, of the Postal Service's action—that homosexuals were virtually without constitutional rights—was all too real, for this was a time when homosexuals were seen as no less a threat to the nation's security and moral fiber than the Communists with whom they were often equated.

The journey from that time to a twenty-first-century America in which gays can marry in at least seventeen states and the District of Columbia, can serve openly in the military, enjoy significant legal protection against discrimination in twenty-one states and countless municipalities, and in which courts, even in the deep South, are becoming increasingly hostile to stereotypical justifications for discrimination against gays, is a remarkable one. Just how did it come about that we went from a nation that a few decades ago felt threatened by the idea of gays even meeting together to a nation in which increasing majorities of Americans support the legal gains that were unthinkable just a few decades ago?

Answering that question is not easy, but I believe the answer begins with gay men and women themselves, for while this book focuses very much on law and politics, this is also an intensely human story about people many of whom, for a long time, were able to live reasonably satisfactory if thwarted lives in a kind of suspended animation. As long as they were willing to keep their secret, they could in effect pretend to be someone else, someone society found acceptable. Human beings, however, being who they are, ultimately need to give expression to their full selves. At its core, the gay rights movement is a tribute to that deep human impulse toward honesty and personal integration.

So, while this book aims to examine the gay rights movement through the prism of legal reform, it does so against the broad canvas of gay history, a history filled with deeply personal drama and conflict which I also try to present as compellingly as I can. Fortuitously, much of that personal drama comes out in simply discussing the factual aspects of the many cases encountered along the way and also in some of the political battles.

Law professors have written literally thousands of law review articles over the last fifty years dissecting virtually every legal issue raised by the gay rights movement. These articles, collectively, are a tribute to how seriously the academic community has taken the subject of gay rights. Such articles, however, by their very nature have focused on specific legal issues without examining how the overall effort for law reform has figured into the broader canvas of gay history. Journalists and historians, on the other hand, have provided compelling narratives of key events in the movement itself but rarely, if ever, focus on law as an appropriate subject of separate examination. This book attempts to bridge this divide. It is aimed at both the general reader and the student seeking a serious introduction to an important subject.

Law reform occurs in two ways: through judicial decision-making and through legislative enactments. Both efforts have been an important part of the gay rights story. In the beginning, before the Stonewall riots, law reform (other than repeal of sodomy laws) was hardly even on the agenda. Legal cases, after all, are a matter of public record. You can't have a lawsuit without litigants willing to come forward, not to mention lawyers willing and able to represent them. There were pre-Stonewall cases, not unimportant ones, in which the rights of gays to meet in bars and to receive publications, even beefcake magazines, were vindicated, and in 1969, the same year as the Stonewall riots, a federal circuit court of appeals held that a homosexual could not be fired from his government job simply on the basis of a revelation that he was gay. Yet, for the most part, the oppression that led most gays to conceal their identities from straight society (and sometimes even from themselves) also kept them from seeking legal relief.

For most gay persons in the 1950s and 1960s, law existed mainly in the form of police officers and prosecutors, and given the public opinion of the time, public exposure often meant personal ruin. This possibility didn't keep underground subcultures from forming, but it does help explain the absence of any organizations publicly devoted to defending gay rights in the courts in any kind of systematic way. That began to change after the Stonewall riots as countless organizations and publications flowered with the aim of improving gay life and raising gay pride and consciousness. In New York, the formation of the Gay Liberation Front and then the Gay Activists Alliance signaled the beginning of a sea change in gay history.

It is helpful to view the post-Stonewall struggle for gay rights as falling into three periods. The first period, lasting from 1969 to the onset of the AIDS crisis, is best seen as a time when gay men and women simply asserted the freedom to be themselves, to live more openly, to be free from harassment, arrest and discrimination, to engage in political combat, and, most importantly, to openly form their own organizations and neighborhoods—in effect to assert and take advantage of the freedoms of which they had historically been deprived and to leave behind the sense of shame and wrongness that society had sought to impose for so long. While a few important cases were litigated during this period, the major battles for gay legal rights in the seventies take place in city council chambers, state legislatures, at the ballot box, and in the struggle to erase the decades of misinformation and stereotyping of what it means to be gay. The seventies was an exhilarating period but also one of conflict and confrontation both within and outside the gay community as liberationists clashed with reformists, gay men with lesbians, and, toward the end of the seventies, the gay community with the religious right. For all its tribulations, it is also a time remembered by many with great nostalgia.

Then came AIDS. The struggle against AIDS was so all consuming that it defines the second period of post-Stonewall history. That struggle placed extraordinary demands on the gay community and totally transformed just about every aspect of gay life, leading to a complete shift in the goals of the gay rights movement, which, in turn, placed the courts for the first time at the center of the gay rights struggle. It is not going too far to say that while the preoccupations of the seventies were a direct reaction to the period of oppression that preceded it, the third post-Stonewall period, beginning with the election of President Bill Clinton, has been shaped in large part by all the ways in which the AIDS crisis transformed the gay community and gay life. During this third period, the focus of the movement shifted dramatically from the desire merely to live a life free from abuse and mistreatment to the demand for equality and complete integration into society, a fight in which the courts began to play a major role.

This book is organized into three parts. Part I, "The Freedom Struggle," covers the pre- and post-Stonewall periods up to the election of President Clinton, and part II, "The Struggle for Legal Equality," the period from Clinton's election to the present. I devote a separate section, part III, "The Right to Marry," to the subject of same-sex marriage because of the issue's centrality to the gay rights movement. The book's conclusion focuses on the special character of the gay rights movement, law's role in it, and prospects for the future.

This project grew out of my research for an earlier book on constitutional law during which I discovered the extent of the campaign against gays and lesbians in post–World War II America. The encounter left me wanting to know how such persecution came about, how and why things have changed so dramatically, and what role law has played in this history. Although my admiration for the gay community and support for gay rights is obvious, I am not unwilling to indicate, particularly in areas involving constitutional law, where it seems too simplistic to think purely in terms of "pro-" or "antigay" results. I also have tried to give voice to those critics within the gay community itself who worry that the equality movement with its white leadership and largely middle-class goals has come at the expense of a vibrant collective identity and the abandonment of broader progressive goals. Most (although not all) gay history has been written by gay men and women. My being straight may have given me a helpful distance in writing this book, but I may also have omitted matters that those more deeply involved in the struggle for gay rights might deem important and for that I apologize in advance.

I hope that by the conclusion of this book, both gay and straight readers will have a much richer appreciation of what the gay rights movement has meant to America as well as to its gay citizenry, how dramatic the personal lives and struggles of so many in the gay community have been, and how law, as an institution and a set of rules, has both shaped and been shaped by that movement. If nothing else, this volume attests to the deep wisdom of Justice Oliver Wendell Holmes's observation that the life of the law is not logic but experience. This book does not deal directly with the experience or rights of transgender persons as a group, not because this topic is unimportant but because it deserves a separate examination beyond the scope of this project.

# PART ONE

# The Freedom Struggle (1945-1992)

For the first two and half decades after the end of World War II, gay men and women were pariahs. As late as 1967, Mike Wallace could begin the *CBS Reports* program, "The Homosexuals," three years in the making, with these words: "The average homosexual, if there be such, is promiscuous. He is not interested or capable of a lasting relationship like that of a heterosexual marriage. His sex life, his love life, consists of a series of one-chance encounters at the clubs and bars he inhabits." Later, although apologetic—"I should have known better," Wallace admitted in 1992—he attributed the program to ignorance, for "that is—God help us—what our understanding was of the homosexual lifestyle a mere twenty-five years ago because nobody was out of the closet and because that's what we heard from doctors" (Kohler 2013). Wallace's reference to the closet is instructive, for there is no question that the gay rights movement could not begin until a critical mass of gay people were willing to abandon the closet and begin to break down the stereotypes to which Wallace alluded. Gays needed to find themselves first in order to confront America.

Coming out in 1950s America took an extraordinary amount of courage, however. The issue wasn't coming out to the straight world. That was virtually unthinkable. Rather, just coming out to oneself and to want to meet others to discuss what it meant to be gay were extraordinary steps. For the most part, all the forces of society were arrayed against such self or group realization. As often occurs, however, some who experienced that oppression began to question it and create the beginnings of a protest movement that would flower in the wake of the 1969 Stonewall riots. I describe all of this, including the extraordinary campaign against homosexuals during this period, in chapter 1. In chapter 2, I focus specifically on Stonewall and attempt a brief assessment of its importance in the gay rights movement. A recent trend has been to question the importance of Stonewall as a transformative moment in gay history, but I believe this view may have gone too far.

The 1970s saw the emergence of a bathhouse, disco, and bar culture to which gays migrated with an exhilaration and sense of freedom that can only be understood against the backdrop of the draconian oppression of earlier decades. Freedom was in the air, and for the time being that was enough for many. It was not, however, the whole story, for many young gay men and women had been deeply politicized by their experiences in the sixties of protesting the Vietnam War, working for civil rights for African Americans, and participating in the nascent feminist movement. For these people, the seventies were all about politics and intellectual ferment. In some cities, gay rights advocates, flying under the radar screen, even secured ordinances prohibiting antigay discrimination; a few courts tentatively moved in the direction of gay rights, and the gay rights movement began its long courtship with the Democratic Party. The end of the decade saw disheartening setbacks as the increasingly powerful religious right secured the repeal of antidiscrimination ordinances passed earlier in the decade in several major cities, but it also saw the first of the major gay civil rights marches, an event that confirmed the breadth of gay organizational activity that had occurred in the seventies and the growing sense of confidence and renewal experienced by many. Chapter 3 examines all of these developments.

Chapter 4 addresses the AIDS holocaust that unfolded beginning in the early 1980s. I tell this story in all its aspects, trying to recapture how frightening and terrifying it must have seemed at the outset, the indifference of straight society, including a conservative national administration, the initial devastation left by the disease, and the heroic response of the gay community itself. From the vantage point of 2013, the most important consequences of the AIDS crisis were how it forced many hitherto closeted gay men, particularly affluent city dwellers previously able to live comfortable closeted lives, to come out and to organize for their own survival; how it led to the establishment of a permanent lobbying presence in the nation's capital to gain needed funds for medical research and protect the gay community from attacks from the religious right; how the emotional impact of AIDS on the survivors began to lead to a reconsideration of personal goals and priorities; and how the crisis forced the gay community to interact with straight institutions in ways that underscored the need for equal rights and the legal recognition of gay relationships. The AIDS crisis also produced two areas of controversy with important legal dimensions: the closing of bathhouses and mandatory AIDS testing. I discuss these developments as well as the important ways in which the AIDS crisis played out (and continues to play out) differently for black males than for whites.

# 1

# Isolation, Oppression, and Emergence (1945–1969)

Imagine that it is the early fifties and you are a teenager living almost anywhere in America. You have a terrible secret that will have absolutely no practical consequence as long as it stays with you. To friends and family who do not suspect that secret, you are completely yourself. They love you for who you are, warts and all, or so they think. You know differently. You know that your secret is so powerful that, if revealed, your friends may shun you and even your family stop loving you. You are also taught that your secret conceals a flaw so abominable that God has decreed (at least if you are male) that you should die if you act upon it. Such a flaw endangers your very soul and doesn't do much for your self-esteem.

How many other people have a similar secret? You have no idea; everyone who can is keeping the same secret. Not only is there no one like you in your town; there is no one like you anywhere—not on television, not on radio, not in the movies. Your best potential role models, your teachers, couldn't possibly share your secret, if they had it too, and still be employed the next day. For that matter, neither could anyone else. You know you have a voice. You believe you are a decent person, but how does that matter when every source of authority you are supposed to trust—family, school, church, the law—says otherwise.

The secret, of course, is your feeling of sexual attraction to persons of the same sex. Is this just a phase that you will outgrow? Why do you have these feelings? Does anybody else have these feelings? You are afraid to ask. Books did not help. One participant in the University of Wisconsin–Madison Archives Oral History Program remembers getting up the courage to sign out some material at her library: "And then what you got was just horror stories about how to change and be changed and that it was a phase" (Biddle 2009). Another participant recalls: "I knew I didn't fit in. I didn't know why, didn't quite know why. There was no literature to tell me—there's no one to tell me what's going on" (Yeardon 2009). The only book written by an actual homosexual that might give you some sense of connectedness is *The Homosexual in America* by Donald Corey, but this was hardly the kind of book that the average gay teenager was likely to know about and, this being the fifties, Donald Corey was a pseudonym for Edward Sagarin, a sociologist, who had a day job and even a wife to protect. The book's theme—that homosexuals were a persecuted minority—was also not likely to make a teenager more open about his fears.

Our isolated teenager is no work of fiction. Consider this observation by John D'Emilio, a leading historian of the gay rights movement: "Pretty much every gay man or lesbian of the Stonewall era came of age believing that we were the only person like us in the world, and that what we were was not good" (D'Emilio 2002, x–xi). Marty Manford recalled that "the newspapers always referred to homosexuals and perverts as if they were one and the same" and that, as a fifteen-year-old, "if you were gay and you accepted those societal norms, then you were at war with yourself" (Marcus 2002, 109). It was the same for young women. In a 1971 interview Barbara Gittings reflected that she had had "a lot of problems coming to terms with myself as a young lesbian" and became active in gay liberation "to help see to it that younger gays don't have to go through the troubles I had when I was coming out" (Tobin and Wicker 1972, 205).

It was no easier in the adult world. In the 1950s and into the 1960s, homosexuals were perceived to be as dangerous as communists, threatening the moral strength and vitality of the nation. Both groups imperiled the nation's future; both represented shadowy conspiracies of like-minded people who sought to undermine and then destroy existing institutions; and both could be combated only with the assistance of a watchful public and energetic government. In the words of William Eskridge, "homosexuals were like the pod people in Don Siegel's *The Invasion of the Body Snatchers*: they were weird aliens who could pass as human and whose goal was to prey on Americans and turn them into pod people" (1996, 710). The fear of communism actually reinforced the fear of homosexuality. At a time when American democracy needed tough, effective men to combat a powerful alien ideology, homosexuality "symbolized the betrayal of manhood—the feminine enemy within men" (Adam 1995, 62).

No boundaries existed when it came to demonizing gays. Pulp magazines ran articles with titles such as "Hidden Homos and How to Spot Them." Mainstream periodicals were no better. *Coronet* magazine, for example, a general interest magazine owned by Esquire, Inc., claimed: "The homosexual is an inveterate seducer of the youth of both sexes, not content with being degenerate himself; he must have degenerate companions, and is ever seeking younger victims. . . . Once a man assumes the role of homosexual, he throws off all moral restraints" (Carter 2004, 14).

Alfred Kinsey's *Sexual Behavior in the Human Male*, published in 1948, underscored the homosexual threat in two ways. First, his estimates (no longer accepted) suggested that there were potentially millions more homosexuals in America than had previously been imagined. Second, Kinsey's descriptions made clear that many homosexuals were not so effeminate that they could, in fact, be easily spotted. Both points fed the public paranoia of a hidden threat to the national well-being. One positive may have emerged from the report, for John D'Emilio believes that the first Kinsey Report, as well as later ones, "by revealing that millions of Americans exhibited a strong erotic interest in their own sex . . . implicitly encouraged those still struggling in their isolation against their sexual preference to accept their sexual inclinations" (1983, 37).

Homosexuals, in the eyes of post–World War II America, were not only immoral and dangerous; they were also sick, and not just in the popular view, but according to the experts, the nation's psychiatrists and psychologists. The only thing to do with them, for their own good as well as society's, was to cure them. Historians have documented the emergence, beginning in the late nineteenth century, of a growing medical consensus that homosexuality was a pathological condition requiring treatment and reversal. In the ensuing decades, mental health professionals saw conversion to heterosexuality as the only possible road to happiness. A series of documents, chilling in their banality, collected in *Gay American History* (Katz 1992), attests to the futility of these "treatment" efforts and the damage they could cause.

The deep prejudice against and fear of homosexuals only partially explain the campaign against them, for there was also something deeply embedded in the psychology of post–World War II America that gave new impetus to the war against homosexuality. A fuller explanation for the postwar paranoia about homosexuals must be sought in a general cultural outlook of the America of the 1950s, which made any kind of deviation a threat.

## Postwar America

William Whyte, in his 1956 best seller *The Organization Man*, captured a key aspect of the fifties when he wrote: "it is the whole man the Organization wants and not just a part of him. Is the man well adjusted? Will he remain well adjusted? A test of potential merit [aptitude tests] could not tell this; needed was a test of potential *loyalty*" (1956, 172). This statement illuminates what gays and lesbians were up against in that era, for, while in the grip of his overwhelming obsession and vulnerability to blackmail, how, in society's view, could a gay man offer the requisite loyalty? Patriotism and conformity were the unchallengeable virtues of this era both at the workplace and home. In the world of *Ozzie and Harriet* and *Father Knows Best*, two of the nation's better-known television sitcoms of the 1950s, with their ideal of the perfect American family, there was little room for toleration of a behavior so different from the norm, one that affronted the whole ideal of pristine uniformity on which the image of domestic happiness, 1950s style, was built. That ideal of domestic happiness, rooted in the institution of heterosexual marriage, had no place for homosexuals and, in fact, required their isolation to reinforce heterosexual norms.

No one, no matter how admired, was safe from banishment or allowed any sympathy once their secret was out. This is what made arrest and exposure the greatest fear of the 1950s gay man. Harry Hay, the founder of the Mattachine Society, remembered: "The moment a person was listed as a homosexual [following arrest], his name appeared on the front page of the newspaper. The moment that happened you lost your job, you lost your insurance, you lost your credit" (Terkel 1995, 304). "Suicides," writes Randy Shilts, "were a common postscript to the raids and exposure as a homosexual" (Shilts 1982, 18). Indeed, it was fear of bar raids that often drove gays to public parks and bathrooms, the back of trucks and other places, although nowhere was completely safe

The story of Dan R., as recollected by Allan Gurganus (1996) in a rich anthology of coming out stories titled *Boys Like Us*, is a particularly dramatic example of how unforgiving midcentury conformist America could be. Dan R. was admired by everyone in North Falls, North Carolina. Thirty-three years old, a great golfer, handy with tools, he had already been elected the 1955 Rotarian Young Man of the Year. Dan R. had a wife who taught third grade and three lovely kids. One day in 1957 he took the children to the cinema in Raleigh, North Carolina (about an hour's drive) to see *Snow White and the Seven Dwarfs*.

While the children were watching the movie, a much different drama was taking place in the men's room of the newly opened J. C. Penney's department store. It seems that a local off-duty police officer was in the habit on weekends of positioning his handsome teenage son near one end of the urinals and having him expose himself in an effort to entrap local homosexuals. The locals were much too knowledgeable and careful to fall for this setup, but Dan R., who had gone in just to relieve himself, found himself momentarily giving way to a forbidden temptation. As he touched the boy's exposed part, he was blinded by the flash of the off-duty police officer's camera. In an instant, according to the local newspaper account, Dan R. "was handcuffed and already on his way to prison." Dan R. served a seven-week sentence and then left the state. Until he sent for his family, his wife went out only to shop for groceries wearing dark glasses. Gurganus never saw Dan again. "My dad," Gurganus recalled, "played eighteen holes a week with him for six years but that was neither mentioned nor admitted. Dan, once considered indispensable, seemed—overnight—not just dead but unmissed" (1996, 59–60). The law had given Dan seven weeks in jail; North Falls had banished him forever and blotted out all memory of his existence.

To a degree impossible to quantify, the fifties war against homosexuals was also abetted by a post–World War II era characterized by two great fears— the fear of nuclear war and the fear of a world communist revolution led by the Soviet Union. These fears were exploited by Senator Joseph McCarthy in a self-aggrandizing domestic war against subversives and potential traitors. A nation extracting loyalty oaths, enforcing blacklists, and rooting out "un-American activities" created an atmosphere that could easily justify a domestic war on a hated and feared group. It was an America that needed a near-perfect self-image to arm itself in the war on communism, one that had no room for homosexuals in the family portrait. Indeed, it hardly had room for divorce. Donna Biddle, born in 1940 and raised in the Bible Belt, where "everything was a sin," had been hiding strong feelings of same-sex attraction from the age of five, but it was the fact that her mother was divorced, "a fallen women," that kept neighborhood kids from being allowed to play with her (Biddle 2009).

American law codified in many ways the moral attitudes of the time and offered little protection against society's prejudices. At this time, adultery was not only a ground (sometimes the only ground) for divorce; it was a crime in most states. Regulation of obscenity too was and remains a recurring issue in constitutional law. Every state prohibited sodomy. The recognition of a constitutional right to sexual privacy was still a decade away. No legal organization stepped forward to protect homosexuals. The most likely candidate, the American Civil Liberties Union, issued a statement in 1957 supporting the constitutionality of sodomy statutes and acknowledging that homosexuality was a relevant inquiry for security clearances.

The degree of isolation imposed on millions of people, gay and lesbian, is almost impossible to conceive. Consider, however, that in 1957, a Chicagoan writing under the pseudonym Valerie Taylor published a lesbian romance titled *Whisper Their Love*. It was her first novel, and over time it sold two million copies (Baim 2008, 59). Two million readers for a novel the heterosexual world never noticed. How could that be? There is only one explanation: for 1950s America, the audience for that book did not really exist. The only major lesbian organization before Stonewall, the Daughters of Bilitis, could hardly attract even a hundred people to its national conferences. The readership for its important periodical, the *Ladder*, probably never broke 500. Two million copies sold, yet when the Daughters of Bilitis first started dancing together in their meetings, they put up curtains across the picture windows so no one would see them (Hirshman 2012, 51).

Those curtains of the Daughters of Bilitis may have been used partly out of fear and perhaps even a sense of shame and guilt, but one thing is clear. That small group wanted to be invisible, and it was exactly that desire for invisibility that almost all gays and lesbians shared that allowed society to be cruel without even acknowledging the extent of that cruelty, an attack on a despised group in which the law unfortunately played a not unimportant role.

## An Attack on All Fronts

The postwar campaign against homosexuals was stunning both in its scope and callousness. It was an assault in which every major political institution was implicated: Congress, the courts, the presidency, major federal agencies, state and local governments. It was not just about overexuberant vice squads, although local police were clearly the infantry in the effort to stamp out homosexuality; this was about a society that had simply decided to place certain people beyond its protection. The most insidious actions happened quietly, often blandly and bureaucratically, in exchanges of information among government agencies and in their administrative rulings, in the drafting of legislation, in legal outcomes, in the disregarding of acts of violence and intimidation, and, of course, in the arrests of persons guilty of simply wanting to explore their own sexuality and meet basic social needs. With the cooperation of local vice squads, FBI offices made lists of bars often frequented by homosexuals.

One case, among many possible ones, shows how closely the police and government could work in their war on homosexuals. The scene is Lafayette Square across from the White House in the early morning hours of October 22, 1963. Two Morals Squad officers see a man in a car pick up another man, drive around the square, and let the man out. Then both men go off in separate cars in the same direction. The officers take it upon themselves to tail the two men a considerable distance, sometimes at high speed, to the parking lot of an apartment complex. There, they question the men, and on the basis of an admission by the man originally picked up that the driver had felt his leg and then invited him to his apartment for a drink, they arrest both men and take them to the Morals Office.

This is only the beginning. For two hours the men are questioned about their sexual histories. It turns out that one of the men (Norton) works for NASA. At 3:00 am, one of the police officers telephones NASA's security chief, who is invited down to hear the last of Norton's interrogation. The NASA officer is then shown Norton's confidential arrest record and allowed "to monitor incognito

an additional twenty minute interrogation of the appellant [Norton] held especially for his benefit." Things, however, still are not over. At this point, the NASA
official identifies himself to Norton and Norton is "invited" down to NASA's
deserted office for a further interrogation that lasts until 6:00 am. On the basis
of these events, NASA later concludes that its employee has made homosexual
advances to the other man and proceeds to fire him (*Norton v. Macy*).

It is a well-recognized mark of a totalitarian regime that an individual is
utterly alone and impotent against the exercise of state power, even in his or her
private life, that no societal institutions exist to intervene on the individual's
behalf. In such a regime, the personal simply does not exist. It is hard to imagine
how Norton could have experienced that night of intimidation as anything less
than the exercise of naked power by the combined forces of state and society.
It is little wonder that gay publications, even in late-1960s San Francisco, had
begun to refer to the United States as "Amerika," sharing the antiwar movement's vision of a fascist country (Ormsbee 2010, 30). Perhaps Norton's treatment may have even affected the judges who heard Norton's challenge to his
dismissal for, in one of the few gay rights victories before Stonewall, the federal
Circuit Court of Appeals for the District of Columbia reinstated Norton to his
position. The case stood (and still stands) as an important precedent that one
can't be fired from a federal civil service position simply because one is homosexual, although the court did make clear that dismissal might be appropriate if, among other things, one were too open about one's homosexuality, thus
causing problems with other employees or the public. We will see this distinction between status and transparency in important later cases.

While gay men were the most frequent targets of the vice squads, lesbians
were hardly immune. Lillian Faderman describes a particularly humiliating incident that occurred in a 1964 raid on a Greenwich Village lesbian, working-class
bar, the kind of raid that could have occurred, and undoubtedly did, throughout
the fifties and sixties in major cities across the country. One patron recalled:
"A large man appeared at the doorway and yelled, 'This is a raid.' Everyone froze;
then like a bunch of sheep we all tromped downstairs and into the waiting
paddy wagons, about forty-three of us." In a subsequent station house search by
a policewoman, they were forced to pull down their underpants and bend over.
Next morning on their way to court, they had to pass through a gauntlet of jeer-
ing policemen. The women had been arrested on charges of disorderly conduct
and disturbing the peace. Since there was no credible evidence against them and
the only peace disturbed had been their own, the charges were dismissed, but as
Faderman observes, "Incredible as it may seem in the context of saner times, they
were forced to endure all that only because they had gone to a public place where
they might meet other people with whom they could be comfortable" (1991, 166).

Make no mistake. This was a war against people, not just conduct. At the federal level, the armed services and government departments, at the prodding of Congress, conducted on-going investigations that led to the dismissal of thousands of civilian employees and military personnel; the State Department actually fired more alleged gays during this period than alleged communists. In April 1953 a newly elected President Eisenhower, in office less than three months, issued Executive Order No. 10450 making sexual perversion a ground for investigation under the federal-security program. More than 800 federal employees resigned or were terminated in the two years following the order because their files linked them in some way with homosexuality. The FBI, working with local law enforcement officials, assisted in these efforts by compiling arrest records at the regional office level that would then be turned over to the Civil Service Commission.

The groundwork had been laid for Eisenhower's order by a 1950 Senate subcommittee report titled "Employment of Homosexuals and Other Sex Perverts in Government." The report found homosexuals to be security risks who "will frequently entice normal individuals to engage in perverted practices." "One homosexual," the report concluded, "can pollute a government office" (Murdoch and Price 2002, 17). Republicans, out of power for almost two decades, saw political potential in the issue; the chairman of the Republican National Committee asserted in April 1950 that "perhaps as dangerous as the actual Communists are the sexual perverts who have infiltrated our Government in recent years" (35). So intimidating was the atmosphere of the early fifties that when Eric Julber, a young attorney just starting out on his own, sought the assistance of the American Civil Liberties Union to defend ONE magazine on First Amendment grounds, the organization refused when it discovered that a homosexual magazine was involved (31).

Hysteria could reach Salem witch trial proportions. In Boise, Idaho, three men were arrested in 1955 for having sex with teenage boys. The hysteria that followed produced a dragnet which resulted in the investigation of the sexual habits of nearly 1,500 men. Countless homosexual men reportedly fled the city for fear of having the secret of their sexual identity revealed. During the fifties and early sixties, "several manias swept Florida" (Eskridge 1996, 727), often triggered or exacerbated by ambitious politicians and a sensationalist media. Public universities were not immune to this contagion. Anyone high in a school administration could mount an antihomosexual campaign with little fear of criticism from trustees or politicians. In the late fifties and early sixties, two separate McCarthy-style purges of gay faculty and students were undertaken at the University of Wisconsin, resulting in numerous dismissals and resignations. Lewis Bosworth, then an undergraduate, recalls his own meeting with the dean of men: "he attempted to get me to admit that I was homosexual. . . . And I denied it. But he also wanted me to give him the names of other homosexual young men, either undergrad or grad, and I refused to do that" (Bosworth 2009).

The systematic attack on gays even infected what was the most important benefit program to emerge from the Second World War. In her pathbreaking study *The Straight State*, Margot Canaday (2009) shows how an entrenched federal bureaucracy trapped homosexuals in a class of inferior citizenship in direct defiance of language in the Serviceman's Readjustment Act of 1944 (popularly known as the G.I. Bill). The act succeeded in reintegrating more than 16 million returning servicemen and women into society by providing them with benefits to pursue a college education and achieve home ownership. By 1948, the G.I. Bill accounted for 15 percent of the federal budget (Canaday 2009, 140). Canaday shows how the Veterans Administration (VA) ignored the explicit direction in the G.I. Bill that its benefits be made available to any veteran who had not received a dishonorable discharge, which meant that the roughly 9,000 homosexuals receiving "undesirable" (not dishonorable) discharges should have been eligible for benefits (141).

Taking advantage of a slight looseness in the language of the statute (the statute referred to discharges under "dishonorable conditions" rather than dishonorable discharges themselves), the VA announced in April 1945 that homosexuals receiving undesirable discharges would not be entitled to benefits since they would be treated as having been discharged "under dishonorable conditions." In response to this deliberate flouting of its intent, a seven-man subcommittee of the House Committee on Military Affairs issued a report strongly protesting the VA's policy. The report declared that the VA had not been given the authority to make moral judgments regarding the behavior leading to blue discharges and reaffirmed the congressional intent that only those receiving a dishonorable discharge could be denied benefits. The distinction between dishonorable and undesirable discharges made perfect sense since dishonorable discharges, unlike undesirable discharges, required a court martial and therefore assured some degree of due process. The report led the military in 1947 to create a new kind of discharge—the general discharge—whose recipients were deemed entitled to G.I. Bill benefits. Remarkably, however, the VA continued to deny G.I. Bill benefits to those discharged for homosexual acts or tendencies, whether the discharge was a general or undesirable one. Congress did not seek to remedy this injustice and, in fact, it became increasingly clear as the homophobia of the fifties took hold, that a major reason for the congressional concern about blue discharges in the first place had been the stigma suffered by heterosexual veterans discharged as undesirable (for drunkenness or insubordination among other things) who might also be assumed by the community and potential employers to be homosexual.

In 1952 Congress enacted the McCarran-Walter Act, a major revision to the Immigration Law, which authorized the immigration authorities to bar "psycho-pathic" personalities from entering or staying in the country. As initially drafted the law had referred to psychopaths and homosexuals: the drafter deleted the reference to homosexuals only after being assured (correctly, as it turned out) that psychopathic personalities would be understood by the courts and immi-gration authorities to include homosexuals. In her book, Canaday also provides a fascinating account of how some psychiatrists in the Public Health Service offered some resistance to certifying homosexuals as psychopathic, but this resistance had little bearing on legal outcomes in the relatively few instances when gay aliens challenged their treatment by the Immigration and Natural-ization Service (INS). As the Fifth Circuit noted in a 1961 case, "Whatever the phrase 'psychopathic personality' may mean to the psychiatrist, to the Congress it was intended to include homosexuals and sexual perverts. It is that intent which governs" (*Quiroz v. Neely*, 907).

The Fifth Circuit's position was sustained by the Supreme Court in *Boutilier v. Immigration and Naturalization Service*, the court declaring that petitioner was afflicted with homosexuality. Clive Boutilier came to the United States in 1955 at the age of twenty-one, where he established himself as a building maintenance man and entered into what became a seven-year relationship with another man. Boutilier was one link in a long chain of stories that were and are the making of America. He was a law-abiding, respected, contributor to society. He, however, made the mistake of wanting to become a U.S. citizen and a further error when he volunteered in his application that he had been arrested on a sodomy charge in 1959. This, in the words of Murdoch and Price, "of course, set off INS alarm bells" (2002, 103) and led to an interrogation in which Boutilier, still apparently proceeding without the benefit of legal counsel, admitted to having had several homosexual counters a year since he was sixteen. At that point, at least as far as the INS was concerned, with its knee-jerk interpretation of the McCarren-Walter Act, Boutilier's fate was sealed.

In August 1965 he was ordered deported. Both the Second Circuit by a vote of 2–1 and the Supreme Court by a 6–3 vote sustained the deportation order. Both courts asserted that they were simply implementing the intent of Con-gress, but William Douglas asserted in conference that Congress's addition of the term "sexual deviates" to the 1965 amendments to the Immigration Law meant that Congress had felt the original language of the statute was not suf-ficient to bar all homosexual aliens (Murdoch 2002, 113). Clearly, a more com-passionately inclined Court could have easily questioned whether Boutilier had had adequate notice that his homosexuality was a ground for deportation, given that he quite justly did not regard himself (as did no one else) as a psychopath.

From the vantage point of 2013, what is remarkable is how untroubled the justices were by a set of facts that cried out for concern from a Court generally so protective of individual rights. That these very decent men of an earlier era, largely free from personal prejudice, simply did not see homosexuals as victims in the same way they saw so many others speaks volumes about the mindset of the times.

As already noted, federal agencies participated in the war as eagerly as local vice squads. The United States Post Office used its authority to combat mailings of obscene materials as a means to identify homosexuals and would even reveal this information to employers. A professor in Maryland and an employee in the Pennsylvania Department of Highways, for example, were both victims of U.S. Post Office disclosures of their homosexuality (D'Emilio 1983, 47). Even the American Civil Liberties Union regarded laws that criminalized homosexual behavior as constitutional, not changing its position until 1964.

Many affluent gays or gays in prominent positions were victims of organized blackmail rings, one of the most notorious being the "Chicken and Bulls" network, which operated in many cities throughout the country and involved young men seeking out well-dressed older men in posh hotels and enticing them into an encounter that would end with phony police officers bashing down the hotel room door and ultimately accepting a bribe for their silence. Admiral William Church, brother of Idaho senator Frank Church, blew his brains out rather than testify before a grand jury that he had been the victim of an extortion plot, testimony that would have revealed his homosexuality (Eisenbach 2006, 8–9).

The catastrophic impact of a revelation also made homosexuals especially vulnerable to blackmail by rogue police officers and also by the Mafia when they controlled gay bars, as they did in New York City during this period. Combating this practice, Hay noted, was one of the original purposes of the Mattachine Society (Terkel 1995, 304). It was also not unknown for arrested homosexuals to be immediately sent for psychiatric evaluation, which could lead in turn to involuntary commitments with little or no due process. More than one lobotomy was performed on nonconsenting homosexuals. Rick Stokes, a lawyer and one of the first gay activists in San Francisco, never forgot the electroshock therapy he had been subjected to because of his homosexuality.

Lobotomies, to say the least, were even more life changing. A caller into an NPR Radio program recalled how a lesbian cousin, after her procedure, "lived in somewhat sheltered situations . . . could never hold a job . . . had no emotion, only showed emotion as she learned it. But it was only because she was a homosexual that they gave her a lobotomy." In a chilling conclusion, the caller remembered: "And she herself told me how and why she had the lobotomy. And at that point in her life, she was in her seventies and she said, 'Oh, well, that was the right thing to do because they told me I was homosexual'" (Mixner 2010). It is difficult to know how many lobotomies and other forms of extreme treatments were imposed on homosexuals during the darkest period of their persecution because many records were destroyed. David Mixner has written: "Families were often adamant about not leaving any trace of the overwhelming shame of having a homosexual in the family and they often erased the gay relative's presence on earth" (2010).

While not the general rule, long prison terms were also possible under state anti-sodomy laws that provided for sentences of twenty years or more, particularly when a judge felt the need to make an example for the good of the community, as one judge did in the case of a local banker in Boise, Idaho, who pleaded guilty to oral sex with a young man he had picked up at the YMCA; he received a seven-year sentence "in order to preserve community purity" (Eskridge 2008, 88). As late as 1965, a gay reverend arrested in Seattle for engaging in sodomy received a ten-year sentence, a sentence that was vacated after he had served more than half of it because it was based on perjured testimony (Eskridge 2008, 154). To appreciate just how vulnerable a gay man might be, consider that in 1945, California amended its habitual offender law, adding sodomy to the list of crimes for which a second offense meant an automatic life in prison. The North Carolina sodomy statute allowed for a sentence of not less than five nor more than sixty years.

## Limited Sanctuary in the First Amendment

Notwithstanding everything I have described, there was one source of protection for gay rights that simply could not be ignored.

Recall the Supreme Court's decision, referred to in the introduction, holding that the distribution of ONE, the first national magazine for homosexuals, was protected under the First Amendment. This was an important decision but not an inevitable one. The Court could easily have denied the appeal of an obscure homosexual magazine without the mainstream press either knowing or caring. Interestingly, there was no written opinion of the Court; rather its reversal occurred in a one-sentence decision that simply cited a major Supreme Court case, *Roth v. United States*, which had just recently set forth a new standard for obscenity. Nevertheless, the decision clearly stood for the proposition that not every magazine aimed at a homosexual audience was by definition obscene.

Because the decision was rendered without dissent, it actually gave a false impression of unanimity. The actual vote in conference had been 5–4

(Murdoch 2002, 46). In 1950s America, this was a tremendous victory. Dale Jennings recalled that when he learned of the Supreme Court's decision on *ONE*, he said, "My God, this is too soon. I'm supposed to be an old man before this happens" (47). It is another measure of the mindset of the times that someone like Jennings didn't think that gays would get to enjoy the simple right to receive a gay magazine in the mail for another forty or fifty years.

A few years later, in *Manual Enterprises Inc. v. Day*, the Supreme Court extended its *ONE* decision when it protected more physically arousing gay beefcake magazines against another attack by the Postal Service. The case was particularly interesting because it marked the first time the Court had actually heard oral argument over a case involving homosexuals and because the government argued that homosexuals, given the nature of their perversion, were more easily stimulated than "normal adults," so allowing homosexuals access to these kinds of magazines would make it more difficult to cure them. The Court rejected these arguments: homosexuals were as entitled to their titillating magazines as heterosexuals.

It is important not to paint too rosy a picture even with respect to the First Amendment. Publishers were still vulnerable to obscenity charges and could face prison sentences for publishing magazines deemed obscene. Much depended on the attitudes of local police and prosecutors. In Philadelphia, for example, Clark Polak, a publisher of gay pornography, was convicted of obscenity charges and faced a two-year sentence before agreeing to suspend his operations (M. Stein 2012, 78).

One other Supreme Court decision, *NAACP v. Alabama*, indirectly benefited the gay community when in 1958 the Court protected the membership lists of the National Association for the Advancement of Colored People from disclosure on First Amendment grounds. Protection of the membership lists was deemed critical to protect the right of NAACP members to work together in a hostile environment, a right of association which the Court has found to be a necessary predicate for the fulfillment of the rights of free speech and assembly explicitly guaranteed under the First Amendment. The state of Alabama had tried to secure the lists in a clear attempt at intimidation, a decision whose underlying principle protected homophile organizations and publishers as well by protecting membership and subscription lists. One group of scholars recently noted that "even though *NAACP v. Alabama* did not involve gay and lesbian plaintiffs, its holding was critically important for homophile groups" (Eskridge and Hunter 2011, 157). At a time when gays and lesbians feared any revelation of their identity, the Supreme Court's decision offered them some degree of comfort that their orientation would not be revealed simply by their joining a homophile organization.

## A Response Begins

One might well ask why a gay man or woman would go out at all, given the potential for catastrophe that hung over any attempt at a social or sexual life. The answer, of course, lies partly in the human desire to have a public social life where one can meet and talk and partly in the innate strength of the sex drive itself. History played its part as well.

To back up just a little, World War II had proved extraordinarily conducive to the establishment of gay relationships among both men and women. Many young men, hitherto isolated in their small towns and rural communities, were suddenly free of the often stifling pressures of home life and social expectations, and, for the first time, they had the opportunity to explore their sexuality in the anonymity of big cities when on leave or off-duty. John D'Emilio has written that "World War II was something of a nation-wide coming out experience. It properly marks the beginning of the nation's and San Francisco's modern gay history" (1992, 77). Stephen Engel has pointed out how the simple fact that the military would ask a prospective soldier whether he had ever felt erotic attraction to other males "ruptured the silence that shrouded a taboo behavior, introducing some men to the concept for the first time" (2001, 22).

The contrast between home life and military life was captured by one twenty-year-old draftee when he wrote to a gay friend: "the army is an utterly simplified existence for me—I have no one to answer to as long as I behave during the week and stay out of the way of the MPs on weekends. If I go home, how can I stay out all night or promote any serious affair? My parents would simply consider me something perverted and keep me in the house (Berube 1983, 94). The war was also liberating for lesbians. The massive numbers of women in the labor force, the absence of men, the sharing of apartments, "forced women to reorient their social lives around female companions" giving lesbians "an increased chance of meeting one another within the cover of the primarily female environment" (Engel 2001, 23). Additionally, roughly 150,000 women participated in the Women's Army Corps (WACS). The story is often told that when General Eisenhower was about to approve a recommendation that a woman on his staff be discharged for homosexual activity, his chief assistant for Corps matters warned him that the discharge would have catastrophic impact on staff morale and likely lead to many resignations, including hers. Eisenhower tabled the recommendation (Gallo 2006, xxviii).

When World War II ended, it was impossible to put the genie back in the bottle. Our youthful draftee, now often a combat-tested veteran, was not about to return to his disapproving mother and stifling small town life. Like thousands of others, he gravitated toward larger towns and cities. Even those who did go home knew for the first time, as a result of their wartime experiences, that they were not alone. Societal norms hadn't changed, however, and, as described, a virtual war on homosexuals began. That war, oddly enough, would produce the beginnings of a gay political culture, for the only public place that gays could congregate with at least some hope of feeling a part of normal society was the gay bar.

Gay bars even enjoyed some degree of legal protection. In 1951, the California Supreme Court held that gay persons had a First Amendment right to associate with each other, and therefore gay bars could not be closed simply because gays happened to congregate there (*Stoumen v. Reilly*). The highest courts in New Jersey, New York, and Pennsylvania all issued similar decisions. These decisions, however, did not produce a harassment- or danger-free zone. In fact, kissing or holding hands or even dancing—perfectly acceptable behavior for heterosexuals—remained grounds for arrest among gays. Approving such arrests in a later case, the California Supreme Court noted that "any public display which manifests sexual desires, whether they be heterosexual or homosexual in nature may, and historically have been, suppressed and regulated in a moral society" (*Vallegra v. Department of Alcoholic Beverage Control*, 912). Rarely has a court issued a more disingenuous statement; nobody was going to arrest John and Jane for holding hands at a bar. In short, under cover of a purported neutrality, California law effectively endorsed the placement of undercover police officers, usually young and attractive, in gay bars to engage patrons in conversation and then arrest them once an interest in sexual activity was expressed. With the importance of the bar scene, it is not surprising that the few efforts at creating protest organizations prior to Stonewall were in response to police harassment, including the Circle of Friends in Dallas and the Society for Individual Responsibility in San Francisco.

Lesbian bars, though not as numerous as bars for gay men, were a significant part of the lesbian subculture of the fifties and sixties. While circumstances undoubtedly differed from city to city, Lillian Faderman, in her study of twentieth-century lesbian history, has emphasized their importance, particularly for young and working-class lesbians, and how they represented the one place where those who had accepted a lesbian sociosexual identity did not have to hide who they were (Faderman 1991, 162).

In a relatively open society, a satisfactory sex life, particularly in the slowly improving atmosphere of the sixties, was not impossible if one knew how to play the game and keep one's identity guarded. Consider this recollection by the writer David Garnes of his life in New York as a young man in the midsixties: "I took full advantage of the gay scene—the bars, the baths, the beaches on Fire Island, and the inevitable weekend parties at friends' houses. At the same time I was careful to maintain a straight façade at school and at my various part-time jobs. . . . This kind of double life was much more the norm than the exception for most gay men in Manhattan in those days, at least those in my particular world" (Garnes 2000, 197). And in Los Angeles, with its beaches, warm weather, and numerous gay neighborhoods pocketing the sprawling region, even congregating outside was not impossible. Indeed, probably the largest public gatherings of homosexuals before Stonewall occurred on the gay beaches of Los Angeles, likely the happiest and most peaceful as well. In an article for *ONE* magazine in July 1958, Jim Kepner, who wrote countless articles for the periodical, describes a day trip to the beach where a friend exclaims, "Doesn't the sight of that crowd just thrill you? Right out in the open, hundreds of our people, peacefully enjoying themselves in public. No closed doors, no dim lights, no pretense" (Kepner 1998, 249).

Other cities also had their public spaces where gays (though always at some risk) could gather. The gay owner, for example, of a nearby coffeehouse remembered that Rittenhouse Square in Philadelphia's Center City as a place where "at any hour of the day or night there would be something going on" and where you could have "15 or 20 friends near you" making jokes and having fun. "You really felt you were on safe ground. . . . There could be two or three hundred people in the park on any given night" (M. Stein 2000, 88).

Politically, however, most gays in the fifties and even the sixties accepted, at least on the surface, their repression as part of the natural order of things. Jim Kepner recalled: "While a few of us grappled with theory about the nature of homosexuality and its relation to the world, the pressing questions for most Gays remained how and whether to tell our parents, how to find and keep a partner, how not to attract attention, how to have sex without getting arrested, and how to be Gay and still religious" (1998, 12). The reasons for this acquiescence are complex, but in a wide-ranging speech given just a few months before his death in 1997, Kepner offered three key reasons for the failure of any major organizing efforts during this period. First, many gays had internalized society's attitudes toward homosexuality: "Most gays felt homosexuality was a sickness, a sin, or both." Self-hatred does not generally serve as a call to action. The second was more subtle but equally important: "Very few [gays] saw our problems as political, i.e. amenable to organizing and most felt that while other social problems might be helped, society will always hate us." In other words, why organize if, in the end, nothing will really change. Finally, there was the simple fact of fear: "A few saw the need for organizing, but were fearful and unlikely to agree on a specific course" (Kepner 2010, 98).

Any effort at organization could be risky. In 1960, for example, a group of lesbians and gay men assembled in a suburb of Philadelphia to organize a local chapter of the Mattachine Society. They had deliberately avoided Philadelphia proper to escape the jurisdiction of the city's police commissioner, Frank Rizzo. It didn't matter. The local Radnor police raided the meeting and arrested eighty-four people (M. Stein 2000, 383).

Slowly, however, a response to the status quo began to emerge. That response took its organizational form in the fifties in the creation of two organizations, the Mattachine Society and the Daughters of Bilitis. The initial impetus for both organizations was as much about self-realization and self-education as anything else. In an interview with Studs Terkel, Harry Hay recalled, "In 1950, when I founded the Mattachine Society, we were interested in finding out who we are, were, as a separate people. We had to reinvent ourselves. Your society had infected us into believing that we are perverts and degenerates" (Terkel 1995, 303). Group meetings could have a profound effect on the participants. One newly arrived member of the Los Angeles Mattachine Society recalled: "Can you fall in love with a roomful of men? I did. Trying for ten years to find another gay in fighting for our rights, here was a roomful. . . . I burst with love and zeal, grateful to be invited into membership. We'd hid in the dark [for] 2,000 years ignorant of ourselves, afraid and persecuted. No more hiding! No more damned hiding! We were on the move, and I was part of it. I loved that roomful of men" (Williams and Retter 2003, 77).

Hay was ahead of his time in understanding that a sense of community was prerequisite for changing the way broader society treated homosexuals. His experience as an active member of the Communist Party led him initially to organize the Mattachine Society into discrete discussion groups, similar to party cells in that they were secret and small. The 1952 arrest, however, of Dale Jennings, later the editor of the first homophile magazine (*ONE*), led the Mattachine Society to organize in his defense. While the Society was not prepared to reveal its own existence, it created an ad hoc group that distributed flyers in the gay bars of Los Angeles. The Jennings trial resulted in a hung jury (eleven had voted for acquittal but one juror held out), and the district attorney decided not to pursue the matter further.

At first, their success in helping defend Jennings encouraged the proliferation of more Mattachine discussion groups, including in the San Francisco Bay Area. This growth, in turn, encouraged Hay to give the Society a greater public profile by incorporating the Mattachine Foundation as a way of reaching out to the wider community. With its new public face, however, came greater scrutiny, and early in 1953, Paul Coates, a columnist for the *Los Angeles Mirror*, revealed that Mattachine's corporate attorney had refused to cooperate with the House Un-American Activities Committee in its investigation of communist subversion by pleading the Fifth Amendment.

In an excellent account, Linda Hirshman describes how Hay and the other leaders of the organization responded to the Coates article by calling a meeting to deal with the crisis, a decision, Hirshman notes, that more experienced and less idealistic leaders would never have taken (2012, 48). Two representatives from each of the discussion groups attended the meeting, during which a real cleavage was revealed. There were those, like the founders, who believed that homosexuals constituted a minority with a distinct culture and that they should emphasize their uniqueness while insisting on their rights. There were others who wanted to emphasize their normality and use the organization to educate the general public that homosexuals were just like everyone else, except for their sexual orientation. As Hirshman points out, "the two factions . . . laid down the terms of argument for the gay revolution from that day forward" (48). In the end, Hay and the other activists decided to resign from the organization, recognizing that their own leftist backgrounds could put the organization at grave risk. Unfortunately, the new leadership at times seemed to buy into the medical profession's dim view of homosexuality. The enthusiasm for the Society quickly withered, and it ceased to be a public force of any kind within a couple of years. The new moderate leadership, by placing acceptance by heterosexual society above self-acceptance, had undermined the very idealism that had proved so intoxicating to the more than 2,500 men who had joined the group before Hay's defeat.

Like the Mattachine Society, the Daughters of Bilitis (pronounced Bill-EE-tis) or DOB, the only other national gay organization prior to Stonewall, would also struggle to define itself and its mission in a hostile world. DOB's initial emphasis reflected the simple desire of a few gay women to connect with other gay women. In 1950s America, these were deeply subversive acts. DOB began when Del Martin and Phyllis Lyon realized that the quality of their own romantic relationship (they had met in Seattle and were struggling to establish themselves as a couple in 1955 San Francisco) was deteriorating because of their isolation from women like themselves. When they were asked to join with a few other lesbians to create a social group that could meet at private homes away from a bar scene that neither Martin nor Lyon found satisfactory, they jumped at the opportunity. The first meeting of the group occurred on September 21, 1955, at the home of another lesbian couple. Four couples were in attendance. By their fourth meeting, the group was ready to give itself a name and think of itself as an organization. Daughters of Bilitis was chosen as the name, partly in homage to a book of lesbian love poems, titled *Songs of Bilitis* and written by Pierre Louÿs, and also because the name had such a conservative ring, reminding one if only subliminally of the Daughters of the American Revolution (Mixner and Bailey 2000, 23).

DOB struggled to define itself in its first year as most of the original members left, but Martin and Lyon, with a few new members, put DOB on an entirely different path when they decided to openly recruit members for the organization. They also issued a statement of purpose—to educate both gay women and the general public about lesbianism and to participate in research—that described DOB's direction as somewhat parallel to that of the Mattachine Society after Harold Hay was forced out. An important vehicle for that purpose was the *Ladder*, the journal of the DOB, which was, in the words of Lillian Faderman, "middle class" in "aspiration and tone" and, among other things, sought to fight the butch image of lesbians among the general public (1991, 179).

Both the *Ladder* and *ONE* were helping to slowly knit together a predominantly middle-class, virtual community out of hitherto isolated individuals. Sharing an experience or writing a letter to the editor could be incredibly empowering. Simply receiving the magazine could take courage. It also raised real worries. In fact, the response to the first issue of the *Ladder* uncovered a widespread a fear among potential subscribers that simply receiving the magazine could have dire consequences. In response, Phyllis Lyon felt compelled to write an editorial titled "Your Name Is Safe."

Both the *Ladder* and *ONE* magazine played an invaluable role in reaching individuals, but the community it created was small and invisible, existing mainly on subscription lists. As important as these periodicals were to those who read them, the simple fact is that not many did read them. Jim Kepner doubts that readership of *ONE* magazine ever exceeded 5,000 and estimated the readership of the *Ladder* at about 500 (1998, 11). For the most part, neither the members of the Mattachine Society nor those of the DOB, who were mainly educated, white-collar workers and artists, were temperamentally made for grassroots organizing. They were individuals who prized their own sense of themselves and largely resisted the gay bar subculture, the natural place, indeed the only place, in which a sufficient number of gays met who could be mobilized as an effective political force.

Unlike the Mattachine Society, which had essentially gone out of business as a national organization in 1961, giving its local chapters complete autonomy, DOB attempted to maintain a national structure that forced most major decisions to be referred to its central organization (see Gallo 2006, 139–146), something that may have inhibited the growth of more local DOB chapters. In any event, DOB never became a large organization, its "national" conventions at best drawing scores, not hundreds of people.

Although DOB and Mattachine saw their missions as primarily social and educational, the two groups did seek to unite around the goal of repealing state sodomy laws that made their basic acts of intimacy a crime. They were not successful. Legislators were unsympathetic, and until the late sixties, there was no doctrinal basis for protection of privacy in the bedroom and therefore no legal strategy that held out the promise of success in court. The political timidity of both the Daughters of Bilitis and the Mattachine Society as organizations should not obscure the individual courage of their members. In seeking, however tentatively, to establish some form of public presence and group identity, these men and women were products and, at the same time, very much ahead of their time.

Timidity was not a problem for Frank Kameny, rightfully regarded as the father of the gay rights movement; Kameny was a casualty of the war against homosexuals who refused to be a victim. He died in 2011 at the age of eighty-six, and his home is now on the National Register of Historic Places. In April 1957, Kameny—a Harvard Ph.D., astronomer, and university professor, who had also fought the Nazis in Europe—joined the Army Mapping Service, a civil service position, to help map the skies for the military. A few months later, the Soviet Union launched the Sputnik satellite, making people like Kameny a national asset. Kameny, however, was not only gay but a man with an arrest record. In 1956, he had been arrested when he responded to a sexual invitation in the bathroom of the bus station in San Francisco where he had just disembarked on his way to an astronomy conference. The incident occurred inside a toilet stall which the vice squad had been spying on through a one-way mirror, and Kameny and the other man were immediately arrested. When Kameny applied for his position with the Mapping Service, he did not conceal his arrest. The arrest came to the attention of the Civil Service Commission. Kameny was fired when he refused to discuss his sex life with investigators. His superior performance rating (Tobin and Wicker 1972, 92) was no protection. A national asset had been transformed into a national liability, even threat, for a characteristic that even the most prejudiced person would have to concede had no bearing on his ability to perform his work.

With his ability to get a job badly compromised, Kameny soon found himself barely able to survive and, in his own words, "living on twenty cents worth of food a day and slowly starving" (Tobin and Wicker 1972, 93). One trip to a bus station men's room to relieve himself had seemingly cost him his entire future and nullified all his past accomplishments. Kameny would spend the rest of his life fighting not only for gay rights generally but for gay pride within the heart of each gay person. It was Kameny who coined the phrase "gay is good." He thought the phrase as important for gays as "black is beautiful" was for blacks. In *Why Marriage?* George Chauncey states, with Kameny's case in mind, that "long before masses of gay people chose to come out of the closet, the national government itself played a crucial role in destroying the walls between people's 'public' roles as workers and churchgoers and their 'private' lives as homosexuals" (2004, 27).

In 1961, the Warren Supreme Court itself, undoubtedly the most rights-sensitive Court in history, unanimously refused to hear (denied certiorari) Kameny's case. In so doing, however, the justices did the gay rights movement a great service. As Murdoch and Price wrote in their revealing study of the Supreme Court and gay rights, "being turned away from the nation's top court without so much as a hearing transformed the once shy Kameny into an astoundingly effective political dynamo" (2002, 60). By way of postscript, in June 2009, the White House Office of Personnel Management issued an official apology to Kameny for his 1957 dismissal. Kameny accepted the apology, which, cheap irony being what it is, had been formally issued by OPM's openly gay director.

Kameny's iconic status derives in substantial part from his indefatigable work on gay rights for his entire life. Not always the easiest person to work with, he was nevertheless always there to provide advice, help guide strategy, and put himself on the line. His contributions stem from two central insights: first, that individual self-respect was the key to unlocking a viable movement of social protest, and second, that nothing would change if gays were not willing to use that new self-respect to confront a hostile political establishment. He prided himself on never backing down from a fight (Tobin and Wicker 1972, 89). To this writer, there are interesting similarities between Kameny and Malcolm X, for, like Malcolm, Kameny wanted gays to recognize that their own negative self-worth had been imposed upon them and was a key tool of their oppression. The kind of questions that Malcolm asked his people—"Who taught you to hate the texture of your hair? Who taught you to hate the color of your skin? . . . Who taught you to hate the shape of your nose and the shape of your lips? . . . Who taught you to hate your own kind?" (Coates 2011, 104)—were also in spirit the kind of questions that Kameny asked of the gay community. In 1972, Barbara Gittings recalled that Kameny was "the first gay person I met who took firm, uncompromising positions about homosexuality and homosexuals' right to be fully on a par with heterosexuals . . . thanks partly to him, I got turned on to gay civil rights issues" (Tobin and Wicker 1972, 213).

As the sixties unfolded, Kameny's growing personal friendship with Barbara Gittings, an early DOB East Coast leader who became editor of the *Ladder* in 1963, became increasingly important. Their coming together resulted, among other things, in the midsixties, in the Mattachine chapters of Philadelphia, New York, and Washington, D.C., uniting with the New York chapter of the Daughters of Bilitis to form the East Coast Homophile Organizations (ECHO). The organization picketed the White House and Independence Hall in Philadelphia. Interestingly, many of the signs used in the White House picketing demanded the right to serve openly in the military. Additionally, the Washington, D.C., chapter of the Mattachine Society, founded by Kameny, convinced the American Civil Liberties Union to support repeal of state anti-sodomy laws (virtually every state had one), which made criminals of every noncelibate gay and lesbian in the country. Significantly, the ACLU embraced this view on the ground that all private consensual sexual conduct, not just heterosexual conduct, should be protected under the privacy right that had been recently enunciated by the Supreme Court in the landmark case of *Griswold v. Connecticut.*

One other organizational effort deserves mention. In February 1966, forty persons representing about fifteen different organizations gathered in Kansas City at a conference formally titled the National Conference of Homosexual Organizations. The conference led to a brief campaign to protest the exclusion of gays from the military, and it ended with demonstrations in several cities on Armed Forces Day.

The sixties also marked the first time that media attention focused on the reality of homosexual life in not wholly condemnatory terms. In July 1962, for example, WBAI in New York, aired a ninety-minute program in which eight gay men discussed their lives. A program about the ordinary lives of gay men was so extraordinary that it received national coverage in *Newsweek*, the *New York Times*, and other publications. Two years later, *Life* magazine published a photo essay titled "Homosexuality in America." Barbara Gittings, founder of the Daughters of Bilitis, recalled, in the film *Before Stonewall*, that "one of the major successes of the gay movement in the 1960's was our breakthrough into mainstream publicity. . . . As much publicity as possible, that was the whole idea, to crack that shield of invisibility that had always made it difficult to get our message across." Gittings herself began appearing regularly on radio and TV shows starting in 1964, at first primarily late at night to protect children from unsuitable fare, later during prime time or day time (Tobin and Wicker 1972, 219). She, along with other activists like Jack Nichols, also began to speak on college campuses.

In addition to the work of Kameny and Gittings, only two developments—one in San Francisco and the other on university campuses—truly prefigured the explosion of political and organizational activity that would follow the Stonewall riots.

## Making Their Presence Felt

In many ways pre-Stonewall San Francisco anticipated post-Stonewall America. The post-Stonewall glorification of gay sexuality had long been a hallmark of pre-Stonewall San Francisco, where Allen Ginsberg's poem *Howl* celebrating homosexuality not only had a rapt audience but was vindicated as not obscene after a celebrated trial that drew national attention. And just as the police had overplayed their hand in New York City in a campaign against gay bars in June 1969, so too had the San Francisco police made a similar mis-take several years earlier when they attacked a gay New Year's Eve dance (not before first openly photographing the attendees) sponsored by the Council on Religion and the Homosexual, a group that included a number of straight ministers from various denominations who witnessed the police action. The attack resulted in negative press coverage for the police; all charges against those arrested were dismissed after the American Civil Liberties Union stepped in. Even in San Francisco, however, an arrest could mean the loss of a job. Evander Smith, an attorney, saw his name in the paper and knew he would be fired. He was right: "When I went to work . . . nobody would have anything to do with me, including my own secretary. Everyone had seen the paper" (Marcus 2002, 102).

A key pre-Stonewall development in San Francisco was the growing alliance with the Democratic Party. Although this alliance would take years to develop nationally, it was well under way in pre-Stonewall San Francisco, aided and abet-ted by a surge in the gay population during the fifties: the number of single-person households in San Francisco doubled in the 1950s and accounted for 38 percent of the city's households by the end of the decade (D'Emilio 1992, 78). San Francisco's popularity was not a new phenomenon as evidenced by Oscar Wilde's famous comment, "It's an odd thing, but anyone who disappears is said to be last seen in San Francisco" (Shilts 1982, 49).

The vehicle for the gay community's growth in political influence was the strong gay bar culture that had emerged in the fifties, out of which emerged two organizations: the Tavern Guild, an association of bar owners, a number of them gay, with the money and incentive to protect their liquor licenses, and the Society for Individual Responsibility (SIR), a group founded to provide a social outlet for the gay community and to insist on its rights. Politically, that meant registering bar patrons to vote and holding candidates' nights. For the commu-nity itself, the SIR sponsored bowling nights, brunches, art classes, and a thrift shop, and even created the first gay community center. In its combination of political and social activities, the SIR very much anticipated the Gay Activists Alliance that followed Stonewall.

From 1965 on, Democratic politicians began courting gay votes, occasion-ally attending meetings of the SIR and even making deals. Jim Foster, for exam-ple, the SIR's political chairman, exchanged his support of two ambitious state assemblymen representing San Francisco districts, Willie Brown and John Bur-ton, for their support of a state bill to repeal California's anti-sodomy law (Shilts 1982, 59). In 1969, the SIR rallied around another aspiring politician, Dianne Feinstein, in her run for a place on the city's board of supervisors. Although she would have won a seat without gay support, with gay support she won more votes than any other candidate (Shilts 1982, 59), enabling her to attain the powerful position of board president. (The board was then elected entirely on an at-large basis, in contrast to the district system in effect when Harvey Milk was elected.) Though police harassment never entirely ceased, the relative safety of San Francisco gay life, in the words of Todd Ormsbee, allowed "a somewhat more open male culture to develop," in contrast to places like Washington, D.C., and New York City, which were marked by federal harassment in the former and Mafia intimidation in the latter (2010, 306).

The second important pre-Stonewall development was the beginning of a significant organizing effort on university campuses. As with so many important movements, it began with a single uncompromising individual. By the age of nineteen, Bob Martin had already led a pretty interesting life. When he was eight, his mother divorced his father and effectively cut off all communication with her two sons, including Robert, for almost a decade. When he was twelve, Bob's father, a naval officer, sent Bob to an elite boarding school in Germany where he began to engage in gay sexual activities (Eisenbach 2006, 52). On his return, he attended a large suburban New Jersey high school, graduating first in his class of eight hundred and then matriculated at Columbia College in the fall of 1965. Martin's mother tried to prevent his enrollment by outing him to the college. Nevertheless, Martin was admitted, but only on the condition that he undergo psychotherapy and "not attempt to seduce other students" (53). His first year was difficult; he had been placed in a dorm suite with three other students but was transferred to a single room in another dorm when his suitemates complained to the administration that they felt uncomfortable with Martin's presence. This incident triggered Martin's decision to organize the Student Homophile League, an organization that he envisioned would finally allow for some semblance of a gay student community.

The Student Homophile League aimed to raise gay self-awareness and encourage gays to come out of the closet. In this it succeeded; indeed, Martin was ultimately elected to the university's student council. Martin's ambitions, however, went beyond the Columbia University campus. His goal was to replicate this success on other campuses throughout the nation, which he indeed did, helped in part by the national controversy stirred by a *New York Times* article that had focused attention on the League's struggle for recognition at Columbia. Spurred by Martin's intense activity and the example of Columbia's success, a loose confederation of organizations of gay student groups had begun to form even before Stonewall, including groups at NYU, Stanford, the University of Hartford, and the University of Minnesota.

In addition to these successes, occasional protests were organized, including demonstrations in several cities in May 1966 protesting the military's exclusion of homosexuals. Nevertheless, as the sixties closed, gays largely remained the objects of scorn and oppression. However their lives may have seemed to themselves, in the words of David Eisenbach, "gays . . . existed in the eyes of the larger society as sinners, criminals, and lunatics" (2006, 68). Then, on a hot June night in New York, a few brave souls showed that they had had enough.

# 2

# Stonewall (1969)

When Peter Finch screamed "I'm not going to take it any more" from his bedroom window in the classic film *Network*, the anguish and frustration to which he gave vent could not have more accurately reflected the feeling of a large portion of Greenwich Village's gay community in the summer of 1969. Four years earlier, Mayor John Lindsay had been elected and had ended the brutal program of repression and entrapment of gays carried out under the administration of Mayor Robert Wagner. In June 1969, however, with another mayoral campaign under way, things seemed to be going in reverse. Several raids on gay bars had already occurred that June, including one at the Stonewall on June 24. The Stonewall, however, had become an object of particular interest to the police. It appeared that Wall Street employees who frequented the bar were being blackmailed for information facilitating the theft of negotiable bonds. For this reason, the police had a different objective for the raid that began a few days later in the early morning hours of Saturday June 28: to close the place for good.

The Stonewall itself was in many ways a typical New York gay bar; it was Mafia controlled and had a clientele not about to complain about the watered-down drinks to Fat Tony (the Genovese crime family owner of the Inn). The physical appearance of the place was dark and depressing, a handyman's special, but the bar was especially important to gay youth and the transsexual community because of its large backroom dance floor and its generally accepting atmosphere. Most of its patrons were working- and middle-class whites, but "there was a significant presence of African-Americans and Latinos as well" (M. Stein 2012, 79). It was, in the words of William Eskridge, "a place where queer was normal, and society's prejudice could be forgotten" (2008, 166). It was also Vito Russo's favorite hangout, "the place," he said, "everyone loved to hate . . . seedy, loud, obvious, and sheer heaven" (Schiavi 2011, 61). Not that it was always a safe place or its appeal limited to outcasts. Martin Duberman, the distinguished historian, made the Stonewall his bar of choice when he came to New York in 1963 and recalled: "in that bar no one was ever sure whether or not he or she would end the night by being arrested and thrown in jail" (1991, 242).

The first night of the Stonewall riots was extraordinary in that it marked one of the rare times in all of the sixties protests, including the anti–Vietnam War and civil rights protests, in which the rioters got the better of the police. This is not the place to describe the first night of the riots in detail—David Carter's book Stonewall does that in gripping fashion, and there are other excellent accounts as well. In brief, the raid had been well planned, with undercover officers canvassing the Inn earlier in the evening. Search warrants had been obtained and, when the police finally raided the place in the early morning hours, it was clear that this was no ordinary raid as officers began to rip benches from the wall and seize alcohol.

But the patrons were in no ordinary mood either. The routine for most raids was well established: patrons lined up, identifications shown, a few arrests made, most patrons released. This time, by all accounts, patrons, particularly the transvestites and marginal street people, were uncooperative, making the whole process take much longer than usual. Then, as patrons were released, they began to mill around the Inn, instead of simply evaporating into the hot June night. A crowd began to grow. It had already been an emotional day with the uptown funeral of Judy Garland, who was adored by many gay men. At this point, police were loading those arrested into paddy wagons. Then, whatever the trigger, the restive crowd turned to action. A stone was thrown against a police car, and then bottles and other objects began to be launched against the Inn.

The police themselves were forced back into the bar. Then matters really turned dangerous as stones turned into Molotov cocktails. The police were trapped, and only the forbearance of the man in charge of the raid, Deputy Inspector Seymour Pine, hardly an advocate of gay rights, who had told his men not to shoot, prevented real bloodshed from occurring. Police reinforcements finally arrived just in time to avert a disaster and the crowd was finally dispersed, but the myth was born. Trapping the police, putting them in a desperate situation, making them feel the same fear and humiliation that was a constant in their lives—all of this created almost unspeakable euphoria within the New York gay community as news slowly spread at what had happened at the Stonewall.

The Stonewall riot did not end that night. The following evening, also a hot one, another crowd gathered. During the day the curious had come to survey the damage, while at the same time people like activist Craig Rodwell, who had been present the night of the riot but not inside the Stonewall, were spreading the word, recognizing the potential political importance of the event. Slogans demanding the end of harassment filled the air, and another stormy night of confrontation with the police ensued. The next few nights were rainy and nothing happened, but on Wednesday a final night of rioting occurred, the most violent yet as both the police and rioters were mentally exhausted. The riots were over but opportunity beckoned.

Stonewall's status should not obscure its humble origins. This was very much an outburst triggered by local grievances. Gays patronizing the Stonewall were simply tired of being harassed, paying the Mafia for lousy drinks, and not even getting the benefit of police protection. The police had not behaved particularly badly on the night of the riot. In fact, one witness recalled that the police had left the paddy wagon holding those arrested unguarded so they could leave the scene (Marcus 2002, 128). People were simply tired of being mistreated. Ray "Sylvia Lee" Rivera recalled: "When they ushered us out, they very nicely put you out the door. Then you're standing across the street in Sheridan Square Park. But why? Everybody's looking at each other. 'Why do we have to keep on putting up with this?'" (127).

Dick Leitsch, president of New York Mattachine, knew that Stonewall had created a moment charged with political possibilities, but his idea for capitalizing on them was to organize a silent vigil in Washington Square Park with the approval of the authorities. That stance, however, was much too passive for a younger generation schooled in the civil rights, feminist, and anti–Vietnam War movements of the decade. Craig Rodwell, founder of the Oscar Wilde Memorial Book Store in Greenwich Village, for example, had left the Mattachine Society when the Society refused to endorse a resolution asserting that homosexuality was just as normal as heterosexuality. Leitsch, at the behest of Michael Brown, one of the younger generation who had migrated from his position on the staff of Senator Hubert Humphrey to become an organizer for the New Left, set up the Mattachine Action Committee, which Leitsch asked Brown to run (Duberman 1993, 216).

No committee, however, could bridge the gap that now separated the two different generations of activists. When Michael Brown and Jim Fouratt urged support for a demonstration for the Black Panthers, Leitsch insisted that the Mattachine Society's name not be associated with the demonstration. Soon after, the rupture was complete and a new organization, the Gay Liberation Front, was born, a name intended to pay homage to the liberation struggles in Algeria and Vietnam (Duberman 1993, 217).

The goal would no longer be acceptance by reasoned conversation but liberation by the exercise of real power. Writing about homosexuals in general in 1951, Donald Webster Cory had lamented: "They never fight back. . . . They accept quietly and willingly, only too happily that they have been spared the humiliation of exposure. They accept with head bowed—angry, hurt and helpless—and often with some sense that perhaps their lot is not entirely without justification" (Cory 1951, 39). It took nearly two decades but Cory's assessment ("they never fight back") no longer held, nor would it in the future. Those who experienced the Stonewall riots would not be the same again. Even Edmund White, then a twenty-eight-year-old struggling playwright who considered the event itself (in which he participated) "rather silly" and "more Dada than Bastille" became immediately active in gay liberation (White 1988, 12).

The riot itself, however satisfying to its participants, would have meant little had not a nucleus of leaders existed to publicize it (the riot itself occasioned relatively little national press coverage in its immediate aftermath) and exploit its symbolic potential. And what better or more American way to celebrate a victory than with a parade? And so a small group of New York gay men—men who had substituted the goal of celebrating themselves for the older one of trying to convince the rest of the world that they were okay—began their planning for a one-year anniversary march, mainly at Craig Rodwell's newly opened Oscar Wilde Memorial Bookstore. The organizers established no litmus test for participation; any group was welcome, and the planners made a conscious effort to spread the word about the parade as widely as possible, informing different cities as well of their plans. As a result, other parades occurred, including an important one in Los Angeles, where more than 1,200 marchers, most of them not affiliated with any organization but just expressing themselves, marched down Hollywood Boulevard with more than 30,000 onlookers, leading the *Los Angeles Free Press* to comment: "In a burst of inspired magnificence, Hollywood's gay community proved once and for all that they are free" (Kenney 2001, 167–168).

No one knew how the New York march would turn out right up to the date itself. In fact, the necessary permit for the march was not issued until the very morning it was to take place. By the time of the parade's kickoff, at about quarter after two, everyone, as Jim Foster put it, was "scared to death" (Duberman 1993, 278). Their fears were not realized. Walking up the left lane of Sixth Avenue, the marchers were met by occasional cheers, puzzled expressions, and an occasional taunt, but no violence. More importantly, more and more people joined in as the parade marched toward its final destination in Central Park. As hundreds, then thousands, collected at the Sheep Meadow, no one could escape understanding the significance of this moment. "So empowering," "incredible," and "into the light" were just some of the descriptions used to describe the day.

Historians of the gay rights movement vigorously debate the significance of Stonewall. Some emphasize the importance of the work of earlier gay activists and see the period after Stonewall as the logical continuation of that work. John D'Emilio has said, for example, that "until the rise of militant AIDS politics in the late 1980s, gay and lesbian activism in the 1970s and 1980s tended to look very much like what Frank Kameny, Barbara Gittings and the members of the Society for Individual Rights in San Francisco were doing in the 1960s. The difference was primarily quantitative" (2002, 227). D'Emilio also emphasizes how even before Stonewall, a gay community life had begun to form, and not just in the largest cities but also in places like Kansas City, Missouri; Rock Island, Illinois; Syracuse and Ithaca, New York; Cincinnati, Dayton, and Columbus, Ohio; Richmond and Norfolk, Virginia; Dallas and Houston, Texas; and Seattle, Washington. He writes: "By the time of the Stonewall riots in New York City in 1969—the event that ignited the gay liberation movement—our situation was hardly one of silence, invisibility and isolation. A massive, grassroots liberation movement could form almost overnight precisely because communities of lesbians and gay men existed" (1983, 107). Even in the heartland, a 1966 newsletter of Mattachine Midwest had begun to use the phrase "gay power" in response to the unrelenting oppression of the Chicago police (D'Emilio 2008, 70).

Still, Stonewall and the commemorative parades that followed seemed to reveal to the gay community for the first time its own possibilities for sustained group action. Philadelphia provides an example of the spreading excitement unleashed by Stonewall and the celebration of gay pride. Philadelphia activists had participated in the Christopher Street liberation activities in 1970 and 1971 but inaugurated their own highly successful march in June 1972. The march began in Rittenhouse Square with a speech by Barbara Gittings, among others, in which she declared, "Gay is good, it's right, positive, healthy, natural and moral. . . . This march may not be a revolution but it certainly is a revelation" (M. Stein 2000, 373). Jeffrey Escoffier remembered the march as "one of the most exhilarating things" he has done (M. Stein 2000, 375). In Philadelphia, the June march was followed by the first Pennsylvania lesbian and gay conference attended by more than two hundred people and sponsored by a number of activist organizations.

That circumstances favored the possibility for a historic moment does not diminish the importance of that moment, for the trajectory of gay life and politics completely changed in reaction to the Stonewall riots, and in that sense they were transformative. It was one thing for there to be a gay subculture operating still, for the most part, below the surface, as it had been in the pre-Stonewall era. It was quite another for gays to be openly debating what it meant to be gay and organizing politically to secure the passage of antidiscrimination ordinances. It was one thing to be negotiating with the establishment to curtail police harassment; it was another to orchestrate confrontations with that establishment, particularly liberal politicians, to end all forms of discrimination. It was one thing to be able to dance the night away on a crowded, pulsating dance floor hidden from public view; quite another to celebrate that same sensuality in the sunlight of a gay pride parade.

In the summer of 1965 the Washington chapter of the Mattachine Society (started by Frank Kameny) had helped organize a series of protests in front of the White House, but though the protests earned a flurry of publicity, the results were ultimately disappointing and the picketing was terminated in October after just a few months. The annual "reminder" protests that followed were important symbolically but hardly presaged the post-Stonewall world of gay organizing. Stonewall's impact can be seen in the fates of two pathbreaking organizations formed in the midsixties, the Dorian Society in Seattle and Mattachine Midwest in Chicago.

In early 1967 in Seattle, Washington, an informal group of gay men (largely white and middle class) decided to develop a formal organization, the Dorian Society, aimed at repealing Washington's sodomy laws. Though it had a political agenda, the Society also cared very much about acceptance by straights, promising in its constitution and bylaws to "encourage socially responsible conduct by all members of the homosexual community" (Atkins 2003, 109). The Society is an example of the kind of organization that was being formed before Stonewall. With its very conservative agenda, the Society unanimously voted in May 1967 to use pseudonyms in all communications and messages and to use false names in all public communications. Most of its members still feared coming out. Then Stonewall happened. and by the fall of 1969, "the impact of the Stonewall riots could not be ignored" (122). Atkins describes how, as the idea of gay liberation moved to the forefront of a new agenda, the Dorian Society, which had seemed so pioneering just a couple of years earlier, now seemed hopelessly passive and its secret membership out of place. In June 1970, a Seattle chapter of the national Gay Liberation Front formed, and within another year the Dorian Society ceased to exist.

Mattachine Midwest was formed in 1965 in Chicago in part to negotiate with the police to end the policy of entrapment. Those negotiations never bore fruit but the organization did not disappear. Instead, it established a newsletter whose circulation was estimated at over 2,000 and which created a real sense of a gay community in the process. The group also developed a telephone helpline that averaged 40 to 60 calls a month and a speakers' bureau that institutions such as the Cook County School of Nursing and the Lakeview Ministers'

Workshop drew upon (Poling 2008, 66). Like the Dorian Society, however, most of the organization's white, middle-aged, middle-class members remained closeted. Not surprisingly, it too saw its influence fade in the aftermath of Stonewall. In his essay on Mattachine Midwest, John Poling states: "In May 1970, during a meeting between Mattachine Midwest and several of the Gay Liberation groups, leaders of the old and new guards looked upon MM [Mattachine Midwest] as a has been. By 1971, the new groups had usurped MM's role as the city's leading gay-rights organization" (68). Although Mattachine Midwest considered disbanding, it decided instead to focus on its role as a social service provider, which it did with some success for another decade.

The fates of the Dorian Society and Mattachine Midwest caution against a narrow view of Stonewall's significance.

Stonewall's legacy even affected communities that had not experienced the kind of oppression felt in the largest cities. Pre-Stonewall Savannah, for example, was remarkably tolerant for its time, with "its own gay counter-culture that gathered in a Stonewall-like club known as the Basement" (J. Miller 2009, 45). Once a year around Saint Patrick's Day, the Basement held what was known as the Sara Awards, when, as recalled by Jack Miller in a brief essay, the bar gave out awards of all kinds to people who contributed to the community, as well as awards of infamy: "The evening was a drag extravaganza and most of Savannah knew about it and loved it" (45). Yet even relaxed Savannah felt the reverberations from Stonewall. At the conclusion of his essay, Miller writes: "Today, Savannah has a robust gay community, several busy gay clubs, and a Pride celebration that draws thousands. . . . Gay life didn't begin in 1969, but it ascended the steps of the Basement Bar and never went underground again" (45).

Although there are strong bloodlines running from the pre-Stonewall to post-Stonewall eras, Stonewall and its aftermath gave something to the gay community, particularly its younger generation, that it had never had: it transformed a shared narrative of oppression into a new narrative of rebellion, which aligned itself perfectly with the ethos of the sixties. Myths matter. In 2013, immediately upon hearing that she had won her landmark case invalidating a key provision of the Defense of Marriage Act, Edith Windsor exclaimed: "I wanna go to Stonewall right now" (Levy 2013).

Historical causation is admittedly a tricky business. Eighteen months before Stonewall, the Los Angeles police had conducted a much more brutal New Year's Eve raid at a bar, the Black Cat, located in the Silverlake neighborhood of Los Angeles, in which they arrested virtually all patrons and injured a number of those arrested. Had the raid occurred in New York, perhaps the Black Cat would be famous and Stonewall just another gay bar. But perhaps not. Maybe the gay left was still too focused on Vietnam and civil rights. One thing, however, is clear. Before Stonewall, magma had been building among gay people for at least a decade below the slowly thinning crust of oppression. With Stonewall, it burst forth, consuming the fears of many and for the first time creating a real sense that the future might be different. In New York, two organizations, the Gay Liberation Front and the Gay Activist Alliance, embodied those hopes as a new era began.

# 3

# Invisible No Longer (1969–1981)

The New York Gay Liberation Front, ushered into existence by the Stonewall riot, was all about visibility and consciousness raising. It also deeply identified with the new left critique of capitalist society, describing itself as "a revolutionary homosexual group of men and women" who believe that "complete sexual liberation" will not occur "unless existing social institutions are abolished." Its sense of universal mission was succinctly captured by the placard "No One Is Free Until Everyone Is Free!!" held proudly aloft by GLF marchers at the first Christopher Street Gay Liberation Day parade. The Front was not interested in legal reform, nor did it keep a close watch on how gays were perceived in the mainstream media, something that became a central focus for the Gay Activists Alliance.

The Front disdained retail politics and had no desire to integrate into straight society. In her introduction to a revealing collection of essays on the Front, Tommi Mecca, speaking of the early gay liberationists, writes: "These early trailblazers were not looking for marriage or corporate jobs or acceptance into the military or the church. . . . They flaunted their difference. They made no apologies. Like their hippie, yippie and countercultural counterparts, they believed in sex, drugs and rock'n roll. Not to mention truth, justice and a redistribution of wealth" (Mecca 2009, xi). The Front was committed to participatory democracy, to letting everyone have their say, to raising consciousness through endless discussion, all of which were worthy values but not necessarily the kind of values that would translate into organizational success or even orderly meetings. It is not surprising that an organization that occasionally needed a softball bat for a gavel and required complete consensus as a predicate to action was not long on concrete results.

Despite the chaos of the organization, those who attended bear witness to just how personally liberating the GLF felt to its participants. According to

John Lauritsen, "there were plenty of mistakes, but it is GLF that transformed the world for gay people" (2009, 112). Edmund White remembers that "we [gay liberation] had these gatherings which were patterned after women's and, ultimately, I think Maoist consciousness-raising sessions. Whether or not our sessions accomplished anything for society, they were certainly useful to all of us as a tool for changing ourselves" (White 1988). And for Arthur Evans, our first Gay Liberation Front meeting "completely changed our lives for everything. Everything was changed after that. . . . I feel a great sense of gratitude to GLF for that" (Eisenbach 2006, 126).

The Gay Liberation Front and the viewpoint it represented did not become the dominant voice of the gay rights movement in the United States. On December 21, 1969, a number of gay activists, including Jim Owles, Arthur Evans, Arthur Bell, and Marty Robinson, gathered in Bell's Greenwich Village apartment to form a new organization, the Gay Activists Alliance. These men were disturbed that the Front's "business" meetings were close to anarchy, but, even more fundamentally, they objected to the Front's concept of the gay rights movement. For people like Owles and Robinson, the gay rights movement was a separate cause, not simply another part of an effort to change the world.

Ironically, many who joined the Gay Activists Alliance and some of its leadership shared the deep critique of society characteristic of the Front; they recognized, however, that their views did not reflect those of many gays. They also recognized that revolutionary rhetoric was no substitute for a concrete program. Nothing so clearly encapsulates the difference between the Front and the Alliance than the definition of activism contained in the Alliance's constitution: "the commitment to bring about change in the present, rather than theorize about change in the future." There was no question among the Alliance's members as to who the agents of change would be and who only theorizers. Given their disdain for the Front's chaotic meetings, it is also no surprise that almost immediately the Alliance adopted *Robert's Rules of Order*.

The liberal establishment, mainly Democratic Party officeholders, which the Front dismissed as worthless, became the very group at which the Alliance directed its energies. Ultimately, the goals of the Alliance and those of the GLF were irreconcilable. The Alliance wanted to use the power of institutions to extract change; the GLF wanted to transform those institutions. The Alliance defined itself by its actions; the GLF by its rhetoric. The Alliance implicitly accepted that institutions could be made to live up to their ideals; the GLF questioned the ideals themselves and the society that defined them. The Alliance dreamed of victories; the GLF of revolutions. In a few short years, both the Alliance and the GLF would disappear, but the Alliance would be, in part, a victim of its own successes and would be followed by other organizations committed to its aims.

With all its failings, the GLF represents the real start of the modern gay rights movement both in its openness and militancy. Not only did it come before the Alliance, but the famous photograph by Peter Hujar of fifteen exuberant gay men and women marching arm and arm up a deserted New York street, almost airborne with happiness, perfectly captures the initial burst of energy that is the GLF's great legacy to the gay rights movement. The photograph, choreographed by Hujar on an early Sunday morning, became the GLF's first recruiting poster, with the invitation *come out!!* in bold lettering across the top. "Come Out" was more than a slogan. The Front's central premise was that "the personal was political and that individuals must be changed in order for the institutions to change" (Tarr 2009, 22).

Nonetheless, it was the Alliance—sometimes with influential allies in the media such as popular talk show host Phil Donahue, who aired numerous programs aimed at creating a more positive image of gay life—which drove the gay rights political movement in the early seventies. The Alliance made liberal politicians their special project. Its "zaps" sometimes took the form of sit-ins and physical demonstrations, other times simply persistent questioning of candidates and politicians anxious to burnish their liberal credentials but who needed a little push to endorse gay rights. As a result of their efforts, every Democratic candidate running for the party's 1972 presidential nomination, other than Edmund Muskie, expressed some degree of support for gay rights.

Because the Alliance cared about politics, it also cared greatly how gays were perceived in the media and began to monitor unflattering portrayals, sometimes insisting on a right of response, on other occasions simply calling attention to inappropriate remarks or jokes, often coupled with a warning that such behavior would not go unchallenged in the future. A searing condemnation of homosexuals and homosexuality in *Harper's* magazine led to a sit-in organized by the Alliance which featured the Alliance's combination of humor and confrontation. The article by Joseph Epstein, had, among other things, declared that homosexuals were "cursed without clear cause, afflicted without apparent cure . . . and an affront to rationality." Epstein also wrote, "If I had the power to do so, I would wish homosexuality off the face of the earth" (J. Epstein 1970, 51). In response, Alliance members invaded *Harper's* offices early one morning. Some chained themselves to the furniture; others offered doughnuts and coffee to a bewildered staff. The surrounding publicity led to an appearance by Arthur Evans on the *Dick Cavett Show* a month later and a three-part series on a local television station which allowed the public to see gays in a more positive light. Gay activists also began appearing on the *David Susskind Show* and the *Tonight Show* with Jack Parr, among others.

The Alliance was not just about politics and media exposure. Its legendary dances at the Firehouse on Wooster Street gave gays a social outlet. There, every Saturday night, a couple of thousand people could be found sweating and dancing, some tripping, all having a blast. It was a far cry from the backroom of the Stonewall Inn. Of course, like the media zaps, the underlying purpose of the dances was to shatter the isolation of individual gays, "the very heart," in the words of Marty Robinson, "of what kept gays apolitical for years" (Eisenbach 2006, 171). In addition to the Saturday night dances, Vito Russo, author of the *Celluloid Closet*, which exposed Hollywood's insidious depiction of homosexuals in film, organized Cabaret Night, a twice-a-month affair that allowed performers the rare luxury of displaying their talent before an all-gay audience. The Alliance also emphasized from the outset the importance of gays feeling free to display their affection in public, kissing hello and goodbye and not being afraid to hold hands (Schiavi 2011, 81).

Although it went about it differently, the Alliance, like the Liberation Front, wanted to change how gays perceived themselves. The purpose of zaps, for example, went beyond trying to influence politicians. A larger goal was, in the words of Arthur Evans, "to reach the existential and emotional life of gay men who were not interested in politics, who did not connect their sexuality with political issues. . . . We wanted to reach their anger and some inspiration with something exciting." Evans believed that, after seeing how the straight world responded to zaps, nonpolitical gays would let themselves feel an anger that would ultimately create a feeling of "class consciousness" and the realization that "assimilation into the heterosexual mainstream is no answer; gays must unite among themselves, organize their common resources for collective action and resist" (Eisenbach 2006, 156–157).

As noted earlier, the Alliance's demise was to some degree a product of its own success. As more and more Democratic politicians began to endorse gay rights, the need for zaps diminished and the Alliance itself began to lose focus, never recovering from the loss of its headquarters as the result of a fire in 1974. Also, as the Alliance gained in prominence, it began to attract increasingly marginal, even unstable persons to its meetings. Ultimately, a number of refugees from the Alliance, along with other prominent activists—New York City health administrator Howard Brown who had just come out, Martin Duberman, and Frank Kameny—formed the National Gay Task Force, later the National Gay and Lesbian Task Force. The Task Force struggled throughout the seventies. "Friction within the Task Force was a constant," recalled Duberman, with board of directors meetings frequently fractious (Duberman 2013, 279–280). Ultimately, however, it became an important and positive force, "cast[ing] its net widely" in the words of John D'Emilio and seeing change "as coming not only through government, but through a range of institutions in American life" (D'Emilio 2002, 105). The Task Force and other lobbying organizations would become extremely important, but the most startling and important triumph of the early post-Stonewall gay rights movement had nothing to do with politics, or at least partisan politics.

## Initial Successes

Doctors, not legislators, provided the most important early success of the gay rights movement when in 1973 the American Psychiatric Association (APA) reversed a position it had taken as recently as 1968 and removed homosexuality from the list of mental illnesses listed in its *Diagnostic Statistical Manual of Mental Disorders* (*DSM*, 3rd ed.). (The first *DSM* had been published in 1952.) Categorizing homosexuality as a malady had long had serious consequences. It was, for example, the original justification for discharging gays from the military, and it allowed gay men to be committed to mental institutions without their consent. In the mid-1950s, however, pioneering research by Evelyn Hooker showed that psychologists simply couldn't distinguish between straight and gay men on standard personality tests, something they should have been able to do if homosexuality were truly a form of mental illness.

There are few straight heroes in the gay rights story but Evelyn Hooker is one of them. Her project began when a gay student (also a friend) challenged her to do research on the topic of the supposedly deeply disturbed homosexual. Hooker began her work at the height of the McCarthy era, with the National Institute of Mental Health's financial support, itself an action also worthy of recognition. In her work, this brave and intelligent woman almost singlehandedly broke through the conventional wisdom that was at the foundation of gay oppression. During her life, Hooker fought and beat tuberculosis and faced the kind of discrimination that went with the territory for a professional woman coming of age in the mid-decades of the twentieth century. In 1992 a documentary on Hooker's work and life, *Changing Our Minds: The Story of Evelyn Hooker*, was nominated for an Academy Award. She died in Santa Monica, California, at the age of eighty-nine.

The APA's decision did not happen by accident but was the direct result of a strategy by gay activists that combined confrontation and dialogue. At the Association's 1970 annual meeting in San Francisco, a group of protesters interrupted a program titled "Issues of Sexuality" by demanding that gays themselves be heard. In response, the APA agreed to hold a panel on homosexuality at its next annual meeting in which gays could participate. When the panel occurred in 1971 it did not attract much attention, but at that annual meeting Frank

Kameny and Barbara Gittings discovered that there was a clandestine organization of gay psychiatrists. After much effort, they persuaded one gay psychiatrist to appear at the panel program the following year, although he insisted on wearing a mask. When he did appear, this time before a huge audience, the sight of a distinguished professional man feeling forced to shield his identity behind a ridiculous mask dramatized better than any words what gay men and women suffered and led the following year to a vote by the APA's board of trustees to drop homosexuality as a class of mental illness, a vote that was subsequently confirmed by a majority of the APA's membership.

In the fall of 1971 the nationally syndicated *David Susskind Show* devoted an entire program to lesbianism. Unlike Phil Donahue, Susskind was not particularly sympathetic and continued throughout the program to defend the current definition of homosexuality as a sickness. Barbara Gittings and six other gay women "tangled for an hour and forty-five minutes with Susskind, who kept the show moving by advancing popular myths about homosexuality" (Tobin and Wicker 1972, 220). The women were, by all accounts remarkably effective in countering him. In fact, one straight woman commented to Gittings after the show, "Why, you homosexuals love each other just the way Arnold and I do" (220).

Another important achievement of the early seventies was the ruling by the U.S. Civil Service Commission that gays could not be fired from federal employment merely because they were gay. This breakthrough can be traced directly to the work of Frank Kameny and the Washington chapter of the Mattachine Society, which Kameny had founded in the mid-1960s to more aggressively promote gay rights. Meetings between gay activists and the Commission had begun as early as 1965. In fact, the first meeting had resulted in a written statement by the Commission in which it attempted to justify the exclusion of homosexuals from all federal jobs (Tobin and Wicker 1972, 182). Beyond specific victories, however, the most important development, in retrospect, of the early seventies was what was happening in the gay community itself.

Once gays began to take control of their own destiny in the seventies, practical necessity dictated a distinctly American strategy: organize, join together, create voluntary institutions. Take advantage of the freedoms you do have. As Alexis de Tocqueville observed in *Democracy in America*, Americans are forever forming associations. We have always been a nation of joiners; the immigrant, the frontiersman, the urban dweller, the farmer, the worker—all have sought personal fulfillment and the advancement of their interests through the creation of organizations. Gays too have followed this pattern. Today, the number and range of organizations dedicated in some fashion to supporting every aspect of gay life are staggering, but this is not a recent development. Within just a few years after Stonewall, more than a thousand gay community organizations had sprung up: "newspapers, magazines, health clinics, churches, multipurpose social centers and specialized businesses—in short a range of institutions that implied the existence of a separate, cohesive gay community" (D'Emilio 1983, 2).

These efforts began to make a real difference in the lives of gays and lesbians. To cite just one example, in Los Angeles, former activists in the Los Angeles Gay Liberation Front helped form the Los Angeles Gay Community Service Center, which initially was intended to provide a place for gay street youth and then expanded to provide a range of services and support for the entire gay and lesbian community. In New York, another important organization, Gay Youth, was begun by Mark Segal. In the words of Stephen Cohen, author of a detailed history of New York's Gay Youth movement in the early 1970s, "Gay Youth's numerous social and political events—dances, movie nights (including a Mae West series), meetings, social get-togethers, and protests—created community settings . . . where one could decipher and define sexual feelings and the meaning of relationships" (Cohen 2007, 45). Like Bob Martin, Segal also wanted to have a national impact and helped organize affiliates of Gay Youth in numerous cities, including Boston, Washington, D.C., Tampa, Detroit, Philadelphia, Seattle, Los Angeles, and Ann Arbor. In retrospect, Gay Youth and its organizations stand as an important precursor to the thousands of Gay–Straight Alliances existing today in public schools throughout the country, both in the needs they filled and the message—the essential worthiness of gay identity—they delivered.

Gay Youth was just the beginning for Segal, who also pioneered the concept of local LGBT newspapers and helped found the National Gay Press Association and the National Gay Newspaper Guild. He also freelanced as a one-man zapping machine. It was Segal who, on December 11, 1973, crashed a live broadcast of the *CBS Evening News with Walter Cronkite*, rushing in front of the camera with a sign reading "Gays Protest CBS Prejudice." In front of millions, Segal perched himself on Cronkite's desk while technicians wrestled him to the floor and wrapped him in wire—all on camera. Later, Cronkite sought out Segal to question him about the reasons for his action and, when Cronkite became convinced of the legitimacy of Segal's complaints about media bias, he arranged for Segal to voice those complaints personally to top management. This led directly to a favorable segment on gay rights on Cronkite's May 6, 1974, broadcast. Subsequently, Segal and Cronkite became friends, and after Cronkite's death Segal issued a moving tribute to Cronkite, noting his important support of gay issues and the fight against AIDS.

As the seventies unfolded, some in America began to see gays in a new light, and as gays began, in increasing numbers, to openly organize in the urban communities where they lived, local legislation forbidding discrimination based on sexual orientation began to be enacted. In 1972, in San Francisco, an ordinance was enacted prohibiting discrimination against gays by city contractors. By the midseventies, municipalities and counties throughout the country, including Boulder, Colorado; Columbus, Ohio; Dade County, Florida; Seattle, Washington; Detroit, Michigan; and San Francisco, California, had enacted antidiscrimination legislation.

On the state level, the seventies saw a significant number of repeals of laws criminalizing sodomy. In May 1975, California became the twelfth state in the nation to decriminalize sodomy followed by Washington state in June. Washington's law went even further than California's in that it decriminalized the solicitation of sodomy as well. Only Hawaii at that point had taken a similar step. Over the next three years, nine more states decriminalized consensual sodomy as part of their adoption of the Model Penal Code recommended by the American Law Institute, a highly influential legal group whose "model" codes have served as a basis for law reform on many subjects in many states. As of January 1, 1979, the sodomy map of the United States looked completely different than it had before Stonewall, with 90 percent of the American people living in the thirty-five states that had substantially decriminalized consensual sodomy by that date (Eskridge 2008, 201).

Not surprisingly, a new breed of activist had begun to emerge. By 1970, a twenty-year-old Minnesotan, Steve Endean, had finally accepted that he was gay and nothing was going to change that fact. Endean also loved politics and wanted to make Minnesota the first state in the nation to enact a lesbian and gay civil rights bill, not an altogether unrealistic goal for a state that had sent Hubert Humphrey and Eugene McCarthy to the U.S. Senate and had nurtured the Progressive Farmer-Labor Party. In the early seventies, Endean became one of the first paid lobbyists in the gay rights movement, drawing a small salary from the Minnesota Committee for Gay Rights, which, combined with tips from his regular five- to seven-day-a-week job checking coats at Sutton's, a well-established gay bar in St. Paul, allowed him to make ends meet.

Endean was not alone. Nurtured in part by the Alliance, which sent out summer caravans to help gays in parts of the country where they were not organized, the gay rights movement began to develop local leaders who then began to achieve success. The rapid expansion of the Metropolitan Community Church beyond Los Angeles also provided a spark for many gay communities and, with its emphasis on social justice, often an aid to organizing efforts. Perhaps most remarkably, out-of-the-closet gays began to run for office and, starting in 1974, even win. These were not high offices—Kathy Kozachinko won a seat on the Ann Arbor City Council and Elaine Noble a seat in the Massachusetts House of

Representatives—but it was a beginning. As important as these early political successes appear in retrospect, however, most gay men prized above all their new sexual freedom, a freedom they exploited in ways that sometimes offended not only the straight community but the lesbian community as well.

## Sex and Freedom

In the early 1970s, troubling divisions developed between the gay and lesbian communities. To a considerable extent these two groups went their separate ways. It wasn't altogether about politics or goals; it was also about behavior. For one thing, gay men were apparently no more sensitive to lesbian women than heterosexual men were to their partners. More than one lesbian activist found gay men's behavior simply revolting. Attempts at organizing joint dances were a disaster. Women were offended by the overt sexuality of the men's dancing. One gay feminist observed: "Most gay men don't understand lesbian women better than most husbands really understand their wives. . . . All said and done, many gay men and lesbians are coming to understand that we have little in common but the society which mislabeled us" (Clendinen and Nagourney 1999, 87). As Tommi Mecca has noted, "Women who suffered a dual oppression, preferred struggling with the homophobia of their straight sisters to dealing with the sexism of their gay brothers" (2009, xii).

The importance of the feminist movement to many lesbians cannot be overestimated. Dorothy Allison has said that "if there had not been a women's liberation movement in the early seventies, I would not only have not started writing. I would not be alive. Because the women's movement told me that my life was not small. That I was not contemptible. That women's lives are not contemptible. That I was in fact important" (Claxton 2012, 42). For the activist Jill Johnson, "lesbians are feminists, not homosexuals" (S. Epstein 1999, 41). While generalizations when it comes to gender are always dangerous, it seems fair to say that for many, perhaps most gay men, the seventies were primarily about sexual freedom, whereas for women, both lesbians and straight women, the era was much more about discovering each other and creating a sense of shared living, in all its dimensions. In the words of one scholar, "lesbian feminists dedicated themselves to building an alternative culture," and in the process forming collective households, running small businesses, and opening up restaurants, coffeehouses, and bookstores (49).

Of course, lesbians and straight women had to struggle to understand each other. Straight women still needed men to satisfy their sexual desires, whereas lesbians could be freer to celebrate sex with each other without suffering the internal conflicts of many straight feminists. This may have been an important reason why Dorothy Allison, with her insistence on frank and open discussion about the realities of lesbian sex and her celebration of radical sexual politics, became a lightning rod for many feminists and more circumspect lesbians.

If many lesbians found community in the feminist movement, many gay men found what they wanted in the protective embrace of a bathhouse culture that, along with gay bars and discos, became central arenas of gay men's social life. Bathhouses had a number of advantages over the bar scenes of the 1960s. First, a not insignificant number of them were owned and financed largely by gay entrepreneurs. They were, therefore, not breeding grounds for blackmail. Also, profits from their operation were potentially available for gay causes, depending, of course, on the attitudes of their owners. Second, bathhouses didn't require liquor licenses so they were not at the mercy of state regulators and were much less vulnerable to vice squad infiltration or having to make payoffs to stay in operation. Third, in the larger cities they could be quite luxurious, featuring disco dance floors, massage parlors, Olympic-size swimming pools, sun decks, game rooms, saunas, and TV rooms. Fourth, bathhouses were, in a strange way, more democratic than the gay bar scene, for, in an atmosphere where sex was a major goal—few gay men went to the baths just to watch TV and swim—social status and where you worked were much less important than how you looked. In the words of one writer, "the baths would foster an environment where people would be judged by their physical attributes rather than by the displays of status, education or wealth that were then prevalent in the gay bars and other areas of gay social life" (Cruz-Malave 2007, 172). One might, of course, argue that the baths simply replaced one form of hierarchy with another, but it was at least a hierarchy that transcended class (though not race) distinctions. I distinguish race here because more than one bathhouse had a policy of discouraging the patronage of men of color, as was also the case with some gay bars.

Bathhouses were not just confined to the largest cities. In his autobiography, *Out of Bounds*, Roy Simmons  an offensive lineman for the Super Bowl XVIII champion Washington Redskins and one of the few professional players to acknowledge, after his playing days, his homosexual orientation—recalled with great fondness a bathhouse he frequented during his college days at Georgia Tech, just a few doors down from the local Arby's. At first he was wary of the bathhouse, but once he got up the courage, Simmons became a regular. He remarked that the bathhouse "changed his life forever," a statement that may seem extreme until one considers what life before Stonewall had been like for men like Simmons (Simmons and DeMarco 2006, 63). That a gay athlete could satisfy his continuing need for anonymous gay sex at a local bathhouse in the middle of Georgia speaks volumes about the transformations that were occurring in gay life as the seventies wore on.

Many young gay men fleeing the oppression and boredom of rural and small town life had no political interests at all. They reveled in their new found sexual freedom and took advantage of it in ways that many people, gay or straight, even today, might find disturbing and dehumanizing. The club 8709, the most infamous of the Los Angeles bathhouses, had a huge orgy room that, according to the reminiscence of one customer, was "packed so tight with bodies you couldn't move" (Faderman and Timmons 2007, 238). In some places, the bathhouses never closed. As John Andriote notes in the opening sentence of his major work on the AIDS crisis, "Being gay in the seventies meant hot men, cool drugs, pounding discos, and lots of sex" (Andriote 1999, 7).

Many gay men had all the gay rights they needed once the police left them alone. They had no interest in creating the gay counterpart to Ozzie and Harriet. Quite the reverse. Philip Gefter, a young New Yorker who in his own words was "shaped by the utopian values of the sixties," recalled that "at one point [during the seventies] I had accrued enough fuck buddies so that I didn't even have to leave my apartment." Gefter also recalled, "I recorded every sexual encounter in my journal as if they were running tallies of my gay identity . . . as if the highest number of sexual encounters meant that I would win in the Olympic sport of 'being Gay'"(Kaiser 1997, 243). Gefter was not alone. In a 1994 essay, the novelist Andrew Holleran described the Greenwich Village of the midseventies as a "mob scene" and a "stampede of promiscuity, [a] gay life that seemed all too often toward the end of the seventies as predictable and conformist as any in the suburbs" (2008, 15). Even acknowledging its excesses, however, many older gay men remember this as an exuberant and happy period for themselves, understandably so given the recent history from which they were emerging and what was to come.

For many gay men, impersonal sex was neither wrong nor something of which one need be ashamed. Indeed, it expressed an honesty about the pure joy of sex, in marked contrast to the hypocrisies of heterosexual society. Patrick Moore, in his defense of the culture of sadomasochism and leather that emerged in the late seventies in places such as the Mineshaft in Manhattan's meat district, writes, "Men who lived in major urban centers in the 1970s love to tell sex stories from the era" (2004, 16). In his moving biography of Vito Russo, Michael Schiavi captures this idea when he writes: "He [Russo] relished the simplicity of meeting a guy under the stars [on Fire Island], making love with him, and then retiring to the dunes for a cigarette and chat if both were so inclined. No pressures, no judgments. Just the kind of unashamed physical rapport that had been one of GAA's founding tenets" (2011, 131). Later, when he worked at the St. Marks Baths, Russo would see this kind of sex in a less positive light (158).

This discussion of gay men's sexual life and lesbians' attitudes toward sex and other women is not an idle detour. On the contrary, it underscores how the first decade of the post-Stonewall period was primarily about sexual freedom for gays themselves, and very little about marriage, military service, and integration into straight society. One cannot appreciate the emotional resonance of the seventies if one loses sight of that simple fact. Of course, in the eyes of religious conservatives, there are rules about whom you sleep with, and when it comes to gays, the answer, even now, is no one. As gay men and women became more open and celebratory about their sexuality in the seventies, battle lines began to be drawn between gay rights activists and the religious right.

## Fending off the Right

Major social change is never easy, and by the late seventies, a backlash fueled by the religious right began to develop, resulting in the repeal of gay rights ordinances passed earlier in the decade, including those in Wichita, Kansas; St. Paul, Minnesota; and Eugene, Oregon. The extent of the backlash was dramatic: in St. Paul, repeal won by 54,090 to 31,690 votes, and in Wichita by 47,246 to 10,005 (Adam 1995, 111).

The most important successful repeal effort, however, occurred in 1977 in Miami. There, in a campaign that made her a symbol and spokesperson of the antigay right, Anita Bryant unleashed a no-holds-barred attack on gays, presenting them in the most inflammatory terms as a threat to the nation's children and basic social institutions. "Some of the stories I could tell you," Bryant told reporters, "of child recruitment and abuse by homosexuals would turn your stomach" (Clendinen and Nagourney 1999, 303). This recruitment was necessary, claimed one newspaper ad, because "since homosexuals cannot reproduce, they must recruit to freshen their ranks" (303). One senses here an antigay campaign staff that had seen one too many *Twilight Zone* episodes, but the strategy worked. On election day, Miami repealed its ordinance by a vote of 202,319 to 83,319. The success of this antigay campaign did not just depend on conservative Republicans. The supposedly liberal Democratic governor of Florida, Reuben Askew (considered by many at the time a possible future president), "went out of his way just before the climactic vote [in Dade County] . . . to announce publicly that he would not want to have a known homosexual teaching his children" (Duberman 1986, 299).

The success of the religious right in repealing municipal ordinances came at a time when many of the young leaders of the Gay Activists Alliance had abandoned politics to focus on their personal lives and careers: "Arnie [Kantrowitz] was struggling to earn tenure at Staten Island Community College;

Jim [Owles] was working for the City Planning Commission in Queens; Marty Robinson had returned to full-time carpentry; Arthur Bell was advising *Voice* readers to forget about gay rights; Arthur Evans was in San Francisco running the Buggery, his Volkswagen repair business" (Schiavi 2011, 155). These men were not alone. "Many gay men," writes Patrick Moore, "who began the 1970s integrated into a political spectrum that included a broad range of left political struggles, found themselves finishing the decade in their own newly developed ghettos, where concerns of class struggle seemed not only far away but beside the point in the more personal exploration of the baths and clubs" (2004, 11).

In the nights following Miami's repeal of its gay rights ordinance, thousands of gays took to the streets in San Francisco, Greenwich Village, and other cities in protest. It was costly, but the gay community had learned a valuable lesson: it could take nothing for granted, as events in California soon showed. There, in 1978, Republican state senator John Briggs, an ambitious man who saw in antigay politics a path to higher office, spearheaded an initiative that would have required the dismissal of not only any gay teacher or public school administrator but also anyone, gay or straight, who advocated or promoted private or public homosexual activity. The First Amendment, as well as the gay community, was now in the line of fire.

For a while it looked as if the proposition (more than half a million people had signed the petition to put it on the ballot) might pass, but Briggs had overreached and the proposition was doomed when former governor Ronald Reagan announced his opposition shortly after meeting with David Mixner and Peter Scott, a meeting arranged by a closeted member of Reagan's staff (Faderman and Timmons 2007, 227). Before Reagan's statement, the Briggs initiative appeared well on its way to victory, but the poll numbers reversed dramatically after Reagan made his position known. On Election Day, Proposition 6 went down by a vote of 58 percent No, 42 percent Yes. In addition to harnessing gay anger, the struggle to defeat the Briggs initiative had a strongly positive effect on gay–lesbian relations. As one lesbian activist exclaimed, "I loved working with those men! Let me tell you, I will *never again* be a separatist" (Faderman and Timmons 2007, 228).

After her success in Miami in 1977, Anita Bryant had sought to expand her campaign by joining forces with right-wing activist Phyllis Schlafly. In a remarkable speech given in 1997, one month before his death, Jim Kepner recalled that "the shock half emptied the nation's middle class gay closets." "It was," he added, "as big a turning point as Stonewall," creating human rights coalitions in many cities (2010, 107). Though, as Kepner points out, many of these organizations were riddled with internal disagreements and power struggles, they all understood that they were engaged in a desperate fight against an increasingly powerful conservative movement. Gays began to mobilize, and Anita Bryant, for one, began to face well-organized counterdemonstrations in, among other places, Houston, Dallas, and New Orleans. Additionally, the National Gay Task Force (now the National Gay and Lesbian Task Force) organized a nationwide campaign with the slogan "We Are Your Children," in response to Bryant's "Save Our Children" campaign. Anti-Anita fundraisers flourished. Tens of thousands of dollars were raised at an "Anita-thon" in Cleveland, an Anita Bryant look-a-like contest in San Francisco, an Orange Ball in Chicago, a Squeeze Anita weekend in New Orleans, and a Disco for Democracy at New York's Waldorf Astoria (Eisenbach 2006, 282).

Another part of the response to Bryant was the first nationally organized gay rights march on Washington, drawing over 100,000 people, although the D.C. police in their estimates of crowd size somehow lost sight of roughly 75,000 of them. The march, however, did not attract the major media coverage that many had hoped for. Amy Hoffman recalls that nationally "newspapers snubbed the event": "Our weekend in the capital seemed to have taken place in some invisible dimension." Back in her hometown of Boston she remembers: "Our contingent arrived back . . . exhausted and euphoric, only to find a crummy one-paragraph note buried in the middle of the *Globe*" (2007, 77). Nevertheless, the march was extremely important in much the same way that the first gay pride parade had been in New York. Those working so hard to raise gay political consciousness owed much to John Briggs and Anita Bryant. Consciousness of gay issues was also rising in the courts as gays began to refuse to accept the kinds of discrimination that they had been fighting on the political front.

## Gay Rights in the Courts

Courts hear cases and controversies. Sometimes rights organizations bring test cases to establish legal rights. For the most part, however, test cases of gay rights were not filed during the seventies, in part because gay rights organizations were themselves in their infancy. A few brave couples sought marriage licenses in several states, including Kentucky, Washington, and Minnesota, but they were a generation and a half ahead of their time and their constitutional arguments were rejected in each case. There were also some successes in getting gay men who had been fired from government jobs reinstated, often with Frank Kameny orchestrating the successful outcome, for *Norton v. Macy* had provided a valuable precedent that the Civil Service Commission had to acknowledge.

Lambda, however, today the leading gay rights legal organization, had "virtually no money" during the seventies and not even an office until 1979, when it found space in the New York Civil Liberties Union premises (Andersen 2006, 28). Few individual attorneys, including gay lawyers, were willing to take on gay rights cases, "largely because they were unwilling to risk being perceived as homosexual" (28). Lambda's initial application for corporate status was actually rejected in 1972, notwithstanding that its papers had been modeled on similar, successful papers of the Puerto Rican Defense Fund (Leonard and Cain 2009, 72). The judges charged with reviewing the application concluded that although they did not doubt that discrimination against homosexuals did exist, the discrimination did not operate to deny them legal representation. It took a decision of the highest court in New York (the Court of Appeals) to rectify this obvious abuse of discretion (*Application of William J. Thom*). Interestingly, when the application was returned to the first set of judges for further review, they granted the application but struck as inappropriate the power to encourage homosexuals to attend law school and assist them once they were there.

Stuff happens, however, and so the decade was not completely devoid of litigation. Gay parents, for example, who wanted to retain custody of their children after the breakup of their heterosexual marriages had no choice but to assert their rights. Gay parents won custody in a number of cases in Michigan, California, Oregon, North Carolina, and Washington, but in several instances courts stipulated that a parent could not live with his or her same-sex partner or socialize with other gays or lesbians (M. Stein 2012, 106). Another success came in the form of a number of decisions by various federal circuit courts (the intermediate federal appellate courts between the federal trial courts, called district courts, and the Supreme Court) protecting gay student organizations on university campuses.

Public university administrations in the seventies were as dependent on democratically elected legislatures for their budgets and their jobs as they are today. Consequently, they were not always friendly to the idea of gay student organizations and in a number of instances did their best to block them. Government entities (including public universities), however, are not allowed to engage in viewpoint discrimination under the First Amendment, which is exactly what these universities were guilty of in their various efforts. During the seventies, the First, Fourth, and Eighth Circuits each sustained the rights of gay groups in clashes with their universities (see, respectively, *Gay Students Org. v. Bonner, Gay Alliance of Students v. Matthews,* and *Gay Lib. v. University of Missouri*).

*Gay Lib. v. University of Missouri* is particularly interesting because the board of curators of the university had based its refusal to accept a gay student organization on the nature of homosexuality itself, finding as established facts, among other things, that (1) "a homosexual is one who seeks to satisfy his or her sexual desires by practicing some or all of the following: fellatio, cunnilingus, masturbation, anal eroticism and perhaps in other ways"; (2) "homosexuality is a compulsive type of behavior"; (3) "homosexuality is an illness and should and can be treated as such and is clearly abnormal behavior"; and (4) "certain homosexual practices violate provisions of Section 563.230 of the Revised Statutes of Missouri" (*Gay Lib.*, 852). The board also accepted the conclusion of the university-appointed hearing officer that recognition of a gay student organization posed a serious danger to the university community and its sexually impressionable students. The Eighth Circuit, however, recognized censorship for what it was. In overturning the board's decision, the court noted that none of the purposes or aims of Gay Lib. evidenced advocacy of present violations of state law or of university rules or regulations. Then, perhaps surprisingly, the court added: "It is difficult to singularly ascribe evil connotations to the group simply because they are homosexuals. . . . such an approach smacks of penalizing persons for their status rather than their conduct, which is constitutionally impermissible" (*Gay Lib.*, 856).

The university cases were important and represent the value of a robust First Amendment. At the time public opinion was unfavorable toward these student groups, so in this instance it could be said that the judiciary was in the vanguard of gay rights, not bringing up the rear. Unfortunately, these cases were the exception to what is otherwise a bleak picture. Let us briefly examine three cases that reveal courts unwilling to recognize the right of gay public employees to keep their jobs even while agreeing that a homosexual could not be fired merely for being homosexual. The mistake of the gay employee in these instances was not in being homosexual but in being too open about it.

In April 1970, young Mike McConnell was offered the job of heading the cataloging division of the University of Minnesota Library, which he accepted in May. On July 9, 1970, the board of trustees voted to withdraw the offer. What had happened between April and July to make a relatively minor position the subject of a vote by the board of trustees? Simply that McConnell and his partner, Jack Baker, had sought a marriage license. The board made no secret that extensive local media coverage of the event had led to a reconsideration of the offer. McConnell sued in federal district court for an injunction prohibiting the university from withdrawing the job offer, claiming that the retraction was premised on his being homosexual and his desire to publicly profess that gays should be entitled to privileges equal to those afforded to heterosexuals. Judge Neville agreed and, citing *Norton v. Macy*, granted the relief sought but stayed the judgment so that the university could appeal to the Eighth Circuit Court of Appeals, which it did.

The Eighth Circuit reversed Judge Neville's decision in terms that reveal how the cultural biases of the time still loomed large in the application of legal principles. Distinguishing the McConnell case from *Norton*, the court first noted that this was not a case involving mere homosexual propensities but a case in which "the applicant seeks employment on his own terms." Then the court showed just what it thought had disqualified McConnell from employment: in seeking the marriage license and arguing for gay equality, McConnell was really claiming "the right to pursue an activist role in *implementing* [the court's italics] his unconventional ideas concerning the societal status to be accorded homosexuals and thereby, to foist tacit approval of *this socially repugnant concept* [my italics] upon his employer, who is, in this instance, an institution of higher learning" (*McConnell v. Andersen*, 196). From the vantage point of 2013, this statement seems both repugnant and absurd, but in 1971, in a cultural and political milieu entirely different than today's, the court was doing what courts often do: reflecting the bias of its own time.

In the second case, in September 1972, the school board of Montgomery County, Maryland, transferred Joseph Acanfora to a nonteaching position after it learned that he was homosexual. Acanfora sued to get his teaching assignment back. Much expert evidence was presented in the case on the question of the appropriateness of homosexuals teaching in public school and their possible impact on children. The federal district judge, in the first part of his decision, could not have written more favorably for Acanfora, asserting: "the time has come today for private, consenting adult homosexuality to enter the sphere of constitutionally protected interests" (*Acanfora v. Board of Education of Montgomery County*, 851). By resting the first part of his decision on a right to privacy, Judge Young was thirty years ahead of his time, and had his analysis stopped there, Acanfora would have won his suit. Judge Young, however, then turned his attention to the fact that both before and after his commencement of a lawsuit, Acanfora had appeared on several radio and television programs. These were all serious programs, and Acanfora said nothing during any of them that the judge found objectionable. Indeed, Acanfora discussed his disinclination to discuss matters of sexuality in the school environment.

These appearances, nevertheless, were Acanfora's undoing, for Judge Young found that though Acanfora had a right to teach even though he was homosexual, he lost that right once he had become so public with his homosexuality that his students would no longer be able to separate his homosexual identity from his position as a teacher. His appearances, wrote the judge, "inevitably sparked additional controversy regarding the subject of homosexuality and the classroom" (*Acanfora*, 856). It was this "*indifference to the bounds of propriety* [my emphasis] which of necessity must govern the behavior of any teacher, regardless of sexual tendencies," wrote Judge Young, which excused the school district from having to rehire Acanfora. In the cultural atmosphere of the early seventies, bad manners could trump the First Amendment.

The third case (*Singer v. United States Civil Service Commission*) showed just how the distinction laid down in *Norton* between status and behavior could work so easily against a gay man. John Singer was a typist in the Seattle office of the Equal Opportunity Commission. After a year, Singer was called before an investigation commission to respond to charges that he was flaunting his homosexuality. The major charges against him were that he had kissed another man in previous employment, applied for a marriage license, and had granted an interview with the *San Francisco Chronicle* in which he identified himself as a homosexual. Such behavior was viewed as sufficiently inflammatory to justify his dismissal because it tended to erode confidence in the Commission.

In each of these cases, we see a timid judiciary reflecting what might be seen as the newly emerging ethos of the times: you can go to your bars and bathhouses and we will pretty much let you alone, but don't you dare remind us of your actual existence, at least if you want to keep your public-sector jobs.

One other case from the seventies, one that made national headlines and landed its chief protagonist on the September 8, 1975, cover of *Time* magazine, deserves our attention. It is a reminder, as the saying goes, that sometimes the worst prayers are the answered ones. It began in March 1975 when Leonard P. Matlovich, after some twelve years of excellent service in the military, wrote to the secretary of the air force, through his commanding officers, that he had concluded that his "sexual preferences are homosexual as opposed to heterosexual." Before sending his letter, Matlovich had consulted with Frank Kameny, who had been looking for an ideal candidate to challenge the military's exclusion policy. Matlovich certainly met Kameny's need in that he had been severely wounded after stepping on a land mine in Da Nang during one of his three tours of duty in Vietnam. He had also been so successful in teaching air force race relations classes that he was sent around the country to perform his duties.

Not surprisingly, Matlovich's letter ultimately led to his discharge from the service. Not surprisingly but also not inevitably, because at the time, the air force did have the authority under applicable Defense Department regulations to waive Matlovich's homosexuality as a ground for separation. Matlovich fought back and won when the District of Columbia Circuit held that it simply could not distinguish Matlovich's case from the ones in which homosexuals had been retained and indeed that it was impossible to tell on what grounds the service had refused to make an exception. Unfortunately, the Matlovich decision led directly to a decision by the Defense Department to change its own regulations, depriving it in the future of the flexibility to grant waivers to serviceworthy homosexuals (Leonard and Cain 2009, 623). Again, it is another marker of the times that the civilian-run Defense Department, although undoubtedly in consultation with the military, thought it better to deprive the armed forces of individuals it might have wanted to retain rather than adopt a set of waiver exceptions that would have provided sufficient guidance to pass judicial muster.

## At Decade's End

The seventies were a troubled time for straight America. Nothing seemed to go right. A U.S. president had been forced to resign in disgrace just a year and a half after amassing the second largest electoral majority in history. Only one state (Massachusetts) had voted for his opponent. As the prosperity of the sixties gave way to the stagflation of the seventies, the United States began to experience a new sensation: powerlessness in the face of events it could no longer control. Blindfolded hostages paraded before television cameras reminded the nation that had led the fight against Hitler that it could now not even protect its own embassies. What was a time of great freedom and exhilaration for gay America was anything but for most of those living in Nixon's and Carter's America.

That weakness translated into timidity at the national level when it came to gay rights. Although President Jimmy Carter (1977–1981) made human rights a centerpiece of his foreign policy, he made little effort to denounce discrimination against gays. Midge Constanza, Carter's director of the Office of Public Liaison (and a closeted lesbian), did facilitate contacts between gay lobbyists and various officials, resulting in some modest successes with the Bureau of Prisons, the Immigration and Naturalization Service, the Federal Communications Commission, and the Internal Revenue Service. (See William Turner's excellent essay in D'Emilio, Turner, and Vaid 2000 for a more detailed description of gay rights during the Carter years.)

The Carter administration's overall indifference to gay issues did not sidetrack the growing relationship between the gay and lesbian community and the Democratic Party. In 1976, there had been no real gay presence at the Democratic National Convention, and the platform made no mention of gay rights. In 1980, there were seventy-seven gay and lesbian delegates at the convention (O'Leary 2000, 92), and the Democratic platform included language, vague though it may have been, supportive of gay rights. Though the Carter forces tried to discourage it, the gay community was even able to nominate a gay African American, Mel Boozer, for vice president, who gave, in the recollection of Jean O' Leary, a major lesbian activist, "an incredibly moving speech."

Clearly, the alliance between the gay community and the Democratic Party was beginning to take shape. In the words of O'Leary, "We were constantly amazed at the successes we had at the 1980 convention. It was such a change from the past. We had gone from being an albatross to a defined constituency, with all the benefits of money, power and votes attached to the definition"

(2000, 92). By way of contrast, the Republican platform included an endorsement of a bill called the Family Protection Act, first introduced by Senator Paul Laxalt in 1979 (Laxalt was a key insider in the Reagan campaign). The bill contained some particularly vicious antigay provisions, including one that would have amended the 1964 Civil Rights Act to provide that actions against gay and lesbian employees, based on their sexual orientation, would never be unlawful.

The 1980 presidential campaign, which Ronald Reagan won in a landslide, served as the high water mark of the Moral Majority. The organization, created and led by the Rev. Jerry Falwell, had been largely successful in making the agenda of the religious right the program of the Republican Party. Notwithstanding Reagan's final margin of victory, polls showed the race very tight going into the last weeks of the campaign. For this reason, it was imperative that Governor Reagan recapture for the Republicans the evangelical vote that President Carter, a Democrat and born-again Christian, had won so convincingly in 1976, allowing him to carry almost all of the former confederate states, including Mississippi, Alabama, Louisiana, North Carolina, Arkansas, South Carolina, and Georgia, in his defeat of President Ford—results that today are inconceivable. (On the Republican side, Ford had carried California and Illinois, outcomes that today seem equally bizarre.) To help Reagan, Falwell had no compunction about exploiting antigay prejudice. In a speech in March 1980, for example, he recalled his astonishment when, during a conversation with President Carter, the president responded to his question about why he had open homosexuals serving on his staff by saying, "I am President of all the American people and I believe I should represent everyone." Falwell claimed to be appalled by the remark (Klarman 2013, 32).

Oddly, given the new freedom the seventies had brought, it appears that the dominant feeling at the end of the decade was one of fear. Looking back, John D'Emilio recalls that by the end of the seventies, the "almost utopian sense of optimism that followed in the wake of Stonewall was fading" (2002, 84). There were a number of reasons why this pessimism was justified. America was still a homophobic society with a population easily manipulated into supporting antigay initiatives, and antigay violence was still very much a part of American life. Moreover, the gay rights movement was still a movement of volunteers, in contrast, for example, to the organizational prowess and financial resources of the Moral Majority, a factor that had permitted an aroused religious right repeated success in repealing antidiscrimination ordinances. In addition to pressure from the right, internal divisions within the gay community "compromised the ability of activists to mobilize their constituents and have the movement speak with a unified voice." National organizations like Lambda Legal Defense and the National Gay Task Force had, in D'Emilio's words, "barely gotten off the ground"

(2002, 75). And for all their newfound freedom, "the vast majority of lesbians and gay men, more than a decade after Stonewall . . . remained 'in the closet.' Many who were willing to socialize within gay and lesbian worlds nonetheless kept their secret from outsiders. Many others even maintained a distance from the social institutions of the gay community" (85).

The gay rights organizations that were beginning to emerge in the late seventies, and indeed the vast army of volunteers in the political battles of that decade, were almost exclusively white and largely middle class, nor were gay neighborhoods characterized by a great degree of social integration. Indeed, gay bathhouses and social clubs could be as racist as any other institution. Deborah Johnson, then an eighteen-year-old activist in Los Angeles, recalls that racism in the gay community "took different forms" but the "most blatant" were the "exclusionary policies at the gay clubs, at places like Studio One." Even in social gatherings or meetings Johnson felt excluded: "But what I kept getting over and over again was that people of color didn't matter and that we were somehow ancillary. And when black people showed up at meetings or social gatherings, they would get the cold shoulder. Nobody would ever talk to them" (Marcus 2002, 191–192). Black isolation from the mainstream of the gay rights movement, particularly the almost complete absence of poor blacks, would have a profound impact on how the AIDS crisis was experienced (and is still being experienced) by the African American community.

As the seventies ended, the political battles of that era would soon seem to fade in significance as a small virus began its horrible work that would alter gay life forever.

# 4

## The AIDS Crisis and
## Its Legacy (1981-1992)

$\mathrm{A}$t the beginning of the 1980s, some began to question how the gay community had used its new freedom. For Larry Kramer, the seventies were a lost decade: "Didn't we see," he asked, "that we should have been fighting for the right to get married or fighting for the right to be noble and live outside in the world instead of fighting for the right to find our love in these tawdry little places? Were the baths the be-all and end-all of what being gay meant?" (Marcus 2002, 247). Kramer's view is not surprising. For him, freedom to engage in anonymous sex had never been the prize. In his freshman year at Yale, in the early 1950s, he had tried to commit suicide by swallowing 200 aspirin after his first sexual experience with a stranger much his senior.

In July 1981, the *New York Times* had reported on a "Rare Cancer Seen in 41 Homosexual Men." The first solid evidence, however, that the disease was sexually transmitted did not come until the summer of 1982 when the Center for Disease Control reported that the disease was likely caused by a single agent transmitted by sexual activity.

There was one tragically lost opportunity for slowing the spread of AIDS during the early years. In the summer of 1982, the Center for Disease Control (CDC) was the one governmental organization with strong contacts in the gay community, owing in substantial part to the fight in the seventies against the Hepatitis B virus, which had involved the CDC with gays in clinics in Los Angeles, Denver, Chicago, San Francisco, and St. Louis. That summer, the CDC warned the blood supply industry that contaminated blood was clearly implicated in the appearance of AIDS among hemophiliacs and transfusion recipients.

The industry, however, failed to act on these warnings, a tragedy given that it was not until April 1985 that a reliable individual test for the presence of the AIDS virus, which had been discovered a year earlier, would be available. There were other problems as well. Pressure from the Reagan administration forced the CDC to resist the kinds of explicit discussions of anal sex that could help prevent the transmission of the AIDS virus. Dependent as it was on a conservative administration peopled by numerous anti-gay-rights conservatives, the agency during this period seemed more concerned that federally funded AIDS education materials not give offense to the squeamish or priggish than that they actually be helpful (see Andriote 1999, 138–153).

It is impossible to understand how the AIDS crisis initially affected the gay community if we see it only through the rearview mirror. Rather, imagine yourself as one of its first victims, or as the friend, parent, brother, sister, or life partner of such a victim. Imagine your own son, brother, or partner slowly mutating into a ghastly skeleton. I say "slowly mutate" because one of the key features of AIDS, one that made strong social support systems so necessary, was the time it took to die. Unlike earlier plagues, whose victims died in a matter of hours or days, AIDS victims lived for years, giving care to others while they could, receiving it when they could no longer care for themselves. In the words of the playwright Scott McPherson, "By most we are thought of as 'dying.' But as dying becomes a way of life, the meaning of the word blurs" (Kayal 1993, 15).

Try to imagine also how it must have felt to worry whether a runny nose might be the first signal of a death sentence. In the early years, there is no name for this horror, no understanding of its origins, no medicine to cure or arrest it, no precedent to compare it to, except perhaps the black plague, and little recognition of its existence by the larger, heterosexual community. No help or even human sympathy came from an administration staffed largely by people who, at best, were merely indifferent to gay issues, and at worst actively hostile.

Shortly after the *New York Times* report on the new gay cancer, Larry Kramer convened a small group of successful gay men in his apartment to chart some sort of course of action. Many in the group had already lost friends and loved ones. The most immediate need was simply to provide some measure of support for the victims. Volunteers, many of them sick themselves, were needed to perform everyday tasks that the worse off could no longer do, everything from shopping, providing transportation, preparing meals, bathing patients, changing soiled sheets, and dealing with the outside world. Above all, the aim was to alleviate the terrible sense of isolation of young men who, just a few months earlier, had been filled with life and energy. As the crisis grew, so did the need for an organization able to coordinate all the different kinds of support the community needed if it was to respond to the crisis in an effective way.

That community organization became the Gay Men's Health Crisis, Inc. (GMHC), which received its corporate charter in the summer of 1982. GMHC was initially a grassroots organization, which was not surprising since the need sprang from every segment of the population. In his 1993 book *Bearing Witness*, Philip Kayal describes an informal organization harnessing a "street level bureaucracy" in a way that effectively tied together volunteers and persons with AIDS, building on "trusted interconnecting social networks" (1993, 3). The spirit of those early days comes through in the statement of one volunteer: "We started out just to find out who was supposed to be dealing with the problems [of AIDS sufferers]. Then we realized no one was: it would have to be us" (15).

As the crisis grew, GMHC grew with it, becoming for a time the eyes and ears of the AIDS crisis for gay communities around the country. While other organizations also became important, particularly the San Francisco AIDS Foundation, GMHC was especially valuable in developing crisis intervention protocols, hot lines, and a buddy system that became models for other AIDS support groups. Some criticized GMHC's hierarchical structure and unwillingness to take on political controversy, but in retrospect this seems unfair—GMHC had enough to do just attempting to alleviate the suffering of men who were losing their jobs, getting thrown out of their apartments, being deserted by their families, and who were desperately in need of the most basic assistance. Ironically, by the time Kayal was writing in 1993, much of the early leadership and many of the original volunteers for GMHC had disappeared, themselves the victims of the crisis they were attempting to ameliorate.

As important as GMHC was as a community organization, its board was basically of a conservative temperament and not geared for political activism. It sought positive relations with the political establishment as the best way to earn acceptance and governmental support. As the death toll mounted, however, without any significant support from any level of government and barely a recognition of the disease in the mainstream press, the need for a more effective political response became increasingly apparent, at least to Larry Kramer. In March 1983 Kramer exploded in print with an article in the *New York Native*, famously titled "1,112 and Counting." No one was spared as he indicted everyone from politicians "who promise us everything for our support and promptly forget us and insult us" to "closeted gay doctors who won't come out to help us fight to rectify any of what I'm writing about."

With his polemical gifts, the article makes for compelling reading even today, as Kramer describes a Center for Disease Control so underfunded that it can't even take case histories of AIDS victims, hospitals so overcrowded and bogged down in bureaucratic rules that victims can't even get the shots of interferon that might provide some limited help, a National Institute of Health so indifferent that it wouldn't even release the very limited research funds within its control, and a New York City Health and Hospitals Corporation so unfocused that it had completely defaulted in its responsibility to educate the public and even those on the medical front lines about the disease. While Kramer indicted everyone, his target audience was the gay community itself. "If this article doesn't scare the shit out of you," he began, "we're in real trouble. . . . Our continued existence depends on just how angry you can get" (Kramer 1997, 578). Kramer's article was not without effect, setting off "the first national tremors of AIDS activism" marked by "candlelight marches in Los Angeles, San Francisco, Chicago, Houston and Manhattan by grim gay men and supporters demanding help from the federal government" (Clendinen and Nagourney 1999, 481).

Kramer was right to get mad. As important as GMHC was, it clearly could not command the resources necessary for medical research, public education to prevent transmission, and a nationally financed system of support services. That battle would need to be fought in Washington. It would not be an easy one. Jerry Falwell and the Moral Majority enjoyed important influence in the Reagan administration. A 1981 fund-raising letter signed by Falwell reveals exactly what that might mean in terms of gay issues: "Recently 250,000 homosexuals marched in the streets of San Francisco. . . . The homosexuals are on the march in this country. Please remember, homosexuals do not reproduce! They recruit! And, many of them are out after my children and your children. . . . Let me repeat, a massive homosexual revolution can bring the judgment of God upon this nation" (Williams and Retter 2003, 162).

AIDS hysteria and antigay sentiment also grew as the crisis unfolded, leading in October 1985 to the formation of what became the Gay and Lesbian Alliance against Defamation (GLAAD) to combat misrepresentations about gays in the media. (One of GLAAD's early successes was to get William Buckley to retract his proposal that all persons testing positively for HIV be tattooed on the forearm and buttocks.) In 1984, President Reagan had been reelected, carrying every state in the union except Minnesota, but not until 1986 would Reagan utter the word AIDS. Reagan's proposed budget for 1986 actually reduced the already small amount of AIDS funding by 10 percent at the same time that the number of AIDS cases was doubling (Miller 2006, 422).

One bright spot, and a hugely important one in its impact on the daily lives of many AIDS victims, was the decision by the Social Security Administration to include AIDS as a disability entitling one to Social Security benefits. This decision was the direct result of work by Virginia Apuzzo, then executive director of the National Gay and Lesbian Task Force (NGLTF), and her assistant, Jeff Levy. In a career of important achievements, this is the one of which Apuzzo is most proud (2004, 87).

While the Reagan administration was not exactly overrun with gay rights heroes, there was one exception. His name was Everett Koop, and fortunately he was also the surgeon general of the United States. Koop was first and foremost a medical professional, and once he realized the importance of condoms in slow-ing the spread of AIDS, he was resourceful and indefatigable in encouraging their use, an emphasis that put him in direct conflict with the abstinence-only views of many social conservatives. Koop's efforts, particularly an October 1986 surgeon general's report directly recommending the use of condoms and a 1988 report titled *Understanding AIDS*, undoubtedly saved lives. The latter report had been authorized by Congress. Koop became the leading spokesperson for the report, which in May and June 1988 was mailed to virtually every household in the United States (Harden 2012, 102).

The entire gay community, of course, supported education about preven-tion, funding for AIDS research, and the Social Security decision on disability; there were other areas, however, that divided the community, none creating more raw emotion than the issue of closing the bathhouses.

## The Bathhouse Controversy

John Brigham, a professor of law, has said that when it comes to the practice of social movements, "we can situate politics by its intensity as well as its place on the political spectrum" (1996, 106). For a brief period in the mideighties, no issue provoked more intense emotion within the gay community than whether bathhouses should be closed as a way of halting the spread of AIDS. Because the issue was essentially a public health question, however, it was hard to place it anywhere on the political spectrum. The question should have been a simple one: what is the evidence that closing the bathhouses will help achieve its pro-phylactic goal? Nevertheless what seemed at stake to many was nothing less than freedom itself. In the words of Victoria Harden, "the bathhouses repre-sented for many in the gay community a civil rights triumph. After years 'in the closet' for fear of losing jobs or being physically attacked, they could openly declare their gay identities and socialize in public at gay bathhouses and bars. Advocates of gay rights vehemently opposed closing the bathhouses" (2012, 109). Randy Shilts, a journalist for the *San Francisco Chronicle*, San Francisco's major newspaper, reported that one influential person in the gay community feared that the entire Castro neighborhood might be ringed by barbed wire as a quarantine measure if he wrote a planned article on the bathhouses. Shilts did come out in support of closing the bathhouses, which led him to be viewed as a traitor by many; friends would not even go out with him to restaurants "because people would come up to the table and shout at me" (Marcus 2002, 269). Cleve Jones, an important gay activist, was spat upon and called a Nazi for expressing the same view (Andriote 1999, 77). Nevertheless, as Shilts also remembered, "the more the gay leaders argued against closing the baths, the more I started coming to the point of view that, 'Gee, this is all stupid and they should be closed'" (Marcus 2002, 269).

What was a no-brainer for Shilts, however, was not the same for historian Allan Berube, who in April 1984 authored an essay titled "Don't Save Us from Our Sexuality" in which he warned, "The closing of all gay bathhouses [in San Francisco] . . . will force casual sex underground, may help spread AIDS, and will invite a wave of political repression" (Berube 2011, 65–66). He praised the few bathhouses that, among other things, were offering free condoms and safe sex literature and forums and urged the public health authorities to encourage the conversion of bathhouses to "safe sex play areas" that could become a model for other cities. Berube's suggestion did not prevent the closing of the bathhouses.

Whether closing the bathhouses was the right decision, the action was clearly aimed at regulating personal behavior. The National Gay Task Force opposed the closings as largely symbolic and perhaps even dangerous if they led to the conclusion that the AIDS epidemic had been contained (Murray 1996, 113; see 110–121 for a forceful argument against the closings). The two cities in which the most controversial bathhouse closings occurred—San Francisco and New York—were also two places where the desires of major political leaders, Mayor Dianne Feinstein in San Francisco and Mayor Ed Koch (and Governor Mario Cuomo) in New York, could be brought to bear on established gay leaders, operating in a context of mutually beneficial relationships. In San Francisco, an effort was made initially simply to ban sex in the bathhouses as a way to avoid closing them, but this proved unsatisfactory to the mayor. Finally, in October 1984, the city's director of public health ordered the closing of nine bathhouses, an order that was ultimately upheld by the judiciary. In New York, two of its most popular bathhouses, the Mineshaft and New St. Mark's, were closed, although others remained open.

What is most disturbing from a distance of three decades is simply how easy it was for the political establishment in certain communities, albeit certainly with some support from gay politicians themselves, to justify closing major gathering places of its gay citizens. What passed for public health decisions appear in the end to have been as much about politics as prevention, where straight politicians, wishing to be doing something, were able to close venues that certainly had little popular support in the straight world and were undoubtedly a reinforcement of popular stereotypes regarding homosexuals and promiscuous sex. There was no denying, of course, that the AIDS virus was transmittable through anal intercourse and that sex with multiple partners increased the risk of becoming HIV positive. What was missing was concrete evidence that closing the bathhouses, admittedly a venue where such activity occurred, would have the intended prophylactic effect, a showing that should have been incumbent on the proponents of closure, given the reasonable arguments of Berube and others and the burden closure placed on the right of gays to meet together, a constitutional right that had been affirmed even during the dark days of the fifties and sixties.

During World War II, in *Korematsu v. the United States* the Supreme Court, without taking a hard look at the evidence, simply deferred to the expertise of the military in security matters to justify the internment of Japanese residents. Similarly Judge Wallach, the New York judge hearing the case on the legality of the New York bathhouse closings, simply deferred to the public health authorities in sustaining the forced closure of the New St. Mark's Baths without any independent analysis or examination of the issue itself, noting with approval an earlier U.S. Supreme Court statement that, when it came to the proper exercise of the police power, "the judicial function is exhausted with the discovery that the relation between means and end is not wholly vain and fanciful, an illusory pretense" (*City of New York v. New St. Mark's Baths*). It is hard to imagine any legislation whose clear aim was to protect public health that could not have met the standard, as set down by the court, of "not wholly vain and fanciful."

This is not to say that Judge Wallach's opinion was wrong but does serve as a useful reminder of how difficult it can be for the judiciary to perform its constitutional function in moments of crisis and fear.

## Fighting Back

As the eighties moved forward, the bathhouse controversy receded in the face of a Supreme Court decision that shocked and united the gay community and a death that provided a new strategic opening in the fight for greater funding for AIDS research and social service support.

In July 1985 Rock Hudson announced that he had AIDS. Rock Hudson had never been a great actor but he had been a great leading man, not just gorgeous but calm and strong, playing opposite attractive, warm-hearted, slightly ditzy women, such as Doris Day in *Pillow Talk*. Hudson seemed to embody everything that a woman could want in a man and everything that a straight man might want to be. His AIDS announcement and subsequent death just a few short months later in October 1985 finally grabbed the attention of a nation. Even though Hudson in the end made no effort to hide that he was gay, for the first time AIDS began to be seen as more than a gay disease. As a *Life* magazine article put it, "Now No One Is Safe from AIDS" (Andriote 1999, 228–229).

Almost a year later, in June 1986, the U.S. Supreme Court in *Bowers v. Hardwick* voted 5–4 to uphold the conviction of a gay man, Michael Hardwick, under a Georgia statute making sodomy a criminal offense. In his concurring opinion,

Chief Justice Burger elevated antigay prejudice to a constitutionally protected tradition, citing among other things, with no sense of irony, that the Romans executed homosexuals. At a time when AIDS victims were beginning to die by the thousands, the Supreme Court in a loud and clear voice said that there was nothing wrong with antigay prejudice and indeed that discrimination was perfectly acceptable.

From a legal standpoint, *Bowers* could not have been a worse decision. It wasn't just its tone. It was a legally damaging precedent. Not long after the decision, for example, the Circuit Court for the District of Columbia upheld the FBI's right to exclude homosexuals from its ranks: "To have agents who engage in conduct criminalized in roughly one-half of the states would undermine the law enforcement credibility of the Bureau" (*Padula v. Webster*, 104). Time and again for the next seventeen years, gay rights opponents would cite *Bowers* to justify their position.

Some movement lawyers and activists questioned whether it would have been better if Hardwick's attorneys had discussed gay sex more frankly and asserted a right on the part of gay people to their own sexual practices, instead of muting gay sexual practices and simply trying to place the case in line with other privacy precedents by the Court. In the long run, such arguments might have been better, but they would not likely have changed the result in 1986, for once the Court decided that the case was about a constitutional right to engage in sodomy, not some broader privacy right or liberty interest, the die was cast. As their own statements revealed, many of these justices were marooned in a much earlier time when it came to attitudes toward homosexuality, a time during which those cases most directly involving sex were "singled out for sanction," as Mary Anne Case concluded in her study of litigation outcomes of gay rights cases (1993, 1694).

While Rock Hudson's death allowed gay lobbyists seeking more money for research and social service support from Washington to emphasize AIDS as a threat to everyone, a "de-gaying" strategy that in the end would reap important dividends, it was *Bowers v. Hardwick* that had the most immediate impact on the gay community. It became, in the words of Deborah Gould, "the last straw," igniting an anger that had been building as the AIDS death toll mounted. Just a week before the *Bowers* decision, widely publicized AIDS caseload projections for 1991 had soared to 180,000 (Gould 2009, 138). It is difficult to overestimate the impact that *Bowers* had on many who had previously remained on the sidelines.

Indifference from the political branches was one thing and not wholly unexpected, but the profound disrespect shown by the U.S. Supreme Court was truly shocking. Angry street demonstrations occurred in Boston, New York, and San Francisco in the immediate aftermath of the Supreme Court's decision.

Troy Perry, founder of the Metropolitan Community Church stated, "I've never seen our people so pissed as they are because of the Supreme Court's decision. I think we're missing the boat if we don't come out of this with a march on Washington" (Gould 2009, 143). Gould, who emphasizes the role that unconscious, nonrational motivations play in individual decisions to engage or not engage politically, believes that *Bowers* spurred the emergence of the direct-action AIDS movement by laying bare "dominant society's hatred for lesbians and gay men" and making transparent "the hopelessness of a strategy for gay rights based on being 'good' lesbians and gays" (141).

Within months of the Hardwick decision, direct-action AIDS groups emerged across the country. Angry protests erupted in major cities in the nights following the Supreme Court's decision, including a defiant "kiss-in" in Boston and a militant demonstration in San Francisco in which John Molinari, a liberal politician, was, for the first time, booed at a gay event when he suggested that the system still worked. The Lavender Hill Mob, an important protest group in New York, formed immediately in the wake of the Hardwick decision (Gould 2009, 123).

As 1987 began, Congress seemed no closer to providing adequate levels of support for research and needed social services. Equally disturbing was the apparently glacial pace of the Food and Drug Administration in evaluating potential AIDS drugs for approval. Insider lobbying by the National Gay and Lesbian Task Force and the AIDS Action Coalition was not producing results. By the end of 1986, the number of people in the United States who had died of AIDS was 24,559—the vast majority gay. Just as he had in his March 1983 article four years earlier, Kramer in March 1987 reprised his role as Cassandra in a searing speech presented at a key meeting of potential supporters of a new direct action group: "In the sobering and indelible climax of the evening, Kramer—unleashing what was by now a familiar stream of harangue and intimidation, drama and breathless hyperbole—instructed two-thirds of the audience to stand and then informed them they would probably be dead in five years" (Clendinen and Nagourney 1999, 547). Few in attendance would forget it.

The new organization, ACT UP (Aids Coalition to Unleash Power), did not take long to act. Fourteen days after Kramer's speech, 250 members of this new organization surged through the streets of New York's Financial District, where they burned in effigy the commissioner of the Food and Drug Administration, chanted "Release the Drugs," and blocked rush-hour traffic. The action produced seventeen arrests and a mention by Dan Rather on the *CBS Evening News* (Clendinen and Nagourney 1999, 547).

Many of the men who formed the leadership for ACT UP included financially successful professional men and artists who had never been in the forefront of, or even very active in, the gay rights movement. These were not men used to being ignored. Until the AIDS crisis, they had been able to live prosperous gay lives, enjoying raucous summer weekends on Fire Island and then returning to their safe lives in the city, where what Andrew Holleran has called the Age of Parties resumed. But a virus makes no class distinctions. It struck Fire Island denizens with the same ferocity as everybody else, and once that happened, remaining in the closet was no longer rational, intellectually or emotionally. As Vito Russo remarked in a 1988 interview, "AIDS has hit people on such a personal emotional level that even basically conservative gay people have been brought out of the closet and into the battle" (Marcus 2002, 293). There was also the simple fact that many of ACT UP's members were HIV positive themselves. For them, there literally was no choice.

ACT UP's goals were to force everyone to recognize the AIDS crisis for what it was, a holocaust—actually the operative word, according to ACT UP, was genocide—and to respond with the kind of urgency that a holocaust deserved. Its slogan of "Silence = Death" was both an implicit rebuke to the more traditional lobbying efforts going on in Washington and a call to arms. As a practical matter, the organization's main goal was to speed up the approval of potentially life-saving drugs and to make sure that those drugs were not prohibitively expensive. It succeeded on both counts. In the short run, its actions helped force Burroughs Wellcome, manufacturer of the only drug then approved for AIDS treatment, AZT, to lower the original price of $10,000 for a year's supply to $8,000 and then $6,500 after a September 1989 protest at the New York Stock Exchange. More significantly for the long run, its actions led the Food and Drug Administration to adopt a whole new set of more flexible policies for the approval of experimental drugs, allowing their use even if their effectiveness had not been firmly established as long as they were not unsafe.

With ACT UP's encouragement, the FDA also began to speed up its review of potential new AIDS-combating drugs, which was critical from ACT UP's standpoint since there was a strong feeling in the gay community that bureaucracy was holding up the approval of effective new drugs that could save lives immediately. This turned out not to be the case, but in October 1988 ACT UP organized a massive demonstration in front of the FDA's building in Washington. Protestors essentially closed down the building for the day, and 176 were arrested. By that time, the death toll from AIDS was closing in on 60,000 people, more than the total number killed in Vietnam. Not long after the protest, the FDA took steps to formalize the process that had been used to expedite approval of AZT, the first of the effective AIDS-fighting drugs.

Sensitizing the FDA to the human costs of delay proved particularly important during the midnineties when the use of a class of drugs called protease inhibitors (in combination with AZT) began to offer real hope to HIV-positive persons. The new drugs blocked the production of an enzyme necessary for the replication of the HIV virus. In December 1995, the FDA approved the use of the first such drug and only four months later—an unprecedented short period of time—approved two additional inhibitors (Andriote 1999, 373).

For a while in the late eighties, ACT UP seemed everywhere. One of the most controversial of ACT UP's confrontations occurred in December 1989 when protestors, many of them clearly victims in various stages of dying, handcuffed themselves to pews at St. Patrick's Cathedral one Sunday, during the performance of mass by Cardinal John O'Connor, interrupting his sermon with shouts of "Stop killing us." Scores more people were arrested outside the building. The deep anger of gays toward Cardinal O'Connor and the Catholic Church arose from the Church's opposition to AIDS prevention education and condom use, a stance many felt was leading directly to the death of young people who simply did not know that use of condoms during anal sex was truly a matter of life or death. Interestingly, while ACT UP's tactics bothered many, including some in the gay community, its emotional impact could be felt in unexpected places. Alice McGillon, a deputy police commissioner who witnessed the demonstration from inside the cathedral, recalls: "People were horrified that they did it—particularly in a very Catholic police department, but I did not think their manner was horrific: these were people who were under control. Some of the protestors were taken out on orange stretchers, and they were so frail. I could have picked them up myself. It was just one of the saddest things I've ever seen" (Kaiser 1997, 323).

ACT UP did not win universal approval within the gay community for its confrontational tactics. For one thing, ACT UP's "in your face, why are you letting us die" approach appeared directly at odds with the "de-gaying" strategy that the lobbyists in Washington had fixed on after Rock Hudson's death. The lobbyists, particularly the newly energized National Gay and Lesbian Task Force, worked hard to develop a good relationship with the Washington power structure, as did the Human Rights Campaign Fund. Theirs was an insider strategy whose weapons were tact and charm and reliable information, trusting ultimately that good relationships would help carry the day. Unfortunately, for most of the eighties, this approach was not producing the kinds of tangible results the crisis warranted. Quiet conversations in the corridors of power don't win headlines, nor do they make particularly good television. ACT UP's direct action tactics did both. They were also cathartic, creating for gay persons all across the country a means of expressing deep anger linked with concrete aims.

By early 1988, chapters of ACT UP had formed in Boston, Chicago, Los Angeles, and San Francisco, and within two years there were more than a hundred chapters worldwide. These local ACT UP groups often focused on their own issues. For example, in Los Angeles, on fifteen different occasions, ACT UP staged sit-ins and die-ins during Los Angeles County Board of Supervisors meetings, leading ultimately to the creation of a separate AIDS ward at the Los Angeles County–USC Medical Center (Kenney 2001, 178).

While ACT UP tactics could occasionally prove embarrassing and even counterproductive (blocking traffic and interrupting operas don't usually win friends in high places), in retrospect ACT UP benefited the more discreet lobbying effort both by underlining the moral urgency of providing funds to fight the disease and by letting the power structure know that the gay rights movement was watching and could make life difficult if working within the system failed. In the words of Patrick Moore, "ACT UP thanklessly provided mainstream AIDS organizations with the 'bad cop' pressure that allowed others to work within the system utilizing a 'good cop' persona" (2004, 130). Ironically, even ACT UP ultimately began to work within the system and develop valuable relationships with those in government.

One payoff occurred in July 1990 when the National Institute of Allergy and Infectious Diseases, the major national institute conducting biomedical research on AIDS, announced that, in the future, AIDS activists would be included on all of the Institute's major relevant committees. In the end, according to John-Manuel Andriote, most of the insider lobbyists he interviewed for his book on the AIDS crisis in Washington ended up feeling that ACT UP actually helped them do their work, in part because in the words of one lobbyist, "it made 'the suits' look suddenly very wonderful and reasonable" (1999, 244).

One event that did unite all elements of the gay community during this period was the 1987 march on Washington. A year in the making, the march drew more than half a million people to participate in the weekend's activities. Politically, the march clearly complemented the efforts of the more traditional lobbying groups. Even the least sensitive politicians know the power of numbers. But emotionally, the high point of the weekend was the mass demonstration (the National Civil Disobedience protest) the next day at the Supreme Court building protesting *Bowers v. Hardwick*. The protest resulted in more than 600 arrests and attracted even greater media notice throughout the country. The AIDS Memorial Quilt was also first unveiled that weekend, a tribute to lives stamped out by the disease and a visible reminder of its cost.

The 1987 march had a meaning beyond political protest. Today, one can see and hear the events of that day through You Tube's collection of film footage on the Gay Cable Television Network. Turn off the sound and it seems like a cross section of white, middle-class America—indistinguishable, for the most part, from any other celebratory parade. Turn on the sound, however, and listen to the emotion in people's voices and you guess you are hearing how blacks might have reacted to news of the Emancipation Proclamation, only here the march itself was the Proclamation.

In her interview in *Making Gay History*, Sara Boesser, just an ordinary marcher except for the fact that she had come all the way from Alaska, recalls the wonder of walking openly among so many people like herself: "I'd never seen people just be themselves on public streets in daylight. Carol [my partner] and I don't even walk in real close proximity here in Juneau. . . . I'd never been so out. I'd never felt so safe" (Marcus 2002, 299–300). The effect of the march, not unlike that of the civil rights march on Washington in 1963, was to galvanize thousands of individuals into action in their local communities. As Urvashi Vaid put it, the weekend in Washington "proved uncontainable . . . striking a chord of self-respect so deep that it could not be ignored" and leading people to return home "transformed, ready to do what seemed unimaginable a few days before" (1995, 99). The National Gay and Lesbian Task Force received a fourfold increase in calls seeking advice and organizing assistance following the march ( 99). Neither the 1979 nor 1987 march has received sufficient credit for energizing the gay rights movement. Urvashi Vaid has remarked on the importance of the former in generating an interest in national organizing and the latter for sparking activism, including the growth of ACT UP chapters, at the local level (117).

Although money was voted for medical research on HIV/AIDS in increasing amounts during the 1980s, reaching more than a billion dollars by the end of the decade, Congress did not pass a comprehensive act aimed specifically at meeting the AIDS crisis until 1990, when it enacted the Ryan White Comprehensive AIDS Resources Emergency Act (CARE). By that time, more than 120,000 Americans had died of AIDS. That Ryan White was a white Indiana teenager who had died of AIDS as a result of a bad blood transfusion served as mute tribute to the National Gay and Lesbian Task Force's "de-gaying" strategy.

Just before Ryan White died, Senator Orrin Hatch, a Utah Republican, renamed the bill in White's memory. It was something of a master stroke. After White died, his mother came to Washington to lobby for the bill, producing eighteen more sponsors for the legislation. CARE provided more than $847 million in its first two years for AIDS services nationwide, and when it was reauthorized in 1996, it provided more than $735 million for that year alone (Andriote 1999, 235–236). Lest we be inclined to lavish too much praise on Congress for finally beginning to address the needs of AIDS victims ten years into the crisis, it bears mentioning that the legislation authorized the spending of HIV funds in every state (and congressional district) in the country, hardly an act of profound courage.

In retrospect, the de-gaying strategy worked but not without cost. For one thing, it made responding to right-wing attacks that sought to use AIDS to demonize the gay community more difficult. The natural response would have been to fight the homophobia that these attacks represented, but this option was essentially unavailable for a strategy that sought to separate AIDS from other gay issues. The de-gaying strategy was also something of a cop-out as gays ceded to others the role of spokesperson. In the words of Urvashi Vaid, "We believed gay people did not carry the same moral authority or influence as public health officials, so we asked the latter to speak for us" (1995, 75). Perhaps, tactically, this was a good idea, but who had greater moral authority to represent the AIDS crisis than the community that was suffering the most? In retrospect, ACT UP's greatest role may have been to represent that moral authority. ACT UP and the NGLTF may have seemed to be working at cross-purposes, but I would argue that the judgment of history shows a greater convergence in their efforts than was visible at the time.

The insider game played by gay rights lobbyists was absolutely necessary on one battlefield that ACT UP simply couldn't engage effectively. By and large, for example, gay rights lobbyists were highly successful in fending off year after year attempts by Jesse Helms and others to require mandatory HIV testing of at-risk persons, particularly those who had been named by HIV-positive individuals as having had sexual contact with them. The NGLTF was not always able to withstand Helms's power, however, most notably when Helms was able to secure legislation preventing the Center for Disease Control from funding any activities that "promote or encourage, directly or indirectly, homosexual activities." The effect of the legislation was to severely circumscribe any programs aimed at encouraging safe sex among gay men. There were also important battles at the state level, particularly in California, where a number of ballot initiatives, including one that would have repealed nondiscrimination laws protecting HIV-positive people, were defeated only after a vigorous fight led by the gay and lesbian community.

While these political and legal battles were important and dramatic, it was the longer-term impact of how AIDS was experienced in the gay community that helped transform the gay rights movement.

## The Impact of the Crisis on Gay Life and the Equality Movement

The AIDS Crisis affected the gay rights movement in profound ways. In the words of Adam Nagourney and Dudley Clendinen, "No other movement has been so reshaped by a plague" (1999, 16).

One of the most obvious effects was organizational. The gay community had virtually no presence in Washington, D.C., when the AIDS crisis began. Even Lambda, today the leading gay rights legal organization, was still just a fledgling.

Such a situation could not continue in the face of the need for federal funding for research and social support, particularly given a religious right that had already become a major force in national politics. There was no choice but to develop a strong lobbying presence, with professionally staffed organizations capable of engaging the opposition in a continuing struggle.

Unlike the local successes of the seventies, the struggles of the eighties forced the movement into a state of permanent political battle. The National Gay and Lesbian Task Force led that fight, with the Human Rights Campaign Fund, created in 1983, giving the gay rights movement its own political action committee capable of providing important financial support to candidates standing up for the gay community. Not everyone approved the national lobbying effort. As one progressive critic of the equality movement subsequently observed, "What was once a movement became an interest group" (Rodriguez 2000, xxiv).

A second important outcome of the AIDS crisis was simply how it forced many gays to reevaluate their individual lives. In *Out of the Past*, Neil Miller describes how the young owner of a small Boston computer firm decided to abandon his evenings of anonymous sex at the Bird Sanctuary along the Charles River after two of his best friends were diagnosed with AIDS (2006, 418). Subsequently, he became involved in a romantic relationship and began questioning how to live. In the end, the young man was grateful for the change: "Sex was such a big part of our identity. You have to redefine things. I had a fairly comfortable self-image and lifestyle that has been radically altered. As it turns out, the things I have changed to are a lot more enjoyable" (418). Another individual recalled: "Until I found out I was HIV positive, I didn't want to be alive anyway because I was so depressed. And then I became HIV positive. . . . It's like, well, you always wanted to be dead, so here you go. Is this what you want? And then I changed my mind. It made me see things differently; it made me make choices differently. Making choices toward living instead of against it" (Kaiser 1997, 316–317).

Individual experiences can coalesce into collective understandings. Certainly that was true of the gay community's experience of AIDS. In the words of Andrew Sullivan, "Where bath houses once brought gay men together, now it was memorial services. The emotional and psychic bonding became the core of a new identity" (2005, 17). It is hard not to believe that the loss of so many friends and loved ones is not partly responsible for the modern equality movement's emphasis on relationship recognition and the gay family.

A third consequence of AIDS was the recognition by gay men of how the absence of any legal recognition of their relationships put them at a profound disadvantage in dealing with state agencies, hospitals, funeral homes, landlords, and parents of dying partners. At the same time, on a human level, barriers between the gay and straight communities were undoubtedly being broken down as gay and straight worlds collided in attacking a virus that affected both of them. Even at the professional level, personal contacts could achieve meaningful recognition. In 1984, Virginia Apuzzo, then a co-executive director of the National Gay and Lesbian Task Force, continually lobbied Ed Brandt, a conservative Republican doctor from Oklahoma and a key figure in Reagan's Department of Health and Human Services, to increase funding for AIDS research. Eventually, he came not only to recommend increased funding to HHS Secretary Margaret Heckler in a supposedly secret memo but is the person likely to have seen to it that the memo ended up in the hands of key players on Capitol Hill. It was, by all accounts, a pivotal moment in the budget battle that year. In the end, Brandt spent his last day on the job at HHS with Apuzzo and later sent her a note saying that he wished he had spent more time with her (Andriote 1999, 224).

The impact of the AIDS memorial quilt in raising the consciousness of the nongay community about the extent and devastation of AIDS should also not be underestimated. Americans in general are not very good at or comfortable with public mourning. The quilt, however, itself symbolic of a heroic pioneer past, was the perfect vehicle for breaking through the public consciousness. AIDS was no longer about numbers but about lost lives, usually young lives. Cleave Jones, the activist who conceived of the quilt, recalls how it provided him and other activists access to places, such as high schools, that might not otherwise have been receptive to a hearing a message about compassion and HIV prevention. "When I go to a high school," Jones said, "I'm welcomed by the teacher, usually the principal is there, with great respect, great deference, and I speak well to these kids" (Andriote 1999, 367).

The public response to the memorial quilt suggested a sympathy for AIDS victims that began to translate, in the words of Martin Duberman, into a "softening of homophobia" that was "real" and could be seen in growing (though still minority) support for gay civil rights measures (Duberman 2013, 299). Although such support is difficult to measure, it takes no great imaginative leap to understand how the suffering of the gay community and the heroic response of so many gay volunteers—often sick themselves—to alleviate the suffering of others could lead to a quiet reevaluation by many of previous prejudices.

The AIDS crisis also produced important changes in how the gay rights movement approached the courts. In her important study of Lambda's history, Ellen Andersen has noted how "opponents of gay rights forwarded the theoretical possibility of HIV transmission as a reason to deny a variety of gay rights claims," including as a reason to prevent gays from forming gay rights groups, having contact with the public, and even retaining or securing custody of or visitation with their children (Andersen 2006, 43). It also greatly complicated the efforts to reform sodomy laws at the state level. As reported by Andersen, AIDS also acted as a "critical event in refocusing Lambda's litigation priorities" as it began to receive a massive number of requests from gay men with AIDS facing homelessness, job loss, and bankruptcy as a result of their condition (44). As a theoretical legal matter, AIDS was not a gay rights issue. As an individual and practical matter, it was the preeminent gay rights issue of the eighties and early nineties.

Another result of the AIDS crisis was that, in part due to the paucity of government resources, gay communities throughout the nation had to create their own social service system. Transporting patients to the hospital, seeing that they were fed, and providing social services and companionship for the lonely and for those no longer able to handle their affairs all became, to some degree, the responsibility of an entire community. Getting political support to fight AIDS may have required a national focus, but the actual fighting of the disease, person by person, required grassroots organizing and a degree of dedication and empathy that clearly tapped the best in a large number of people, something that, though again hard to quantify, has made for a gay community powerfully aware of the benefits of mutual support and understanding. Things were materially different in poorer African American communities and neighborhoods, which often lacked the resources, connections, infrastructure, and manpower that characterized the larger, more middle-class, and increasingly less closeted white gay community.

The AIDS crisis also affected gay–lesbian relations. For most gay women, whatever differences had existed between the gay and lesbian communities seemed trivial in the face of AIDS. These bonds were made even closer by the lesbian baby boom of the late 1980s, as artificial insemination became an increasingly routine procedure, often resulting in coparenting arrangements between lesbians and gay men (Miller 2006, 420). I don't mean to imply that there were not significant differences among gays and lesbians during this period and that all tensions evaporated—they certainly continued to exist—but clearly bridges were built and relationships created that benefit the gay community and gay rights movement even today. The admiration that lesbians gained from their work was reflected in Charles Kaiser's remark that AIDS "would convert a generation of mostly selfish men, consumed by sex, into a highly disciplined army of fearless and selfless street fighters and caregivers. Since lesbians were never at much risk for infection, the depth of their commitment to this battle was even more impressive" (Kaiser 1997, 284).

While the AIDS crisis produced its share of divisions and acrimony within the gay community, ultimately its response to the crisis became a justifiable source of pride. A minister in the eighties in Provincetown, Massachusetts, Kim

Crawford Harvie, recalls that "we were so good to each other. There were ten thousand acts of kindness a week" (2010, 148). In his historic 1992 campaign speech to gay and lesbian supporters at a Los Angeles dinner, presidential candidate Bill Clinton took special note of the community's courage and compassion during a time when no one seemed to care and then concluded, "What I came here today to tell you in simple terms is, I have a vision, and you're part of it" (Clendinen and Nagourney 1999, 572).

While generalizations are difficult, it is hard not to trace both the confidence and the skill with which the gay rights community has advanced its goals in the last fifteen years and the goals themselves to lessons learned and aspirations kindled in the course of the AIDS crisis. There is one group, however, to which much of this discussion does not apply and for whom the fight against AIDS is experienced even today in a much different way.

## The African American Experience

From the vantage point of 2012, the history of the fight against AIDS is a positive one. By 1996, the introduction of protease inhibitors had begun to transform an HIV-positive result into a manageable condition, not a death sentence. It did not take long for AIDS to begin to fade as a galvanizing political issue. Some activists even began to work with the pharmaceutical companies to assist in their drug investigations. So striking was the change that, according to Richard Canning, gay writers had begun, by the late nineties, to treat the AIDS epidemic as a historical event and then to ignore it altogether (Canning 2011, 27).

The history of AIDS in the African American community, however, has not been so triumphant. Indeed, the struggle against AIDS, from its inception, has underlined, not transcended, divisions of race and class in American society, divisions that made African Americans disproportionately vulnerable to the transmission of HIV. Recent Center for Disease Control (CDC) statistics now show that gay sex accounts for only a little over half of new infections, heterosexual sex for just over a third, and injection drug use for a little more than a tenth. These statistics help explain an even more stunning set of statistics from the CDC showing the rate of infection today to be eight times higher for African Americans than whites.

A key to the fight against any communicable disease is halting its transmission. The good news about the HIV virus for the gay community was that the vehicle for its transmission among its members, unprotected sex, could, by definition, be protected against if the people spreading the virus could be reached and educated and habit patterns altered. In the case of the white gay community, particularly in the larger cities, this is exactly what happened. Even before the medical breakthroughs of 1996, the incidence of new cases had stabilized among white gay Americans. The success of that effort, however, required resources and a social infrastructure that was simply lacking in many poorer minority communities. This might not have been a huge problem had the relationship between the African American and white gay communities been closer, but gay black Americans were generally as segregated from the white world as their straight brothers and sisters.

There was another factor at work, one emphasized by Stephen Inrig in his study of HIV in North Carolina but undoubtedly relevant elsewhere. Inrig concluded that "the structure of sexual networks proved to be one of the most important biosocial factors that increased the risk of HIV transmission in North Carolina's African American community." It was simply a question of mathematics: "Since sexual networks in the state—both gay and straight—were segregated along racial lines, networks among minorities were smaller and more contained, meaning an individual within those networks was far more likely to have sexual contact with someone who had many sexual partners regardless of his own number of partners" (Inrig 2011, 22). Since a person with many sexual partners was very likely to have a sexually transmitted disease, such as syphilis or gonorrhea, and since such diseases dramatically increase the transmissibility of HIV, the vulnerability of African Americans to HIV was greatly heightened.

It wasn't just about math, however. Inrig describes how cultural factors within the African American community often led to a deep sense of shame among black gay men about their homosexuality, a shame that kept many from acknowledging their orientation even to themselves; the unfortunate result was that many gay African Americans did not consider themselves part of an at-risk population. Inrig concluded that this reluctance to acknowledge the presence of the disease meant that there was a relatively short interval between diagnosis and death and therefore a much shallower sense of a community crisis. "Their more rapid demise," Inrig speculates, "may have prevented their loved ones from connecting individual illnesses to larger trends; too few people in a position of knowledge could recognize a collective threat or generate a collective response on their behalf" (2011, 19–20).

One strategy that might have made a real difference in African American communities and elsewhere would have been a mandatory testing program. Here we come up against an important divide, for almost all gay organizations strongly resisted any testing that might reveal the names of HIV-positive persons. For many, any mandatory testing program would be the first step toward quarantine. Talk of concentration camps and comparisons to Nazi Germany fueled an intensely emotional debate. Part of the problem was that mandatory testing was just what social conservatives like William Buckley were advocating. Buckley even went so far as to advocate tattooing HIV-positive persons on the buttocks, a suggestion he later apologized for.

Nevertheless, most public health professionals also believed that some sort of testing would be enormously beneficial. There were just too many HIV-positive people who, unaware of their condition, were infecting other equally oblivious sexual partners. Whether mandatory testing would have worked as well as many professionals hoped—there were fears expressed that testing would actually be harmful by driving the most at-risk persons farther underground—the lack of such testing closed off the one avenue that might have helped the African American community realize the extent to which HIV was affecting its own members. This is not to say that the deepest fears of some in the gay community were totally fanciful. In 1986, when irrational fears regarding AIDS were at their height in the straight world, Californians even voted on a Proposition 64 that would have quarantined thousands of AIDS victims and forced thousands more HIV-positive persons to leave their jobs. Although the measure lost, proponents had had no problem securing the 683,000 signatures that put the initiative on the ballot in the first place.

Whatever preventative effect mandatory testing might have had, AIDS would still have been a health crisis of incalculable proportions. Even today, there is no known cure for AIDS but instead an effective set of medical strategies for dealing with it. The disease has caused and continues to cause immense human suffering.

## The Human Cost

By 2004, more than half a million Americans had died of AIDS. We have discussed AIDS, as we must, in macro terms, citing numbers and discussing political and social consequences. To understand and feel this story in its most human dimensions, however, we need the help of gifted writers. Two of the best, in this author's view, are Andrew Holleran and Christopher Bram. In 1988, Holleran published a remarkable set of essays that were reissued as *Chronicle of a Plague, Revisited* in 2008. In the introduction to the volume, Holleran writes of his own experience rereading the original:

> It was like opening a tomb to come upon quotes from people whose voices, scattered through the essays, I'd not heard in more than twenty years. I'd forgotten my roommate's telling me, 'I don't like looking at pictures of dead people.' I'd forgotten a friend saying, 'I wasn't doing anything everyone else wasn't.' Or another friend whispering to me at the

baths, the germs don't need me. But it was these voices of the dead that summoned up for me that awful time when no one could see the way out (Holleran 2008, 2).

Many of Holleran's themes are universal—death, lost friendships, fate, memory—but always a by-product of the need to observe and report, to somehow come to terms with the unimaginable, when sex itself became lethal and discretion a matter of survival.

Yet this is still only part of the story, for another universal theme is how life goes on even in the midst of tragedy, a thought captured by Christopher Bram in his beautiful 1992 essay "Perry Street, Greenwich Village," in which he quarrels with the depiction of the West Village as a ghost town and marvels at how "everyday and commonplace" gay life goes forward: "Attractive men still notice each other on the street, although they're not as quick to go home together as they once were; there's more conversation nowadays, more flirtation" (2009, 12). Bram then offers an observation suggestive of the ways in which the AIDS crisis politicized life for all gay people: "On our stoop, we continue to talk about old movies and Motown's greatest hits, but we also talk about AIDS and politics. We run into each other at memorial services . . . and protest rallies. I was startled to realize how 'in the life' I am, and how political that life has become" (13).

If Bram's feelings are at all representative, then perhaps the most telling consequence of the AIDS crisis was simply how it forced the realization for many that political and legal outcomes mattered and that only direct engagement could bring about desired results. There were no guarantees of success, but indifference meant failure. The stage was set for a new era of activism.

# PART TWO

# The Struggle for Legal Equality (1993 to the Present)

In the early 1990s, two unexpected events occurred that helped set the stage for the major political and legal battles of the next twenty years.

The first event was the election of Bill Clinton as president in 1992. With Clinton's election and Democratic control of both houses of Congress, gay rights groups had every reason to expect President Clinton would easily redeem his promise, made during the campaign, to allow gays to serve openly in the military. A federal law banning discrimination in employment on the basis of sexual orientation also seemed a real possibility. How could they not succeed when Clinton's inauguration had occasioned the first-ever gay inaugural ball at the National Press Club, where more than 1,500 gathered to sing, dance, and celebrate, and when the newly elected president had sent a letter to the National Gay and Lesbian Task Force (although not appearing in person) thanking them for their support in the recent campaign?

The second event was the shocking decision by the Hawaii Supreme Court (*Baehr v. Lewin*) in which it treated the prohibition of same-sex partners from marrying as a form of gender discrimination under the Hawaii Constitution. With the Hawaii decision, suddenly it seemed that marriage—this most cherished of social institutions—might become a reality for same-sex couples in at least one state. Remarkably, these two goals were coming within apparent range only a few years after the Supreme Court's decision in *Bowers v. Hardwick* had reaffirmed the right of states to make homosexuality and felony synonymous.

With these two events, the legal, political, and social struggle for the integration of gays into American life began in earnest. The goal was no longer just freedom but true equality. It would no longer be enough simply to meet without fear of arrest or to know that their basic acts of intimacy were no longer criminal. (By 1992, anti-sodomy laws were rarely enforced even in the decreasing number of states that had them.) Now, the goals would be the right to have gay emotional relationships and ties treated with equal respect, the right for gays to serve openly in the military, the right for gays to be free from discriminatory treatment in all phases of life, the right for gay couples to walk the streets without fear, and the right for young gay persons to enjoy an accepting and safe educational environment.

In this part, I describe the struggle to achieve each of these goals. I have arranged the material covering the goals of the modern gay rights movement into separate chapters because each of these objectives has had its own special dynamic, and each has posed different legal and political problems. The danger of this approach is missing the forest in the trees. In an effort to minimize this difficulty, I begin this part II with two introductory chapters. The first, chapter 5, traces three major developments that I believe are broadly responsible for the remarkable success of the equality movement. Chapter 6 then examines some of the larger issues that divide those favoring and opposing gay rights, focusing especially on the issue of whether gayness is a matter of choice and whether there are legitimate public reasons for opposing gay rights. These two chapters provide context for the discussion of the individual gay rights goals that follow in chapters 7–11. Collectively, these chapters tell a remarkable story, with judicial decisions and legislative enactments playing a crucial role in the daily life of gay men and lesbians: at home, school, the workplace, the streets, and family life.

In considering the events of the past twenty years (or even forty years, for that matter) it bears mentioning that the term "gay rights movement" is misleading to the extent that it conveys the sense of a centralized movement inexorably going forward along a variety of preconceived fronts. Opponents of gay rights, even Supreme Court justices, abet this misconception by introducing the specter of an ominous-sounding "gay agenda" as if there were some secret plan directed from a central headquarters buried beneath a remote mountaintop. Nothing could be further from the truth. There is no secret plan and certainly no central headquarters, although it is fair to say that the movement, when viewed as a totality, has been led and its goals chosen by a predominantly white, educated, middle-class leadership.

The "movement" is best viewed as a series of efforts to achieve specific goals—involving different strategies, facing different obstacles, fought in different fora, and achieving different results, united only by the common aspiration of integrating gay citizens into our civic and social life on equal terms with everyone else. Separating these different goals into separate chapters more accurately reflects the true nature of what the gay rights movement has been all about. Interestingly, that aspiration toward equality and integration—the defining quality of the "movement"—is not shared by all within the LGBT community. We examine those dissident voices in the final chapter of part II.

# 5

# Three Key Developments

In a constitutional democracy, success comes in three sometimes interrelated ways: by convincing one's fellow citizens; by persuading lawmakers; and by resorting to litigation to vindicate constitutional and legal rights.

The extraordinary way in which gay rights advocates have been winning the battle for the hearts and minds of their fellow citizens is a key development of the past two decades. The fact is that no longer is there any issue involving gay rights, including same-sex marriage, in which a majority of the nation does not support the gay rights position. Perhaps even more extraordinary is that, for the first time, polls indicate that a majority of Americans do not find homosexuality morally objectionable.

We do not, however, live in ancient Greece. We are a republic and, as such, we elect representatives to enact laws. In a functioning democracy, there should be a correlation between public opinion and the laws that are enacted, but few would dispute that public opinion often plays second fiddle to powerful special interests and the perceived needs of career politicians to protect themselves and curry favor with the most ideological of their constituents. In the late nineties, for example, there was a groundswell of support for providing protection for gays under federal hate crime legislation, but nothing happened in the face of Republican opposition. Also, public opinion has for decades approved of legislation to protect gays from employment discrimination, but no such employment legislation at the federal level has passed.

So winning hearts and minds, though important, is not a guarantee of success. It must be translated into political power, and political power requires engaging in the political process, which in turn means continuing to engage with the two major political parties. It is not surprising then that a second key development during this period has been the way in which the two major parties have aligned themselves with pro- and anti-gay-rights forces. That pro-cess did not begin in the early nineties but it certainly accelerated at that time. Today, it is not going too far, particularly at the national level, to characterize the Democratic Party as the party of gay rights and the Republican Party as the opponent, although one senses a growing rebellion against reflexive anti-gay-rights positions within the GOP.

A third development has been the key role that litigation has played at both the state and federal levels in shaping the gay rights movement. I cover much of this litigation in the separate chapters examining the individual goals of the movement. I also reserve examination of the litigation over same-sex marriage for part III. In this chapter, I examine two critical decisions by the U.S. Supreme Court, which represent key victories in the gay rights movement, and some other important decisions as well.

## Winning Hearts and Minds

In June 2013, the Pew Research Center released the results of a survey under-taken a month earlier showing dramatic changes among the general public over a remarkably brief period. Whereas a 2004 *Los Angeles Times* poll had revealed that 60 percent of Americans would be upset—and 33 percent *very* upset—if they had a gay or lesbian child, those percentages in the 2013 Pew survey had dropped to 40 percent and 19 percent, respectively, meaning that in less than a decade, one in five Americans had decided that having a gay child was not really a big deal after all. The importance of this development for gays them-selves cannot be overestimated. In a second Pew Center survey of attitudes of self-identifying gays, lesbians, and bisexuals, the importance of family reaction was a consistent theme of those describing the coming out process, for, quite naturally, the greatest fear is losing the love and support of those closest to you.

There is no question that members of the LGBT community are increas-ingly open about their sexuality and feel increasingly accepted. According to a December 2012 *USA Today*/Gallup Poll survey, more than three out of four people from the LGBT community were generally open with others about their orientation. More than 90 percent of those polled responded that the larger society had become more accepting in recent years.

In the 2013 Pew survey described above, 77 percent of gay men and 71 per-cent of gay women said that all or most of the important people in their lives are aware of their orientation. As more gays have come out to families, friends, and co-workers, negative stereotypes about gays have become harder to main-tain. Randy Boyd said it as well as anyone when he stated: "The more openly gay people there are, the harder it is for people to hate us. Because you can't hate faces. You can hate organizations. You can hate 'them,' but when you realize that 'them' is my son or my sister or my next-door neighbor, then it's hard to hate" (Marcus 2002, 414). Senator Rob Portman, Republican from Oregon, was simply acting like countless others when he announced that he was switching his position to support same-sex marriage shortly after his son revealed to him that he was gay. There is, in fact, a strong statistical correlation between having a close friend or family member who one knows is gay and support for gay rights. The Pew survey of the general public's attitudes toward same-sex marriage found that more than two-thirds (68 percent) of those who reported knowing a lot of gay men or lesbians favored same-sex marriage, while only one-third (32 percent) of those who reported not knowing any gay or lesbian supported it. All of this might help explain why, for example, Gallup Poll surveys showed an increase in support for same-sex marriage nationally between 1993 and 2010 from 27 percent to 53 percent.

The changing attitudes of the public on same-sex marriage may also reflect something even deeper, for fully 60 percent of the American public now says that homosexuality should be accepted by society (up from 47 percent a decade ago), and only 31 percent say it should be discouraged (down from 45 percent a decade ago); 54 percent report having a favorable opinion of gay men (up 16 percent from a decade ago) and 58 percent of lesbians (up 19 percent from a decade ago). The increasing acceptance of homosexuality in general has undoubtedly been influenced by the remarkable changes in how gay characters and gay love are portrayed in the media and mainstream America. As a result of movies like *Brokeback Mountain* with its Academy Award–winning portrayal of the relationship of two gay cowboys and television programs like *Queer Eye for the Straight Guy*, whose cast was invited in 2004 to throw out the first ball at Fenway Park for a regular-season Sunday afternoon game, gays now occupy a place in the national consciousness inconceivable even twenty years ago.

There are few celebrities more popular than Ellen DeGeneres, and the coming out of her character in 1997 in *Ellen* was a huge event, watched by tens of millions and talked about by many more. The mere fact that a major network had been willing to bring forward an important and sympathetic lesbian character was itself mute testimony to the new era that had begun. The fact that Ellen herself came out as a real person at the same time turned a television moment into a moment for the entire world. One forty-seven-year-old gay man participating in the 2013 Pew survey commented, "Ellen DeGeneres is my hero! She has done more for this country than many presidents have." While *Ellen*, the television program, lasted only one more season with Ellen as an openly lesbian character, it broke a barrier that already seems long in the past. The program *Glee* took another important step in 2009, not only featuring a sympathetic gay character but showing exactly the kinds of a prejudice that a gay teenager had to navigate. *Modern Family*, one of the nation's most popular television shows—Governor Mitt Romney confessed it was his favorite program—has featured Cameron and his partner Mitchell seeking to adopt a second child. What is most remarkable is how little controversy these and many other programs have occasioned. The television world is, in fact, becoming one in which Ozzie and Harriet can coexist with Ozzie and Ozzie and Harriet and Harriet.

In addition to the mass media, another key reason for changing public attitudes has to do with the literally thousands of organizations of all kinds whose purpose is to defend gay persons from unfair treatment and enhance the quality of gay life. Although their purpose is often to provide internal support for gays, they end up engaging every element of straight society, collectively comprising a de facto army: articulate, resourceful, and determined.

For law, the leading organization has been the Lambda Legal Defense and Education Fund, initially organized by a group of gay lawyers in New York in the early seventies but now a multi-million-dollar organization with a thirty-person legal department, including support staff, as well as a separately staffed Education and Public Affairs Department. In addition to Lambda, other key legal organizations include the National Center for Lesbian Rights (a public interest law firm founded in 1977), the Gay Rights Project of the American Civil Liberties Union, Gay and Lesbian Advocates and Defenders (a legal rights organization focusing on the New England states), and the Servicemembers Legal Defense Network, which focused, during the era of Don't Ask, Don't Tell, on defending gay servicemen and -women.

Litigators themselves are very aware of the subtle role that public opinion can play in influencing judicial outcomes. To cite just one example, lawyers for Lambda, according to Ellen Andersen, spent significant resources to educate the public in New Jersey about same-sex marriage in the year before it filed suit claiming same-sex marriage to be a right under New Jersey's constitution, including holding town meetings across the state (Andersen 2006, 214). The New Jersey Supreme Court in *Lewis v. Harris* ultimately held that gays were entitled to civil unions but not gay marriage.

Politically, the gay rights movement, through the Human Rights Campaign (HRC) and Victory Fund, has developed an important national political presence—the HRC for lobbying and fund-raising, the Gay and Lesbian Victory Fund to support gay candidates. In its fiscal year 2011, the HRC had a budget of $38 million and a staff of 179 people. One organization that has played a pivotal and colorful role in the history of gay rights is the National Gay and Lesbian Task Force, a history that John D'Emilio sees as unique in the way that the organization has reinvented itself at different times for different purposes under different leadership, sometimes emphasizing national issues like federal funding for AIDS research and support, sometimes more involved at the state and local level with antiviolence and local organizing projects (see D'Emilio 2002, 99–119). On the state level, the Empire State Agenda (New York), MassEquality (Massachusetts), and Equality California advocate broadly for gay rights, seeking to change public opinion and, when appropriate, lobby their respective legislatures. Equality Foundation seeks to build strong statewide organizations throughout the nation.

The national organizational infrastructure reaches far beyond legal and political concerns. Since 1985 GLAAD (the Gay and Lesbian Alliance against Defamation) has been watching over the media to guard against negative stereotyping of gays and the gay community. It too has become a major force in protecting the gay community. GLSEN (the Gay, Lesbian, and Straight Education Network) supports and encourages the creation of Gay–Straight Alliances in public schools throughout the nation. PFLAG (Parents, Families, and Friends of Lesbians and Gays) provides additional support for gay youth and gives parents struggling with their child's homosexuality an important resource. SAGE (Services and Advocacy for GLBT Elders), a national organization founded in 1978, with numerous affiliates throughout the country, acts as both a social services support network for elderly gays and an advocacy group; in 2005 it became the first official gay community delegate at the White House Conference on Aging. The Family Equality Council provides a national voice and source of support for gay families throughout the country. Pride at Work seeks to connect the union movement and gay rights concerns of wage workers, including discrimination protection in collective bargaining contracts and reduction of homophobia among co-workers. Out and Equal Workplace also advocates for equality in the workplace; its 2011 annual Workplace Summit, cosponsored by scores of major corporations, drew over 2,600 participants in 2011. The Metropolitan Community Church, started by Troy Perry in his Los Angeles living room before Stonewall, has inspired the creation of more than 250 independent congregations worldwide. There are now more than 120 gay community centers throughout the country, with an umbrella organization, CenterLink, providing important support.

Perhaps just as important in influencing public opinion are the countless community and professional organizations ranging from gay bowling and softball teams, to local HIV-AIDS support groups. There is hardly a professional group that doesn't have its own gay organization. The National Lesbian and Gay Journalists Association, to cite just one example, includes a score of chapters throughout the country.

In summary, the increasingly favorable view of gays and increasing support for gay issues have resulted from the convergence of many factors, but certainly three of the most important are the increased unwillingness of gay persons to remain in the shadows, the positive depiction of gays in the media, and the vast organizational infrastructure that now protects and enhances gay life and promotes gay visibility in so many ways.

Winning hearts and minds is one thing. Translating them, in our complex politics, into tangible change is something quite different, particularly when one major party has generally come to stand for gay rights and the other against them.

## The Parties Choose Sides

In 1992, speaker after speaker at the Republican National Convention seemed to demonize a culture that would even consider the idea of gay rights. Not only did the convention do the incumbent president, George Herbert Walker Bush, little good, but it marked a fork in the road for the GOP that arguably led to the reelection of an embattled Democratic president twenty years later, for, according to the 2012 exit polls, gay voters may well have made the difference in many of the swing states that produced President Obama's margin of victory. Nationally, the polls showed that while straight voters were evenly divided between the president and Mitt Romney, the 5 percent of the electorate who identified themselves as LGBT gave the president more than three-quarters of their vote, with many, as noted, in important swing states (Cohen 2012, A20).

Politically, the major story of the modern gay rights struggle is undoubtedly how the movement has tied its fortunes to those of the Democratic Party. In one sense, this development is not surprising, for the gay rights movement has been engaging in a continuing dialogue with the Democratic Party on gay rights for forty years. Sometimes the relationship has been warmer than others. Slowly but surely, however, the gay community has become family within the Democratic Party. The Gay Activists Alliance put pressure on liberal politicians, almost exclusively Democratic, to support gay rights initiatives because they felt that Democrats would at least listen to them, and by 1980, the party's national platform had issued a vague but pathbreaking endorsement of gay rights.

Clearly, with its historic championing of minorities and its emphasis on equality, the Democratic Party was a natural point of focus for the gay rights movement. Yet the Republican Party might have also provided a solid ideological foundation for the movement had the party itself been more receptive. The basic demands of the modern gay rights struggle are, after all, about the freedom to serve one's country, hold a job without fear, lead a violence-free life, and marry whom one wishes. None of these goals asks the federal government (or state governments, for that matter) for a dime. What has kept Republicans from embracing gay rights has nothing to do with party ideology and everything to do with the Republican Party's perceived need to appease the religious right at every turn when any issue of gay rights is on the table.

The turning point in the gay movement's relationship with both parties can be traced to the watershed moment at the 1992 Republican National Convention when Pat Buchanan declared a culture war on liberal ideas, including gay rights. It wasn't just his words but his whole demeanor that genuinely alarmed gays of all political stripes. Here on display at a major party's national convention was a rancor and anger not just over issues but obviously directed at gays as people; for many it was an attitude that could not help but recall the darkest days of the fifties and sixties. Buchanan's speech might not have been so significant had it been an anomaly at the convention, but it wasn't. Speaker after speaker echoed his themes. No one, including President Bush, made an effort to repudiate or even soften them. The convention was a disaster for the Republicans. The public understood what it had been seeing, and certainly the gay community did as well. According to gay activist David Mixner, "support [for Clinton] crystallized overnight with Pat Buchanan's speech. It created a voting bloc and tripled the money" (Bawer 1993, 52). Interestingly, Ross Perot, a serious Independent candidate who participated in all of the televised debates, made no attempt to court the gay vote, asserting at one point that he would not hire gays or lesbians for his cabinet because the "American people wouldn't like it." What nation he actually thought gay citizens hailed from he did not indicate.

As noted in the introduction, Clinton's election promised real change, but that change went largely undelivered; it also resulted in the passage of two damaging pieces of federal legislation: the Defense of Marriage Act and Don't Ask, Don't Tell. From 1992 on, the Republican Party has consistently adopted anti-gay-rights positions, almost always in the name of protecting traditional families and institutions. In 1993, to cite one example, Senate minority leader Bob Dole warned the newly elected President Clinton in private discussions that the Republicans' job, in his view, was to see that the president failed, so he could be replaced; it was not to make deals with him. At the same time, Dole told Clinton that he intended to keep the gays in the military issue alive precisely because he believed that it trapped Clinton "on weak ground" (Branch 2009, 7).

This strategy did not help Senator Dole when he ran against President Clinton in 1996, but it might have been key to the reelection of President George W. Bush in 2004 against Senator John Kerry. In that year, as part of a deliberate strategy to bring out its conservative base, which had extreme misgivings about some of the president's domestic policies, the Republican Party spearheaded drives to put constitutional amendments banning same-sex marriage on the ballot in eleven states, including Ohio. Had Senator Kerry captured Ohio, he would have won the election. He didn't, however, and many observers in Ohio asserted that the huge turnout of evangelicals in Ohio was the direct result of the ballot question on same-sex marriage, which passed with 62 percent of the vote (Rosenberg 2008, 378). The ballot strategy may also have tipped the balance for Republican U.S. Senate candidates in Oklahoma, South Dakota, and Kentucky (see Rosenberg 2008, 373–374).

Democrats, however, did not retreat from their gay rights positions as a result of the 2004 election. The election of President Obama in 2008 in fact only seemed to underscore the partisan divisions that gay rights aroused, even outside the marriage question. Partisan votes in Congress on the inclusion of gay-bias crimes in the hate crimes legislation of 2009 and the repeal of Don't Ask, Don't Tell in 2010 attest to the depth of that divide.

Legislation adding sexual orientation to the list of hate crime motivations was signed into law by President Obama in October 2009. One might have thought this would be the least contentious of all the gay rights issues, particularly considering the overwhelming bipartisan majority by which hate crimes legislation (which identifies and targets hate crimes based on racial and other forms of bias) had originally passed. Nevertheless, only 3 Republican senators out of 40 supported the measure, 28 opposed it, and 9 didn't vote on the measure at all. In the House of Representatives, the vote was a little more mixed, primarily because the legislation was attached to a military appropriations bill that contained provisions to which some liberal Democrats objected. The final vote in the House was 281–146: 237 Democrats supported the bill (15 opposed it), and 131 Republicans opposed it (44 Republicans supported it). A similar result occurred on the final vote that repealed Don't Ask, Don't Tell, with 235 out of 250 Democrats voting for repeal and 160 out of 175 Republicans voting against it. In the Senate, 8 Republicans supported repeal, a higher number than expected, but still well below the 31 Republicans who voted against it.

There was at least one time when a sufficient number of Republicans to make a difference stood up to their leadership to defend a gay rights initiative. It occurred in 1998 when the Republican leadership attempted to overturn President Clinton's executive order prohibiting a person's sexual orientation from playing any role in federal employment decisions. For weeks, during the summer of that year, Tom DeLay, then majority whip in the House of Representatives, Senator Jesse Helms, and the religious right had filled the air with antigay rhetoric. Though the campaign had the support of the Republican congressional leadership (Trent Lott and Newt Gingrich), on August 4, sixty-three House Republicans joined the Democratic minority to defeat what was called the Hefley Amendment, which would have reversed President Clinton's executive order. Among those speaking against the amendment were Dana Rohrabacher

(R-CA) and Tom Bliley (R-VA), both of whom had 100 percent positive ratings from the American Conservative Union.

Occasionally, a responsive Republican could present a real dilemma for gay political organizations in deciding whom to support. The most famous instance involved Alphonse D'Amato, a two-term U.S. senator from New York, a conservative, and a genuinely annoying person (he seemed to relish that attribute). D'Amato, however, had been helpful on almost all gay rights issues, so the Human Rights Campaign decided to endorse him over Congressman Chuck Schumer (who won the election). In the words of its then executive director, Elizabeth Birch, "people were apoplectic over this decision"; "we lost some major donors who were furious with us" (Marcus 2002, 411).

Even President Obama's overwhelming gay support in 2012 was by no means a sure thing. With Obama's victory in 2008 and a strongly Democratic Congress to work with, the gay community's initial hopes for success in 2009 on its major issues had been extremely high. Six months into Obama's presidency, however, many felt betrayed. Urvashi Vaid captured the mood when she accused the president in June 2009 of having made "a cold calculation to throw gay people under the bus by opposing same-sex marriage, by inviting Rick Warren to the Inauguration, by opposing elimination of Don't Ask, Don't Tell, by treating us as trinkets and tokens" (Vaid 2009). Things did not improve in the ensuing months. By February 2010, the cover for that month's issue of the *Advocate* pictured a half-shadowed, half-lit portrait of an unsmiling Obama with the word "Nope?" running in large letters along the bottom, a play on the disappointed hopes of so many.

The perception of Obama began to change when, in April 2010, he issued an executive order requiring all hospitals receiving federal aid to allow visitation of gay patients by their partners, but the major breakthrough occurred at the end of 2010 when the president was able to push through repeal of Don't Ask, Don't Tell in favor of open military service, a development I examine in more detail in part III. Nevertheless, as 2011 began, the administration remained committed to defending the Defense of Marriage Act in court, and the president himself remained on the fence respecting same-sex marriage.

The definitive history of how and why the administration and President Obama came to reverse these positions has yet to be written. The common perception is that the vice president's clear endorsement of same-sex marriage during a television news show forced the president's hand. If it had not been discussed beforehand and was truly a spontaneous declaration, the vice president ultimately did the president a favor, for it was Obama's subsequent endorsement of gay marriage coupled with the administration's decision not to continue to defend the constitutionality of the Defense of Marriage Act which cemented his support within the gay community.

Population statistics partially explain why each party is likely to maintain its current stance for the foreseeable future. Actual LGBT numbers are a matter of considerable debate. Gary Gates, a scholar at the Williams Institute of UCLA Law School, has estimated the gay and transgender community at 3.8 percent of the American population, and this seems a reasonable percentage, suggesting a self-identifying gay population of roughly 12 million people, located primarily in metropolitan areas (Gates 2012, 693). It is an interesting number in that it is large enough, particularly in states with lots of electoral votes, and with constituents affluent enough, to explain why the Democratic Party now regards the gay community as a not insignificant part of its voting and financial base but still small enough to suggest why the Republican Party has been unwilling to risk sacrificing any portion of its much larger base of social conservatives.

The alignment of the parties on gay rights has been as important at the state as at the national level. Nothing shows that more clearly than the configuration of states that have passed and failed to pass legislation protecting gays from employment (and sometimes other forms) of discrimination. Twenty-one states currently have such laws. Each of them voted for President Obama in 2008 and 2012. Put another way, with the exception of Indiana and Montana, which provide protection for public employees, no state that voted for Mitt Romney has a state law protecting against discrimination on the basis of sexual orientation. Every state that allows same-sex marriages or civil unions also voted for President Obama twice.

## Finding a Friend on the Supreme Court

As important as President Obama has proved to be for gay rights, one Republican may have been even more important. His name is Justice Anthony Kennedy, the author of three landmark Supreme Court opinions, two of which—*Romer v. Evans* (1996) and *Lawrence v. Texas* (2003)—we now discuss, reserving the third for part III.

In *Romer*, gay rights advocates successfully challenged Amendment 2 to the Colorado State Constitution, which prohibited the passage of any laws protecting gays from discrimination and had the effect of repealing gay rights ordinances already enacted in Denver, Boulder, and Aspen. The citizens of Colorado had enacted Amendment 2 by ballot initiative in 1992. The state was not unusual in simultaneously having a statewide majority against gay rights but more tolerant municipalities in which gays, by their larger presence, could organize successfully to obtain nondiscrimination legislation, which is precisely what had happened in Colorado. In *Romer*, Amendment 2 was challenged on the ground that it violated the Equal Protection Clause of the Fourteenth Amendment.

The Court in *Romer* might have declared that, to pass constitutional muster, laws discriminating against gays, like laws discriminating against blacks
and women, were subject to much greater scrutiny than were ordinary laws.
Had it done so, *Romer* would have been a far-reaching decision, pointing toward
broad constitutional protection for gay rights goals, including marriage. That,
however, was not the Court's decision. Rather, the Court simply said that the
amendment served no legitimate state purpose because its sole goal was to put
a class of citizens in an unequal position vis-à-vis all other persons. In other
words, legislation intended solely to make one class of persons less equal than
others was so arbitrary that it did not meet the most minimal standard—a rational basis—that any piece of legislation is required to meet under the Equal Protection Clause.

*Romer* was still an important psychological victory. For the first time in its
history, the Court had implicitly found the gay community worthy of constitutional protection. Just as important, *Bowers v. Hardwick* now had to contend
with a new kid on the block, one that allowed gay rights advocates to point to
their own Supreme Court precedent to say that gays are in fact worthy of having
their rights recognized, that they too had a right to have their views heard on
terms equal with everyone else, and that they too had the same opportunity for
success.

Unlike *Romer*, *Lawrence v. Texas* (a 6–3 decision) went to the heart of gay
sexual practice. In *Bowers v. Hardwick* the Court had held that states could
criminalize sodomy. While the statute at issue in *Bowers* made no distinction
between heterosexual and homosexual acts of sodomy, the Texas statute in *Lawrence* criminalized only homosexual sodomy. Thus, *Lawrence* could have been
decided on simple equal protection grounds since *Romer* had made clear that
statutory distinctions based on nothing more than animus to homosexuality
violated the Equal Protection Clause. This was, in fact, the position that Justice
Sandra O'Connor took in her concurring opinion. For her, as for the majority
in *Romer*, legislative distinctions had to be based on more than, in her words,
"mere moral disapproval of an excluded group" (*Lawrence*, 585). The majority
opinion, however, written by Justice Kennedy and joined by Justices Ginsburg,
Breyer, Souter, and Stevens, seemed to rely primarily not on the Equal Protection
Clause but on the liberty interest of the Fourteenth Amendment's Due Process
Clause. As a practical matter, sodomy statutes had not been widely enforced for
years. The fact, however, that the Supreme Court had given these statutes constitutional sanction in *Bowers*, in effect permitting the state to criminalize normal gay sexual activity, hung ominously over every legal and political argument
in favor of gay rights. After all, what right did a group have to claim protection or
recognition when their basic act of intimacy was criminal? *Lawrence* blotted out

that line of argument because the majority held that homosexuals were entitled to respect for their private choices.

Sometimes the Supreme Court effectively overturns a precedent by simply ignoring it. Even when the Court formally acknowledges that it is overruling a prior decision, it often does so quietly and even with respect, explaining how changed circumstances or difficulties in application have rendered the earlier decision no longer worthy of effect. No such excuses were offered for *Bowers v. Hardwick.* "Bowers was not correct," wrote Justice Kennedy, "when it was decided, and it is not correct today. It ought not to remain binding precedent. *Bowers* should be and is now overruled" (*Lawrence*, 578).

The tone of Justice Kennedy's opinion might well have been an unconscious response to the gratuitously demeaning, homophobic tone of *Bowers v. Hardwick*, which had conflated homosexual conduct with incest and adultery. Writing for the majority in *Hardwick*, Justice Byron White, a former professional football player and Kennedy appointee, had asserted, "it would be difficult, except by fiat, to limit the claimed right to homosexual conduct while leaving exposed to prosecution adultery, incest and other sexual crimes even though they are committed in their home" (*Bowers*, 195–196).

This was the mindset that *Lawrence* rejected. While Justice Kennedy disclaimed any intent in *Lawrence* to give "formal recognition" to any relationship that homosexual persons seek to enter, the logic of his reasoning belied his disclaimer when he spoke of the deeper relationship which intimate sex often signifies: "When sexuality finds overt expression in intimate conduct with another person, *the conduct can be but one element in a personal bond that is more enduring.* The liberty protected by the Constitution allows homosexual persons the right to make this choice" (*Lawrence*, 567; my italics). The Court acknowledged the religious convictions that led many to oppose gay marriage but quoted from an earlier Court decision: "Our obligation is to define the liberty of all, not to mandate our own moral code" (*Lawrence*, 572)

The tears flowed among onlookers as Justice Kennedy read his opinion to a hushed audience. For the first time, the Court—and not just any court—was recognizing the right of gays to the same measure of privacy and dignity as their fellow citizens: "The petitioners are entitled to respect for their private lives. The State cannot demean their existence or control their destiny by making their private sexual conduct a crime. Their right to liberty under the due process clause gives them the full right to engage in their conduct without the intervention of the government" (*Lawrence*, 578).

The Supreme Court rarely issues an apology. It came close to doing so in *Lawrence.* If *Bowers v. Hardwick* had been the gay community's *Dred Scott* decision, as Thomas Stoddard, then the executive director of the Lambda Legal Defense and Education Fund had called it, then *Lawrence* was its *Brown v. Board of Education*. Gays were no longer presumptive criminals. As important as *Lawrence* was to the gay community, it needs be added that sodomy reform was always both a gay and heterosexual issue. Indeed, there were never more than ten states that had allowed heterosexual sodomy but prohibited homosexual sodomy (Andersen 2006, 61). From a legal perspective, *Lawrence* still left open some key questions, most importantly, how would the Court decide cases involving disparate treatment of gays and heterosexuals in which the liberty/privacy interest was not at issue?

The answer was not long in coming. Matthew Limon, an eighteen-year-old, had been tried as an adult for the felony of having oral sex with a fifteen-year-old and was sentenced to seventeen years in prison. Limon had made the mistake of choosing a same-sex partner. Under Kansas law, had his partner been female, he would have been guilty only of a misdemeanor and his maximum sentence would have been fifteen months. Shortly after *Lawrence* was decided, the U.S. Supreme Court vacated, without opinion, the judgment of the Kansas Supreme Court, which had upheld Limon's conviction at a time when *Bowers* was still good law and ordered that the conviction be reconsidered "in light of *Lawrence*." Ultimately, the Kansas courts reversed the conviction, finding that the disparate treatment of homosexual and heterosexual sex violated both Kansas's and the U.S. Constitution's Equal Protection Clause. But for *Lawrence*, Matthew Limon would likely be getting out of prison just about now.

Lawrence also had its impact on family law. A year after *Lawrence*, for example, the Idaho Supreme Court in *McGriff v. McGriff* rejected a rule that had previously prevented a gay person from being awarded custody of a child, reasoning that *Lawrence* had made the practice of homosexuality "a protected practice under the Due Process clause" and consequently "sexual orientation, in and of itself, cannot be the basis for awarding or removing custody; only when the parent's sexual orientation is shown to cause harm to the child, such that the child's best interests are not served, should sexual orientation be a factor in determining custody" (*McGriff*, 117).

There are, very occasionally, cases that create an atmosphere well beyond the importance of the individual issue decided by a court. *Lawrence* was one such case, giving renewed confidence to the gay community and its allies. It was also just a few months after the *Lawrence* decision that the Massachusetts Supreme Court declared same-sex marriage a constitutional right under the Massachusetts Constitution. Even though *Lawrence* did not apply directly to a state constitutional issue, the Massachusetts Supreme Court at the very outset of its opinion quoted Justice Kennedy's recognition of the right of gay persons to dignity.

The decision in *Lawrence* had important precursors at the state level, including a key New York case, *People v. Onofre*, in which the New York Court of Appeals (the state's highest court) in 1980 found that the state's sodomy statute violated the U.S. Constitution on grounds both of equal protection and privacy. More than two decades before *Lawrence*, one of the most watched state high courts in the nation had rejected claims by the state that concerns for public morality provided a legitimate basis for criminalizing private conduct. It was a major victory for Lambda, which had brought the case, and the first time a court had found a sodomy statute unconstitutional in the context of same-sex activity (Andersen 2006, 32).

Gay rights litigators did not win every battle before the Supreme Court. In 2000, the Court, in a 5–4 decision (*Boy Scouts of America v. Dale*), reversed a New Jersey Supreme Court decision and held that the First Amendment right of association prevented a dismissed gay scoutmaster from basing a discrimination claim against the Boy Scouts of America on a provision of the New Jersey Civil Rights Law forbidding discrimination on the basis of sexual orientation. The Court has long held that individuals have a First Amendment right to band together for expressive purposes, and a group so formed has a right to control its own message. In this case, the conservative majority agreed that the Boy Scouts had a clear message that homosexuality was morally wrong and therefore Dale's dismissal was constitutionally protected. The dissent, among other things, argued that, all things considered, no one would confuse membership in the Boy Scouts with an endorsement by the Boy Scouts of homosexuality, particularly if acceptance of the scoutmaster was required by state law. The dissent also asserted that the majority had accepted the Boy Scouts' assertion about its message much too readily. *Boy Scouts v. Dale* was not the first case to involve a conflict between the First Amendment and a claim of gay rights.

A few years earlier, the Court had unanimously held in *Hurley v. Irish-American Gay, Lesbian and Bisexual Group of Boston* that the organizers of the St. Patrick's Day parade were within their rights to prohibit a gay organization from carrying its own banner in the parade. The case was a relatively easy one for the Court since the parade itself was treated as a form of speech with a clear right of the sponsors to control its message.

One might think, based on the *Boy Scouts of America* and *Hurley* cases, that a student chapter of a Christian group would be well within its First Amendment right of expressive association to require members to sign a Statement of Faith that was intended to exclude anyone who engages in "unrepentant homosexual conduct" or holds religious convictions different from those in the Statement of Faith. Nonetheless, in another 5–4 decision (*Christian Legal Society v. Martinez*) the Supreme Court in 2010 held that Hastings Law School could constitutionally deny the Christian group's application to become a registered student organization, based on the school's policy requiring all student organizations to allow any student to join them. The Court distinguished *Boy Scouts of America v. Dale* in part on the ground that the school's policy did not compel the Christian group to accept a member who did not share its views but merely made such acceptance a condition for receiving registered status. The constitutional acceptability of the school's all-comers policy turned on the Court's conclusion that the policy was viewpoint neutral (gay groups, e.g., would have to accept Christian fundamentalists) and reasonable in light of the overall purpose of having student organizations at a law school.

Constitutional law cases often raise the question of which of two competing constitutional principles deserves priority based on the facts of the case. To interpret constitutional law cases as purely pro- or antigay on the basis of their result is to fail to recognize their broader importance. To cite just one example, a case such as *Boy Scouts of America v. Dale*, which was perceived as antigay at the time it was handed down, embodied a principle—the right of an organization to protect its expressive message—that protects all organizations, including gay ones.

The North American Gay Amateur Athletic Alliance (NGAAA) found this out when its rule limiting the number of nongay players on any team to two was challenged. The state of Washington, the site of the controversy, has a law prohibiting discrimination on the basis of sexual orientation, a law similar to the one whose application to the Boy Scouts was deemed unacceptable. And just as the Supreme Court had protected the Boy Scouts' message, the federal district court, relying on the Supreme Court's decision, found that the First Amendment protected the NGAAA rule from attack since it was related to the organization's message of promoting and demonstrating the participation of gay athletes in sports (*Apilado v. North American Gay Amateur Athletic Alliance*).

It should also not be surprising that an ideologically divided Court can still render unanimous decisions when the application of constitutional principles seems clear, even on matters relating to gay rights issues on which the Court is usually divided along ideological lines. This is what happened in *Rumsfeld v. Forum for Academic and Institutional Rights, Inc.* When Don't Ask, Don't Tell was in effect, a number of universities sought to bar military recruiters from their campuses since the military clearly did not comply with their policies prohibiting campus access to employers who practiced discrimination on the basis of sexual orientation. In response, Congress enacted the Solomon Amendment, which denied federal funds to universities denying campus access to military recruiters. A group of universities, represented by the Forum for Academic and Institutional Rights, sued claiming that the Solomon Amendment violated their

First Amendment rights. On the basis of past voting in cases involving gay rights litigants, one might well have expected another 5–4 or 6–3 Supreme Court decision. Nevertheless, the Court in a unanimous 8–0 decision upheld the Solomon Amendment, finding that since Congress could directly require campus access under its Article I, Section 8, power to raise and support armies, it could exercise that power indirectly through the threat of withholding federal aid.

In this chapter we have examined three major developments since 1992 that have contributed to the success of the gay rights movement: the favorable evolution of public opinion; the adoption by the Democratic Party of most all of the goals of the gay rights movement; and the recognition by the Supreme Court that gays and their relationships are entitled to constitutional dignity. We have not, however, discussed the general debate over gay rights. That debate has two aspects: the debate between proponents and opponents of gay rights; and the debate within the gay community over whether the struggle for equality has not come at the cost of a vibrant and cohesive gay community and a more progressive agenda. We examine the first debate in the next chapter, chapter 6, reserving the second for chapter 11, following examination of how the individual goals of the equality movement have fared.

# 6

## The Debate over Gay Rights

Gay rights issues can divide communities into warring camps. The smaller the town, the more wrenching the division can be. In *The Stranger Next Door*, Arlene Stein describes one such battle. It began in 1993 when a group of Christian conservatives in Oregon sought passage of a law in as many counties and local jurisdictions as possible that would prohibit the passage of any antidiscrimination legislation protecting gays. The previous year Oregon voters had rejected a similar law intended to apply statewide. Timbertown was one of the towns that had been targeted for this new effort. (This was not the town's real name but was used by Stein to protect the identities of some of those she interviewed for her book, an effort that failed shortly after the book was pulished when a journalist revealed the town's true name.) At first, the city council, hoping to deflect such an emotionally charged question, tried to keep the proposed charter amendment from appearing on the ballot, putting it on only after being advised by state authorities that it was under a legal obligation to do so.

In 1993, Timbertown was not the same place it had been thirty years before. In the fifties and sixties, the timber industry there was thriving; it was a good place to raise a family, as it had been for generations, creating a close-knit community where virtually everyone knew everyone else, a community based on shared values of a deep Christian faith and all that went with it, including a strong commitment to rearing children into responsible, god-fearing adults in families defined by clearly delineated gender roles in which the wife obeyed the husband and nurtured the children and the husband was the sole breadwinner and respected authority figure. Many in the community still clung to those values in 1993, but by then a deep recession in the timber industry and increasing automation at the remaining mill plants had created an economic reality in which fathers were no longer the sole breadwinners, which undermined their authority, and women no longer able to stay at home full time, which undermined their nurturing role.

In her work, based on numerous interviews with every facet of the Timbertown community, Stein describes two sets of perspectives that help explain Timbertown's ultimate passage of the anti-gay-rights city charter amendment (57 percent to 43 percent). First there was the resentment of the working-class white men, who felt that their own social pain and economic plight were being ignored in favor of a vocal minority (A. Stein 2001, 116). Then there were the evangelical Christians, who saw gays as "the antithesis of moral individuals, the embodiment of a world in which rules, order, self-discipline and stability are severely lacking" (106). Rules, order, discipline, and stability, of course, are precisely what most evangelical Christians believe to be at the very heart of a good Christian life.

The people and perspectives that Stein so richly captures form the core of the opposition to gay rights throughout the country. I begin this chapter by referencing Stein's work because it is a useful reminder that attitudes toward gay rights, including those of its most virulent opponents, are formed out of life experiences and deeply held personal values. The gay rights movement today operates within the context of those realities.

## The Debate

If one had to encapsulate the political debate about gay rights into one question, it might be this: Should gays, gayness, and gay relationships always receive the same respect as heterosexuals, heterosexuality, and heterosexual relationships? The debate remains intense more than four decades after Stonewall because for many people (although certainly a declining number), acceptance of gays and gay relationships represents a threat to the moral teachings and underpinnings of society. Essentially two visions are in competition with the gay rights view very much in the ascendancy.

Gay rights proponents argue that there is absolutely no intelligible basis for treating gays differently than anyone else for any purpose because sexuality is a private matter, gays have the same needs as anyone else for society's blessing and support, gays are as fully capable as heterosexuals in every sphere of activity, gays have long-term loving relationships that are equally worthy of society's acceptance and support, and gays pose no threat to the larger society since gayness is just as right and natural for gays as heterosexuality is for heterosexuals and you can't persuade someone to be or not to be gay. While even most evangelicals agree that sexuality is a private matter—indeed they draw a clear boundary between private behavior and public acceptance—opponents of gay rights disagree with gay rights proponents on every other point. For them, gay rights often amount to claims of special privilege that threaten to undermine society's most important institutions: marriage and the family. Many opponents of gay rights do not accept the idea that "gay is good." For them it is unnatural and something to be condemned. There is a divinely established order, and homosexuality simply lies outside it; any other stance undermines that order.

Some opponents fight gay rights no matter the issue. Others do not oppose efforts at preventing employment and housing discrimination but draw the line at relationship recognition. For example, many evangelicals and Catholics who rated homosexuals less than 50 on what is called the feeling thermometer (signaling basic distaste) still supported policies to protect gays and lesbians from job discrimination, although they were very much against gay marriage or civil unions (Shames, Kuo, and Levine 2004, 35). Interestingly, the Mormon Church, which strongly opposes same-sex marriage and was a strong financial supporter of Proposition 8 in California, endorsed the passage of an antidiscrimination ordinance in Salt Lake City; the ordinance exempted religious organizations from the obligation not to discriminate.

At the outset, we must distinguish this debate from the more academic question whether gay sexuality itself is an intrinsic aspect of a person's being that has existed across time (often called the "essentialist" view) or instead is a product of social and cultural forces dependent on time and place (often called the "constructivist" view). Constructivists, in the words of John Boswell, believe that "people consider themselves 'homosexual' or 'heterosexual' because they are induced to believe that humans are either 'homosexual' or 'heterosexual,'" but "left to their own devices . . . people would simply be sexual" (1989, 17–18). Boswell himself takes a different view, believing, for example, that gay men in ancient Greece did have a gay identity even though Greek society at the time was not imposing or constructing such an identity for them. In a fascinating law review article written in 1993, Daniel Ortiz pointed out that "all the participants agree that taking a side in this controversy commits one to a whole set of positions on other issues of critical importance to gay theory and politics, issues like the possibility of gay history, the existence of gay community, and the very meaning of notions like gay identity" (1993, 1834). We shall see in chapter 12 how these issues have affected gay attitudes toward the gay rights movement itself, but certainly the larger society assumes that gay persons exist and that they are defined by their sexual orientation. The question for public debate is whether society can express its disapproval over that orientation, and if so, where, how, and to what extent.

## The Choice Question and Its Significance

One scientific question has loomed large in the debate over gay rights, namely, how fixed same-sex attraction is and how easy it may be to change. The implications for the gay rights debate are significant because if one assumes that (*a*) heterosexuality is preferable to homosexuality and (*b*) homosexuality can be discouraged, then permitting differentiation on the basis of sexual orientation arguably has a rational basis. Why, for example, recognize civil unions or domestic partnerships and why not allow discrimination if gayness is essentially changeable and wrong? Justice Antonin Scalia's statement during the oral argument in *Lawrence v. Texas* that a school district would be within its rights to prefer heterosexual over homosexual kindergarten teachers because otherwise children "could be induced to follow the path of homosexuality" makes sense only if children can be induced to be gay.

Constitutionally, the issue of choice matters because if gays constitute a genuine minority (as opposed to people who simply have voluntarily chosen a particular behavior), then laws that discriminate against them might require a higher degree of governmental justification than ordinary laws to meet the requirements of equal protection under the U.S. Constitution's Fourteenth Amendment. A law that discriminates on the basis of race, for example, is subject to what is called strict scrutiny and will be found unconstitutional unless it serves a compelling governmental interest and there is essentially no other way to achieve that compelling interest. A law that discriminates on the basis of sex is subject to what is called intermediate scrutiny; it must serve an important (but not necessarily compelling) governmental interest crafted narrowly (but not necessarily as narrowly as possible) to achieve that interest. Most laws, however, must simply be rationally related to a legitimate government objective in order to pass equal protection muster.

Courts that see homosexuality merely as a behavior may not accord any special protection for gays as a class of persons where equal protection is concerned. This position was succinctly stated by the Ninth Circuit in 1990: "Homosexuality is not an immutable characteristic," the Court declared; "it is behavioral and hence fundamentally different from traits such as race, gender or alienage, which define already existing suspect and quasi-suspect classes. The behavior or conduct of such already recognized classes is irrelevant to their identification" (*High Tech Gays v. Defense Industrial Security Clearance Office*, 573–574). This distinction is made by citizens as well as judges, so it has strong political as well as legal ramifications. "Some people say that homosexual behavior is the same as being black," voiced one voter in the midst of a campaign to repeal a gay rights ordinance, but "Does anyone really believe that? This makes no sense to me. We need to stop this in Cincinnati" (Dugan 2005, 77). Notice the key words "homosexual behavior" and "being black." I should add here that laws that burden a fundamental constitutional right are also subject to strict scrutiny. This is important because, if *Lawrence v. Texas* created a fundamental right to sexual autonomy, then laws that burden that right are subject to challenge whether or not being gay is a matter of choice.

If polls are at all reliable, there has been a sea change on how the public views the issue of choice just in the last half decade, one that may well help explain the growing support for gay legal rights. While a 2007 CNN/Opinion Research Corporation poll found that 42 percent of those questioned thought that homosexuality is a result of upbringing/environment as opposed to 39 percent who believe that it is something a one is born with, a March 2013 ABC/*Washington Post* poll showed that 62 percent of those questioned thought that being gay was not something one chose, as opposed to 24 percent who thought that it was a matter of choice.

The public's emerging view is certainly shared by most professionals. While there are considerable differences of opinion among scientists, psychologists, and other professionals as to the causes of a gay orientation, almost all agree that one's sexual orientation is determined at an early age and is not simply a matter of choice or lifestyle, a phrase many social conservatives like to use.

Perhaps surprisingly, in a paper titled "The Top Ten Myths about Homosexuality," Peter Sprigg, a senior fellow for policy studies at the Family Research Council, an anti-gay-rights group, writes, "Homosexual *attractions* are clearly not a 'choice' in the vast majority of cases" (2010, 9). This appears to be a considerable concession, given that Sprigg also insists that "the research does not show that anyone is born gay" (4). Indeed, Sprigg lists "People are born gay" as the No. 1 Myth perpetuated by the gay community. I suspect that social conservatives like Sprigg resist the idea that someone is born gay, even when conceding the strength of same-sex attraction, because if someone is born gay, then reparative therapy involves tampering with God's creation, whereas if gayness can be traced to other factors, such as developmental conflicts in the family, there is no such tampering. It also means that change is presumably more possible than if one were born gay. Even here, however, Sprigg's claims are surprisingly modest: "This is not to say that change is easy, that it is typically accomplished through prayer or will power alone, or that success of reorientation therapy can be guaranteed" (13). Interestingly, the change that Sprigg envisions is not so much a change in innate attraction but in the possibilities of behavior modification leading to heterosexual adjustment or chastity.

It is at this point that the debate becomes heated and emotional, because gays view reparation programs as both insulting and dangerous, not to mention implicitly accepting of the notion of gay persons as inevitable sinners. The mental health establishment expresses virtual unanimous concern that behavior modification programs pose real dangers to its participants, particularly among young people, often enrolled at their parents' behest. In contrast to the religious right, the American Psychological Association, in its 2007 report titled "Appropriate Therapeutic Responses to Sexual Orientation," concluded: "Same-sex sexual attractions, behavior and orientation per se are normal and positive variants of human sexuality" (2).

Because gay rights can be such an emotionally charged issue, the results of honest inquiry, even by a distinguished psychoanalyst, can be sensationalized. In May 2001, Robert Spitzer presented to a symposium of the American Psychiatric Association the preliminary findings of a study he had conducted among a group of men and women who claimed that they had successfully changed, to varying extents, their sexual orientation from gay to straight. Spitzer's report was modest and accompanied by many disclaimers, including that his group of subjects was far from a representative sample and that the kind of changes that he was reporting were not likely except among a very small percentage of the gay population. He made no effort to hide the fact that his subjects were largely recruited from persons who had learned about his study from groups endorsing conversion therapy and that a majority of the subjects (78 percent) had spoken in favor of efforts to change homosexual orientation, often at their church (Spitzer 2006, 41). Spitzer also made a point of saying that his study did not in any way decide whether the benefits of reparative therapy to those who wanted it outweighed the risks. For that discussion, Spitzer stated, "What is needed is a prospective outcome study of reparative therapy in which a consecutive series of volunteer individuals are evaluated before starting therapy and after several years." In essence, Spitzer's study amounted to little more than a finding that he believed that some of the subjects he interviewed believed that the therapy had been successful (57).

Spitzer, who had been a pivotal figure in convincing the American Psychiatric Association to drop its classification of homosexuality as a mental disorder in 1973, was vilified in portions of the gay community for his study. The reaction of the gay community, unfair in this writer's view given the many qualifications in Spitzer's study, was itself an understandable reaction to the exaggerated claims for Spitzer's study by those groups, such as Focus on the Family, that simply ignored the measured nature of Spitzer's remarks and pretended that his study proved that conversion therapy worked.

In the May 2012 issue of the *American Prospect*, Gabriel Arana, the progressive magazine's web editor, reported on an interview with Spitzer in which he stated that at one point he spoke with the editor of the *Archives of Sexual Behavior* about writing a retraction, but the editor declined. Then, at the end of the interview, Arana writes: "Spitzer was growing tired and asked how many more questions I had. Nothing, I responded, unless you have something to add. He did. Would I print a retraction of his 2001 study 'so I don't have to worry about it anymore'" (Arana 2012, 54). Subsequent to the *American Prospect* article, Spitzer himself issued a formal apology to the gay community.

More and more, the evidence is accumulating for a biological basis for sexual orientation. In 2011, Simon LeVay, a highly respected British neuroscientist and author of an important textbook on human sexuality, published *Gay, Straight, and the Reason Why* in which he surveyed the existing literature on the origins of sexual attraction. He summarized his findings this way: "Taken together, the multitude of research studies published since 1991 have greatly strengthened the idea that biological factors play a significant role in the development of sexual orientation—in both men and women. More than that, they tend to bolster a particular kind of biological theory. This is the idea that the origins of sexual orientation are to be sought in the interactions between sex hormones and the developing brain" (LeVay 2011, x). Interestingly, these research findings are strengthened by other studies showing that, on average, pre-gay children (children prior to puberty who later identify as gay) tend to exhibit traits not conforming to their gender type at an early age, in other words at an age when external factors (overbearing mother, absent father) are not likely to have had a major influence. These findings too support the view that "sexual orientation is influenced by factors operating early in life" (LeVay 2011, 14).

The fact that one's sexual orientation is determined at an early age is not equivalent to saying that everyone is either exclusively gay or heterosexual. In his famous 1948 report on male sexuality, Kinsey developed a seven-point scale of sexual orientation, with exclusive heterosexuality at one extreme (0) and exclusive homosexuality at the other (6). The usefulness of Kinsey's continuum, indeed the whole subject of bisexuality, has long been a subject of interest for researchers. In his review of the literature growing out of that research, LeVay concludes that the concept of a continuum seems to have more relevance for lesbianism than it does for gay male relations. For LeVay, the research indicates strongly that men generally fall into the category of gay or straight in their basic attraction, whereas "sexual orientation in women has a more dimensional quality," with women being "distributed in a continuum across the spectrum of sexual orientation" (2011, 18).

Human sexuality is an extraordinarily complex phenomenon, but one understandably blurred by supporters of gay rights since, from a political standpoint, gays as a group must be brought into sharp focus. In the words of the writer Susie Bright, "when you march on Washington, you can't hold a sign with a paragraph explaining your sexual persona. You need sometimes to say, *Hey I'm Gay, Get Used To It,* and that is typically when you are making a political point" (Bright 2000, 41).

Since gay rights opponents believe same-sex relations are sinful, then reducing their incidence effectively reduces the amount of sin in the world, a good thing from a fundamentalist standpoint. And what better way to discourage that sinful conduct than by continuing expressions of disapproval. For fundamentalists, the message is clear: more tolerance leads to more sin. Their fixed conception of the nuclear family—deeply and sincerely felt—also feeds into their hostility to gay rights, for if heterosexual marriage and children define the only acceptable mode of life, then the "homosexual lifestyle" is as threatening in its otherness as the sexual behavior it represents is sinful.

In July 2013, the newly chosen Pope Francis shocked everyone, including presumably his closest advisers, when he asked, Who am I to pass judgment on gay priests? The statement was made in the course of an hour-long informal press conference toward the close of his extraordinary trip to Brazil. It was held on board a plane in which the pope stood facing reporters much as a modern day politician might. The reporters could ask anything they wanted. As welcome as the pope's comments were to many, they were personal and represented no change in church doctrine as expressed in a 1992 statement of the Congregation for the Doctrine of the Faith, describing homosexuality as a "moral disorder." "As in every moral disorder," the Church avers, "homosexual activity prevents one's own fulfillment and happiness by acting contrary to the creative wisdom of God" (para. 3). The Vatican statement affirms in clear terms that gays and lesbians are entitled to the same measure of dignity and concern as all other persons, but separating the disorder from the person is not easy and, indeed, at one point the statement seems to blame gay rights advocates for the hate directed against them, arguing that "when civil legislation is introduced to protect behavior to which no one has any conceivable right, neither the church nor society at large should be surprised when other distorted notions and practices gain ground, and irrational and violent actions increase" (para. 7).

The phrase "behavior to which no one has any conceivable right" is, of course, today the polar opposite of the view expressed by Justice Kennedy in *Lawrence v. Texas* that protecting the right to engage in private homosexual activity is vital to protecting the dignity of homosexuals as human beings. For the Catholic Church it is the choice not to engage in homosexual activity that would fulfill the homosexual's human potential and "What is at all costs to be avoided is the unfounded and demeaning assumption that the sexual behavior of homosexual persons is always and totally compulsive and therefore inculpable" (para. 8).

In its most quoted passage, the paper concludes: "Sexual orientation does not constitute a quality comparable to race, ethnic background, etc. in respect to non-discrimination. Unlike these, homosexual orientation is an objective disorder . . . and evokes moral concern. . . . Homosexual persons who assert their homosexuality tend to be precisely those who judge homosexual behavior or lifestyle to be 'either completely harmless,' if not an entirely good thing and hence worthy of public approval" (para. 10). The same Catholic Church that wishes to recognize the dignity of homosexuals as persons comes close to asking them to return to an invisibility that would undo the entire course of gay history of the last half century, including a modern gay rights movement that has been all about visibility.

## Public Reasoning

Fundamentalists and the Catholic Church have a right to their opinions; the problem is that they are not what the philosopher John Rawls has called "public reasons." In Rawls's view, citizens in a constitutional democracy must give reasons for their positions based on reasoning, which itself is based on the shared values of a constitutional democracy. Arguments rooted in biblical interpretation are not public reasons. Opposition to gays in the military, for example, on the ground that gays are unacceptable in the eyes of God is not a public reason for opposing open service of gays. On the other hand, an argument that gays in the military would make the military less effective is a public reason rooted in a shared assumption that an effective military is a good thing.

There are some who question whether any ostensibly public reason for opposing gay rights can be anything more than a rationalization for a deep hostility to gay sexuality. In her book *From Disgust to Humanity: Sexual Orientation and Constitutional Law*, Martha Nussbaum, a professor of law and ethics at the University of Chicago, argues that opposition to gay rights is inspired primarily by feelings of disgust and repulsion toward homosexuals, feelings that, she concludes, deserve no recognition in public law. She refers, for example, to the Defense of Marriage Act as a "hate-inspired law" (2010, 209).

In a review of Nussbaum's book, Mary Anne Case, a feminist constitutional scholar also at the University of Chicago Law School, asks: "If disgust is out-of-bounds, is there, in Nussbaum's view, a more appropriate emotion for opponents of homosexuality to mobilize in aid of their opposition? Or is Nussbaum in effect demanding nothing short of complete capitulation from them?" (Case 2010b, 90). Case then asks two additional questions: "To the extent that the opponents' arguments are now on their face being made with ordinary public-regarding reasons, what difference if any should it make whether disgust underlies them? And is it the case that there is no feasible intermediate stopping point in law and policy between attaching moral opprobrium to homosexuality and embracing it fully as morally acceptable?" (104).

These are fundamental questions, ones that have been and continue to be of profound importance in legal philosophy, with important practical implications as well, for gay rights is only one of a number of issues, including regulation of obscenity and prostitution, in which the question of sexual freedom and the right of society to impose its vision of morality on private lives arise. In 1957, the Wolfenden Commission proposed that British law decriminalize sodomy between men over the age of twenty-one. The report gave rise to intense debate about the legitimate reach of the law. H.L.A. Hart, among others, argued in *Law, Liberty and Morality* (1969) that there was a private sphere into which the law should not reach; Lord Devlin, by contrast, asserted in *The Enforcement of Morals* (1968) that society had a perfect right to enforce its vision of morality through democratically determined laws. To some extent, the issue in this country was resolved on a constitutional basis by *Lawrence v. Texas*. Yet, clearly those who advocate that discrimination against gays can appropriately express society's feelings about homosexuality and the right to express its disapproval of same-sex relations swim comfortably in the waters charted by Lord Devlin and those advocating for protections against such discrimination in the seas favored by H.L.A. Hart and, going back far enough, by John Stuart Mill.

With this overview in mind, we begin our examination of how individual goals of the gay rights movement have fared by examining the workplace where gay persons, like everyone else, spend a major part of their lives.

# 7

# The Workplace

The gay rights movement has focused on three things respecting the workplace: (1) encouraging the creation of an accepting work atmosphere; (2) providing same-sex couples through domestic partnership recognition with the same benefits as opposite-sex couples; and (3) fighting discrimination.

Public employees, however, enjoy certain protections not applicable to private employees. The most important difference is that the Equal Protection Clause of the Fourteenth Amendment, which says that no state shall deny persons the equal protection of the laws, means that gay public employees have a level of protection against irrational or arbitrary discrimination that their private-sector counterparts do not always enjoy. Additionally, public employees in many states enjoy civil service protection requiring the government to justify its termination of an employee. None of this is true for private-sector employment, where, under a principle known as employment at will, an employee can be fired for any reason or no reason at all unless the discharge would violate the terms of either an applicable collective bargaining agreement or individual contract or an applicable nondiscrimination law. The distinction between public and private employment obviously becomes less important in states (or municipalities) that have included sexual orientation in their antidiscrimination laws covering private employment.

In the employment/workplace context we see both the importance and the limits of what law can achieve, for on the one hand law cannot legislate social acceptance, while on the other hand legal protections against discrimination and harassment can at least assure civilized behavior and fairness.

## Workplace Culture

Surprising as it may seem, even in large corporations with clear antidiscrimination policies, many gays continue to conceal their sexual orientation at work. The 2013 Pew survey of LGBT Americans reported that only one-third of participating employed LGBT adults stated that all or most of their co-workers knew of their sexual orientation; approximately half said that virtually no one knew of their orientation. Lack of openness has its costs. Office gossip and simple questions like "What did you do this weekend?"—for most a welcome diversion—become a difficult terrain for the closeted gay employee.

There are a myriad of reasons why gay employees are less candid in the workplace than elsewhere. Consider these statements of three participants in the 2013 Pew survey when asked to describe the experience of coming out: "All my friends know about my sexual orientation, but I keep it private at work. I do not want it to influence my career"; "The only people I don't share my sexual identity with are my employers and coworkers because of previous harassment and misconception"; "Being able to answer questions about my significant other at work is something I still struggle with because I fear people will behave differently towards me."

Remaining in the closet comes with costs. For many years, gay employees reported fears of excelling. Whether this is as true today is hard to judge. In his account of coming out in a large corporate environment in the early nineties, Rick Schroder, an employee of the Shell Oil Company, describes how he worried about doing his job too well. Shell, then and probably now, awarded outstanding employees with trips to desirable vacation spots. Schroder recalls: "My colleagues relished the opportunity to win—for me it was horrifying. The last thing I wanted was visibility that might cause my social and professional lives to collide" (Schroder 2008, 25). Even today gay employees are reluctant to declare themselves, so it is not surprising that, as late as 1990, a time long past the explosion of gay community organizations, there were only ten gay employee networks among the Fortune 1000 corporations (Raeburn 2004, 25). For 2011, the Corporate Equality Index, conducted by the Human Rights Campaign, shows that more than 80 percent of the 477 employers participating in the survey have some form of officially sanctioned group or diversity council that includes LGBT issues.

The growth of employee groups within large corporations is certainly partly attributable to the Corporate Equality Index begun in 2002 by the Human Rights Campaign. The index, by giving potential employees, consumers, politicians, and the public a standard for measuring employer attitudes, provides an important incentive for corporations to improve their standing

with the LGBT community. Of the 293 Fortune 500 companies that were officially rated in the 2013 survey, 252 received a 100 percent rating. The 2013 index
also rated 201 Fortune 500 employers who had chosen not to participate in the
survey although directly invited to do so. This group achieved only a 14 percent approval rating. These results are extremely interesting and merit more
research; they suggest that there are not only red and blue states but red and
blue corporations as well.

Why have a majority of Fortune 500 companies been so receptive to gay
needs? At least three key forces seem to be at work. First, these corporations
compete for the best employees, so it only takes one company within an industry
to set a standard that its competitors may feel they must follow. The Corporate
Equality Index makes clear just which employers in a particular industry, and
even which industries, provide the best support for its gay employees. Second,
there has been a growing recognition that closeted gay employees simply are
not as effective or productive as their more open counterparts; consequently,
astute employers will build an environment in which coming out creates as little
stress as possible. Third, and perhaps most important, large corporations abhor
controversy. As the gay community has grown stronger, more visible, and more
organized, the incentive for large corporations to foster good relations with it has
grown as well, particularly in the absence of push back from organized opposition. A corporation perceived as hostile to equal rights can quickly find itself
the object of a consumer boycott, as Target did in the fall of 2010 when it was
revealed that the company had made a big donation to a group backing a Minnesota gubernatorial candidate opposing gay marriage, hardly a radical position.
Target quickly tried to explain its donation, noting that it had never knowingly
donated to legislation or referenda whose aim was to undermine equality for all.

The dynamics at work are much different in other environments. In businesses with a relatively small number of employees, the factors that have led
large corporations to adopt gay friendly policies are not present. Allies are harder
to find, and much depends on the attitude of the owner of the business and one's
co-workers. It seems clear that when a gay man is known as a good worker, if he is
respected for his character, then his decision to come out can be a good one not
only for the gay individual but for the working environment as well.

As for the more rarified worlds of the arts and sports, the setting makes all
the difference. In fields encompassing the arts, coming out, as a general rule,
seems almost a nonissue. Film, theater, and music celebrities have limited
ability to control information about their private lives and, with today's more
accepting atmosphere, less incentive to do so. Moreover, the arts in general
prize individual freedom and harbor, hopefully, fewer stereotypes than other
professions.

The exact opposite, of course, has been true for professional sports and particularly the major team sports, where coming out could easily jeopardize acceptance by one's teammates, not to mention, for top athletes, loss of endorsements. Nevertheless, even here the closet has begun to open. On May 29, 2013, star soccer midfielder Robbie Rogers became the first openly gay athlete to participate in a major team sport when he entered a game in Carson City, California, between the Los Angeles Galaxy and the Seattle Sounders in the seventy-seventh minute of the game. He was greeted with cheers by the 25,000 fans in attendance. Even more significantly, in early 2014, Michael Sam, an all-American defensive end at the University of Missouri and a sure N.F.L. draft pick, announced to the world that he is gay. His teammates had known for a year and supported him completely. In his new locker room, he will be just one more all-American. The world will be watching how he fares.

Leading a double life can take an enormous toll. Consider the story of Rick Welts, the president and chief executive officer of the National Basketball Association's Phoenix Suns, as reported by Dan Barry in the *New York Times* of May 15, 2011. Welts had known he was gay from a young age. Living in Seattle, he was lucky to get a job as a teenager with the professional basketball team the Seattle Supersonics. He was so well thought of that Lenny Wilkins, the Sonics coach, once visited him at his fraternity house at the University of Washington, an event that undoubtedly sent his prestige soaring. His association with the Sonics ultimately led to a highly successful career in management, first with the corporate National Basketball Association itself—among other things Welts dreamed up the idea for the NBA all-star weekend—and then as an executive with the Phoenix Suns. When Welt's longtime life partner died of AIDS, he had to grieve alone since he had never been able to share his personal life with anyone at work. At a time when he most needed the understanding of his colleagues and the time simply to collect his emotions, he was given neither. Sometime after the death of his partner, Welts began a new long-term relationship. This one ended badly a couple of years before Welts made his decision to come out. The breakup resulted from the fact that Welts's partner could no longer accept that Welt was not yet ready to share their relationship with the world, at least Welt's work world.

## Domestic Partnerships

Domestic partnerships are the nonalcoholic beverage (the near beer, if you are of a certain age) of the gay rights movement. They don't provide much in the way of an emotional jolt but are very important in certain jurisdictions and will continue to be in the future. Domestic partnerships should be thought of as any legal recognition of relationships short of marriage. Some jurisdictions offer gay couples (and sometimes heterosexual partners) the opportunity to register as domestic partners without actually offering specific benefits. At the other end of the spectrum are civil unions, which are in effect domestic partnerships on steroids.

The history of domestic partnerships is inextricably linked with the history of the gay rights movement. Indeed, in the 1980s the push for domestic partnership benefits in San Francisco mirrored the conflict that has been playing for decades between religious groups and gay rights advocates. It began in 1982 when the San Francisco board of supervisors enacted a domestic partnership law. Mayor Dianne Feinstein, however, vetoed the legislation under intense pressure from the local archdiocese. There the matter stood until 1989 when a similar ordinance was passed, this time with the approval of Mayor Art Agnos. Just as with same-sex marriage, however, social conservatives immediately gathered the necessary signatures to put the new law before San Francisco voters, who voted to repeal it. A modified, somewhat less expansive version of a domestic partnership law was then drafted by Harry Britt, the gay man who had replaced Harvey Milk on the board of supervisors after Milk's assassination. This time, despite continuing opposition from religious groups, the modified law passed.

In states providing for same-sex marriage or broad civil unions, employers, both public and private, are generally required to treat domestic partners the same way they treat heterosexual married couples (Hertz and Doskow 2012, 17). Domestic partnerships, however, can be enormously important in other states. They will determine, among other things, whether a gay employee can cover his or her same-sex partner under the company's health policy and whether the employee can take a leave in the event of a partner's illness.

We need to recall the distinction between public-sector and private-sector employees. In non-same-sex-marriage, non–civil union states, private-sector employers generally have complete discretion over whether to grant domestic partner–type benefits to their employees with one important exception. A number of cities and counties, including Philadelphia and Miami Beach, have what are called equal benefits ordinances, which require employers wishing to contract with the city to offer the same benefits to employees with same-sex partners that they offer to married employees. For private-sector employers dealing with union-represented employees, recognition of domestic partnerships is a matter for collective bargaining, but with respect to nonrepresented and management employees, it is a matter of corporate policy whether to provide such benefits. Public-sector employers, however, live in a different legal universe, one in which laws can be passed limiting the authority of public employers to grant such benefits but also one in which such benefits may be required by state high courts interpreting their own state constitutions, something we have already seen at work in the marriage context in a number of states.

Religious conservatives have opposed domestic partnerships with almost the same intensity that they have opposed same-sex marriage: any recognition of gay relationships is anathema to them. Indeed, one of the less remarked upon stories of the past decade—one that runs counter to the general trend of public opinion on gay rights issues—has been the number of states that, during this period, have enacted constitutional amendments with language broad enough to be interpreted as not only barring same-sex marriage but also denying recognition to civil unions and domestic partnerships. Between the year 2000 and 2008, Nebraska, Louisiana, Arkansas, Georgia, Kentucky, Michigan, North Dakota, Ohio, Oklahoma, Utah, Kansas, Texas, Alabama, Idaho, South Carolina, South Dakota, Virginia, Wisconsin, and Florida enacted such amendments

Remarkably, most of these states had already enacted statutes barring same-sex marriage, so the subsequent constitutional amendments were intended to broaden the scope of the prohibition to include civil unions and domestic partnerships and to provide protection against judges finding the existing anti-gay-marriage statutes unconstitutional. Often the language in these amendments is ambiguous as antigay forces faced a dilemma in putting the amendments on the ballot, desiring on the one hand to bar any recognition of gay relationships yet also aware that some opponents of gay marriage did not want to prohibit all relationship recognition. As a result, there has been and will continue to be important litigation on the reach of these amendments. Wisconsin and Michigan provide prime examples.

In Wisconsin, in June 2009, Governor Jim Doyle, a Democrat, signed a law giving limited domestic partnership benefits to same-sex state employees. Just a few days later, a lawsuit was filed seeking a declaration that the new law violated Wisconsin's Marriage Protection Amendment, which prohibits not only gay marriage but also any "legal status identical or substantially similar to that of marriage." Ultimately, the Wisconsin Court of Appeals, an intermediate court but one whose rulings are binding throughout the state, had the final say on the issue when the Wisconsin Supreme Court refused to hear the case. In December 2012, the court upheld the Domestic Partnership Law. Interestingly, the court did not reach the question whether domestic partnerships are "substantially similar" to marriage, determining instead that, as used in the amendment, the term "legal status" itself was not intended to prevent at least some benefits being offered to domestic partners. The court, among other things, placed great weight in reaching its conclusion on statements made by proponents of the Marriage Protection Amendment exactly to that effect (*Appling v. Doyle*).

In Michigan, the battle has played out with particular drama, both political and legal. In 2008, the Michigan Supreme Court held that the state's ban on same-sex marriage and civil unions prohibited public or private employers from providing benefits to same-sex couples based on recognition of their relationship (*National Pride at Work v. Governor of Michigan*). Notwithstanding the court's ruling, Democratic governor Jennifer Granholm worked out an agreement, through the State Civil Service Commission, with two state employee unions to provide health insurance benefits to live-in partners, regardless of whether the employee and partner were in a same-sex or heterosexual relationship.

Republicans took issue with the agreement and, after assuming complete control of the legislature and the governorship, enacted a law in 2011 barring public-sector employers from providing domestic partner benefits. This would have undone the Granholm agreement, except that the State Civil Service Commission then voted to amend its contract so as to no longer refer to partnership status in any way but instead to allow an unmarried employee to enroll in the employee's health plan one "Other Eligible Adult" with whom the employee had been living at least a year. In January 2013, an intermediate state appellate court upheld the commission's action on the ground that the contract provision did not refer to gender in any way and therefore was not based on recognition of a domestic partnership. The attorney general vowed to appeal the court's decision. In Michigan, political football is almost as interesting as its Big Ten counterpart, at least to non–sports fans, and just as entertaining.

Court victories for gay rights advocates can be undone. In 2005, the Alaska Supreme Court ruled that under the state constitution's Equal Protection Clause, public employers have to offer the same benefits to same-sex domestic partners as they do to married couples (*Alaska Civil Liberties Union v. State of Alaska*). In 2006, the voters of Alaska enacted a constitutional amendment not only barring same-sex marriage (Alaska already had a statute to that effect) but broadening the language to prohibit any relationship recognition.

To the extent that the United States Constitution has something to say in this area, it will supersede state constitutional amendments. Thus, the domestic partnership case with the widest implications involves a ruling by the Ninth Circuit Court of Appeals (*Diaz v. Brewer*). In that case, the court invalidated under the Equal Protection Clause the attempt by Arizona to prevent gays from receiving domestic partnership benefits. The case had an interesting wrinkle. The Arizona Domestic Partnership Law, which allowed both qualified same-sex and heterosexual couples to receive its benefits, was enacted only half a year before the voters of Arizona in November 2008 declared marriage to be only a union of a man and a woman. Less than a year later, Arizona, by statute, took away the domestic partnership benefits it had previously granted. Gay employees sued claiming that the federal Equal Protection Clause was violated because, under Arizona law, heterosexual couples could qualify for benefits by marrying, an option not available to same-sex couples in Arizona. The trial court and later the Ninth Circuit agreed. The Ninth Circuit specifically rejected Arizona's claim that the statute had a rational basis, namely, a desire to save money. While money was being saved, it amounted to such a small amount in comparison to the state budget that the court dismissed it as a pretext for the real motive—to penalize an unpopular group.

Litigation over domestic partnership benefits is almost exclusively a fight between two sets of litigators: those representing the views of religious conservatives and those advocating for gay rights. Religious conservatives have not been very effective in opposing corporate recognition of same-sex relationships. In fact, the extent to which major corporations now provide benefits to same-sex partners is one of the major equality victories of the past two decades. Very few companies offered domestic partnership benefits in the early nineties. Today, according to the 2013 Corporate Equality Index survey, 62 percent of the Fortune 500 companies offer domestic partner health benefits.

While the fight over domestic partnership benefits has spilled over into the courts, particularly with respect to public employees, the extension of those benefits in the private sector has been much more about shifts in societal attitudes, the assertiveness of the growing networks of gay employees within major corporations, and the recognition by corporations that such benefits are vital if they are to hire and keep the best gay employees. The fight against discrimination and harassment, on the other hand, is very much a legal battle, one on which red and blue states clearly divide, a subject to which we now turn.

## The Fight against Employment Discrimination

Efforts to secure protection against discrimination in employment decisions such as hiring, firing, and promotion have taken place on two fronts: legislative halls and the courtroom. In both arenas there has been significant success, but more remains to be achieved.

The most significant failure of the equality movement has been its inability to persuade Congress to enact federal legislation that would add sexual orientation to the list of proscribed forms of discrimination under Title VII of the federal civil rights law. Federal legislation to accomplish that purpose was first introduced by New York's Bella Abzug in 1974. The 1974 legislation prohibited discrimination in housing and public accommodations as well as employment.

After two decades of futility, the Employment Non-Discrimination Act of 1994 (ENDA) was introduced covering employment discrimination only. While it may be easy to lay this failure at the doorstep of the Republicans, the fact remains that Democrats controlled both houses of Congress and the presidency during the first two years of both the Clinton and Obama administrations yet still failed to secure passage of ENDA. This was partly a question of priorities and partly a reflection of the difficulty of securing passage in the Senate in view of the filibuster rule requiring sixty votes to bring legislation to the floor, although again the Democrats had a filibuster-proof majority in the first year of President Obama's first term until the election of Republican Scott Brown to fill Senator Ted Kennedy's seat in Massachusetts.

Although no federal legislation has been enacted prohibiting discrimination on the basis of sexual orientation, the federal Civil Rights Act of 1964 does prohibit employment discrimination on the basis of sex. Distinguishing between discrimination based on sex and discrimination based on sexual orientation is not easy, and indeed in many instances is arguably a distinction without a difference. Take *Dillon v. Frank*, for example, a hostile work environment case brought under Title VII of the federal Civil Rights Act. Dillon, a mail handler at a bulk mail handling facility of the U.S. Postal Service, was taunted, ostracized, beaten by one person, and subjected, in the words of the Ninth Circuit, to a "full orchestral assault of verbal abuse" (*Dillon*, 1). After years of accepting this abuse, Dillon finally resigned on the advice of his psychiatrist.

Dillon argued that his suit was not based on the fact that he was homosexual. Rather, he argued, he was subjected to abuse solely because he was a man and therefore was a victim of sex discrimination under Title VII. The Sixth Circuit rejected this argument, finding that the fundamental cause of the abuse was his orientation not his sex. Interestingly, however, the court left the door open to a possible future suit when it found that Dillon's argument was "unpersuasive, primarily because he has not shown that his co-workers would have treated a similarly situated woman any differently" (*Dillon*, 9). This is a rather extraordinary statement though quite logical as a matter of formal reasoning. The court is saying that if only there was a well-treated lesbian at the facility, he might have a case. Suppose there were an open lesbian at the facility; an employer acting purely in its own self-interest would be in the odd position of desiring Dillon's co-workers to be equally cruel to her to avoid a sex discrimination claim. Somehow all this seems a rather counterproductive way of interpreting a federal remedial statute.

*Dillon* could have ended with a different result had the Sixth Circuit looked to the spirit, if not the letter, of the Supreme Court's decision in *Price Waterhouse v. Hopkins*. In *Price Waterhouse*, the Court upheld the sex discrimination claim of a woman who had been denied partnership status with Price Waterhouse based in part on sexual stereotyping. In his plurality opinion, Justice Brennan wrote, "we are beyond the day when an employer could evaluate employees by assuming or insisting that they matched the stereotype associated with their group" (*Price Waterhouse*, 251). This case has had a major impact among lower federal courts, and indeed, five circuits now recognize a significant overlap between sexual orientation and gender discrimination on the one hand and sexual stereotype discrimination of the kind condemned in *Price Waterhouse* on the other (Pizer et al. 2012, 746; see, for example, *Prowel v. Wise Business Forms, Inc.*). At the risk of editorializing, the notion that harassment based on gender nonconformity is not based on sex (and is therefore not sex discrimination under Title VII) seems wrong, at least in the case of an effeminate gay man, since clearly those same traits exhibited by a woman would have been completely acceptable. It is hard to imagine the Supreme Court not weighing in again on this issue at some point, if only to establish a uniformity among the circuits.

The gay rights movement has been much more successful at the state and local levels. Twenty-one states plus the District of Columbia and more than two hundred municipalities located in thirty-five states currently prohibit employment discrimination on the basis of sexual orientation (Pizer et al. 2012,757). Sixteen of those states also bar discrimination based on gender orientation (meaning that they protect the transgender community). While these numbers are impressive, there are still vast swaths of the country in which there is no protection. No southern or border state prohibits discrimination based on sexual orientation (many of these states have no antidiscrimination laws at all), nor do the Plains states. Ten states (Alaska, Arkansas, Idaho, Mississippi, Montana, Nebraska, North Dakota, South Carolina, Tennessee, and Wyoming) offer no protection at either the state or local level (Pizer et al. 2012, 757). Local laws providing protection against discrimination are obviously of special importance where there are no state antidiscrimination statutes. Cities in this group include Phoenix, Tucson, New Orleans, Miami Beach, Tampa, Detroit, Ann Arbor, Louisville, Cleveland, and Austin.

State antidiscrimination laws represent some of the most important political successes of the gay rights movement because they have been won state by state against real opposition. Unlike many city antidiscrimination ordinances that passed in the early 1970s, these statewide victories did not come in under the radar, for the first state antidiscrimination law was not enacted until 1982, when the religious right was already emerging as a major political force. Part of the explanation for the success of these efforts is simply that Americans do not like discrimination in any form, a feeling best captured by one focus group participant in Oregon at a time (1992) when an antigay ballot measure was before the voters: "I don't think being gay is right. It's immoral. It's against all religious beliefs. I don't agree with gays at all, but I don't think they should be discriminated against" (Vaid 1995, 20).

The experience of Cincinnati not only measures the change in opinion that has occurred respecting discrimination against gays but illustrates how framing issues can be of fundamental importance in shaping the gay rights debate. The story begins in 1991 when the Cincinnati city council, responding to intense lobbying from several local gay rights organizations, enacted an ordinance protecting gay city workers from discrimination. Cincinnati was not a path-breaker on this issue; several other Ohio communities, including Columbus and Akron, had previously enacted similar ordinances (Dugan 2005, 2). The following year, the Cincinnati city council enacted a general Human Rights Ordinance protecting all residents of Cincinnati from employment and housing discrimination on a number of grounds, including sexual orientation. Soon, Christian right organizations had succeeded in placing on the ballot a city charter amendment to repeal the existing ordinance and to prohibit the city council from enacting any such legislation in the future. The initiative passed with a two-thirds majority. As described by Kimberly Dugan in her study of the campaign, the opposition was able to convince many voters that discrimination protection for gays was a matter of special not equal rights.

Eleven years later, gay rights advocates in Cincinnati placed on the November 2004 ballot an initiative to repeal the 1993 antigay law. This time, Dugan reports, the gay community was united on strategy and presented the issue as one of fundamental fairness, not equality. The strategy worked as the voters reversed themselves and repealed the 1993 ordinance. The following year, the city council reenacted discrimination protection for gays. Once again, opponents mobilized to place a repeal initiative on the ballot, but this time they could not secure the requisite signatures in sufficient time. It appeared that the initiative was likely to fail in any event, for a decade had quietly produced a sea change in voters' attitudes.

Cincinnati wasn't the only city where its citizens had a change of heart. You may recall that in 1977, Miami voters repealed their gay rights ordinance by the huge margin of 202,000 to 83,000. In 1998 the Miami city council once again passed a protective ordinance, and once again in 2002, repeal was sought by the religious right through a ballot initiative. This time, however, the initiative failed by a margin of 53 percent to 47 percent.

The fight for state antidiscrimination laws becomes more difficult as attention has turned to more conservative-voting states. In 2009, Delaware became the twenty-first state to pass antidiscrimination legislation, while the Idaho and North Dakota legislatures rejected similar legislation. The most interesting and

surprising victory for gay rights has come in Salt Lake City, where the city council unanimously approved a bill, after the Mormon Church endorsed it, banning
discrimination based on sexual orientation in housing and employment. The
law contains strong provisions protecting the right of religious organizations to
discriminate in furtherance of their religious principles, a key to the Church's
endorsement.

Another area in which progress has been made over the past two decades
involves the evolution of the federal case law on constitutional protections for
gay public employees. We have already discussed the Acanfora case from the
early seventies, illustrating how a school teacher could be fired simply for publicly defending his right to be rehired to a position to which he had been illegally
fired. This judicially imposed code of silence was indeed a consistent theme of
important court decisions throughout the seventies and eighties. In another
important case, for example, a young guidance counselor, Marjorie Rowland,
in the joy of a new lesbian relationship, momentarily let her guard down and
expressed her happiness to a fellow employee. She had picked the wrong person
to confide in. On being informed of the guidance counselor's sexual orientation, the principal promptly transferred her to a new post and her contract was
subsequently terminated.

Rowland contested her termination and, as in *Acanfora*, the federal district
court judge found in her favor, but the court of appeals reversed, making clear
that Rowland had no constitutional right to discuss her homosexuality since it
did not relate to a matter of public concern (*Rowland v. Mad River Local School
District).* Interestingly, Justice William Brennan issued an unusual public dissent when the Supreme Court refused to hear Rowland's case. Justice Brennan
pointed out that the Court had never addressed whether the constitutional
rights of gay litigants had been violated and argued that it was time to do so.
(Given that just a few months after Rowland, the Court handed down its decision in *Bowers v. Hardwick*, perhaps it may have been just as well that the Court
did not take the case.)

Even when it came to clearly protected speech, gay employees were vulnerable when speaking out publicly in ways that revealed their orientation. In 1993,
reviewing the existing case law, Patricia Cain concluded, "To win, an employee
must have remained as closeted as possible. Speaking out publicly can result in
loss of employment despite the fact that such speech warrants a certain degree
of First Amendment protection. Generally speaking, public employees are limited by the legitimate interests of their employers in protecting the public's
image of the employer" (Cain 1993, 1604).

By the end of the 1990s, however, things had begun to change, as illus-
trated by this 1998 decision of a federal district judge in Utah in the case of

*Weaver v. Nebo School District.* The case involved a highly regarded teacher and volleyball coach, Wendy Weaver, who, when asked by one of the girls on the volleyball team whether she was gay, answered affirmatively. As a result, Weaver was admonished not to make any further statements about her sexual orientation or lifestyle and was removed as the volleyball coach. Judge Bruce Jenkins was appalled by the school's directive and found that it violated Weaver's First Amendment rights. Judge Jenkins also held that Weaver was entitled to reinstatement as volleyball coach, declaring that "if the community's perception is based on nothing more than unsupported assumptions, outdated stereotypes, and animosity, it is necessarily irrational and under *Romer* and other Supreme Court precedent, it provides no legitimate support for the School District's decisions" (*Weaver*, 1289).

In addition to the First Amendment, the Fourteenth Amendment's Equal Protection Clause also protects against discrimination by a government employer. In 2012, for example, the Kentucky Cabinet for Health and Family Services was held accountable for violating a gay employee's equal protection rights when it fired him for sending inappropriate e-mails, when a heterosexual married woman who sent exactly the same kind of e-mails was never even considered for termination (*Stroder v. Commonwealth of Kentucky Cabinet for Health and Family Services*).

In another case, in 2011, a federal judge in the Northern District for Ohio upheld the right of Shari Hutchinson, a lesbian, to pursue a discrimination claim against her county employer, rooted in disparate treatment under the Equal Protection Clause. Unlike Stroder, Hutchinson had no direct evidence of discrimination but believed she had been passed over a number of times for promotion because of her sexual orientation. Through discovery, Hutchinson's attorney had produced enough evidence of disparate treatment to suggest that her employer's stated reasons for not promoting her were pretextual. She was therefore entitled to go to trial, where she would have a reasonable chance of winning, because under *McDonnell Douglas Corp. v. Green*, a Supreme Court case establishing the basic framework for analyzing Equal Protection claims, the burden of proof in discrimination cases shifts to the defendant to explain the discrimination once the plaintiff establishes that the discrimination occurred. Since *Romer v. Evans* teaches that animus is not an appropriate basis for discrimination, Hutchinson's county employer would now have the burden of proving another motive for its discrimination. In *Scarborough v. Morgan County Board of Education*, the Sixth Circuit found that evidence showed that just such animus had motivated the Morgan County school board when it refused to rehire an employee based on his affiliation with an event attended by homosexuals.

Many judges today clearly view the right of gay persons to defend themselves in public and be more open about their orientation in a markedly different way than they did just a couple of decades ago. Their evolution has gone hand in hand with the changes in the broader culture, reflected in, among other areas, a much greater public sensitivity to the kinds of violence and bullying to which extreme homophobia can lead.

# 8

---

# Freedom from Violence;
# Freedom to Serve

In 1987 a Reagan Justice Department report concluded that gays "are probably the most frequent victims" of bias crimes (Vaid 1995, 11). Violence against gays ranges from horrific homicides to the day-to-day school experience of being bullied and humiliated. Bullying of public school students who are gay or perceived to be gay remains a major problem in our nation's schools, but this is an instance where the legal system has played a helpful role in trying to stop it.

## Freedom from Bullying

For too long, the gay student was completely alone in facing often unrelenting assaults on his personhood and safety. Sometimes simply not believing complaints, sometimes blaming the victims, sometimes simply laughing them off with statements like "boys will be boys," school administrators in many places rarely investigated complaints and even more rarely took action. The result was often an escalation of terror as natural bullies realized they could continue their actions with impunity. For many, suicide seemed the only way out. In recent years, things have begun to change, and as with so many steps forward, this one began with one brave individual who endured almost unimaginable suffering throughout his public school career, and then, even more remarkably, having somehow managed to survive and even to begin to thrive, decided to sue.

Jamie Nabozny decided to pursue legal action primarily to ensure that what had happened to him in the Ashland, Wisconsin, public school system would not happen to any other gay student in Ashland or anywhere else. His suit, begun in the fall of 1993, is a case study in how the law can move public policy forward. At the time of his suit under the Fourteenth Amendment's

Equal Protection Clause, there was little legal precedent to suggest that he would be successful. Remarkably, however, once the full extent of the misery he had suffered became apparent (a simulated rape, a beating leading to hospitalization for internal bleeding, and an incident in which he was urinated on were just three major incidents in a never-ending campaign of harassment), as well as the administration's indifference to his plight, the need and essential rightness of his suit became obvious. As the three-judge federal court of appeals panel noted in its unanimous opinion (all three of the judges, incidentally, had been appointed by Republican presidents), it was "impossible to believe that a female lodging a similar complaint would have received the same response" (*Nabozny v. Podlesny*, 454–455). Therefore, it was clear that Jamie Nabozny's constitutional right to equal protection of the laws had been violated, unless the school could show a rational justification for its differential treatment.

In the end, the school district paid out close to a million dollars to settle the case. The more important impact, however, was to finally arm bullying victims everywhere with a legal weapon with which to fight back. While emphasizing that bullying is still a major problem, Carlos A. Ball, in *From the Closet to the Courtroom*, a book that brings to life five key law suits in the history of the gay rights movement, states that "*Nabozny* laid the legal foundation that has permitted many other victims of antigay harassment and abuse to turn to the courts for help. . . . the settlement agreements that have sometimes been reached in those lawsuits have required school districts to adopt policies, procedures and training programs specifically aimed at addressing and preventing harassment of LGBT students" (2010, 97).

There is bullying and then there is extreme bullying. In the case of the latter, Title IX of the Education Amendments of 1972 affords some measure of federal protection. The kind of bullying experienced year after year by DP in the Hudson Area School District was just as repulsive as that experienced by Nabozny in Ashland. It began in the seventh grade and finally drove him out of the public school system by the beginning of what would have been his sophomore year. In *Patterson v. Hudson Area Schools*, the Sixth Circuit Court of Appeals reversed a federal district court decision that had dismissed DP's suit against the school district on the ground that DP had not established the deliberate indifference on the part of the district that DP would need to prove to establish liability. The case is important because it underscores that a school system cannot just impose what in many cases was perfunctory punishment against bullies and expect to be shielded from liability.

Outside of the school context, a major victory in the legal fight against violence occurred in the fall of 2009 when President Obama signed into law the Matthew Shepard and James Byrd Jr. Hate Crimes Prevention Act. The act expanded the definition of a hate crime under the 1969 Federal Hate Crimes Law (18 U.S.C. Sec. 245) to include crimes motivated by a victim's sexual orientation, gender identity, or disability. Matthew Shepard was the young University of Wyoming college student who had been brutally murdered in Laramie, Wyoming, eleven years earlier; James Byrd was a black man murdered and dragged by truck through the streets of a small Texas town.

The new law also significantly strengthened the 1969 law. The 1969 Hate Crimes Law was only triggered if the victim was engaging in a federally protected activity such as voting or jury service. The new law dropped this limitation, meaning that the Department of Justice can now step in and prosecute a hate crime no matter the circumstances under which it is committed. Passage of the legislation marked a major legislative triumph of the gay rights movement. Lobbying was spearheaded by the Human Rights Campaign and the National Gay and Lesbian Task Force. The legislation also marks the value to the gay movement of creating alliances, for removal of the federal activities limitation was clearly of interest to many civil rights and civic organizations, not just gay rights groups. For this reason the legislation was endorsed by literally hundreds of organizations, including the International Association of Chiefs of Police, the NAACP, the YWCA, many church organizations, and the National District Attorneys Association.

The federal legislation is important, as a practical matter, because at the time of its passage eighteen states offered no protection against hate crimes based on sexual orientation. There was also the symbolic importance of the first piece of federal legislation explicitly protecting gays and transgender people. Notwithstanding the widespread support of the bill among so many organizations, 131 House Republicans and 28 Senate Republicans opposed it. The Republican Speaker of the House, John Boehner, vehemently opposed the bill, characterizing it as radical social policy that was "wrong" because "it's going to add further charges to someone based on what they may have been thinking." Boehner's position, of course would mean that the original 1969 Hate Crimes legislation was as wrong as its 2009 expansion, and if prosecuting a hate crime is wrong because it represents some kind of effort at thought control, then perhaps the FBI shouldn't even be reporting on the number of hate crimes, something it has been doing since 1990 under the Hate Crime Statistics Act of 1990 signed into law by the first President Bush.

Speaker Boehner was also apparently unaware that his First Amendment concern had been considered and unanimously rejected by the Supreme Court in 1993 in *Wisconsin v. Mitchell*, a case that considered the constitutionality of the Wisconsin hate crimes statute. In upholding the constitutionality of the statute,

Chief Justice William Rehnquist, hardly a leftist, found that "the Wisconsin statute singles out for [penalty] enhancement bias-inspired conduct because this conduct is thought to inflict greater individual and societal harm" (*Wisconsin*, 487–488). Those harms included, according to the state of Wisconsin, the tendency of hate crimes to provoke retaliatory crimes, inflict emotional harm on their victims, and create community unrest. Rehnquist found that these justifications provided "an adequate explanation . . . over and above mere disagreement with offenders' beliefs or biases" (488).

Chief Justice Rehnquist was right. Hate crimes legislation is necessary because hate crimes threaten social stability within a community and create fear by singling out a particular segment of the community in a way that other crimes do not. Its victims are not just those immediately attacked but all those who are part of the group inspiring the attack. Hate legislation also draws a line in the sand: you may have and express any beliefs you want under the First Amendment but you act on them in the form of criminal behavior at your peril. I don't believe this would strike the average citizen as radical policy or a form of thought control, particularly since the legislation bars any prosecution based on an individual's expression of "racial, religious, political or other beliefs" and also states that nothing in the law should be "construed to diminish any rights under the First Amendment to the Constitution." Hate crimes, it should be noted, target more than just individuals. The Metropolitan Community Church, for example, experienced a total of eighteen fires during the church's first twenty-five years (Clendinen and Nagourney 1999, 183).

Hate crimes legislation protecting gays has a special justification (as it does for blacks) because of the historically brutal nature of many of the crimes committed against them. Homophobia has always presented a particularly vicious face, almost as if its perpetrators were desperately trying to exorcise their own demons. Speaker Boehner's concern about penalizing people because of what they might be thinking seems somewhat out of place in considering this hate crime: "a shy [gay] man, too devoted to his parents to leave their small town in Alabama, is invited from a pool tournament to his death by two men. They had decided ahead of time that they would murder him. After beating him, they stuff him into the trunk of his own car and drive him out to a boat ramp. . . . There they beat him further with an axe handle and then slit his throat. They pour kerosene on some tires, set them on fire, and then throw his body on top, creating a pyre" (Senak 2003, 240). I include this description not for sensationalism but to underscore why legislation condemning violence motivated by hate does serve a legitimate purpose and why gays are especially in need of its protection.

## Freedom to Serve

Hate-motivated violence doesn't just occur in the civilian world. In July 1999, two young men, boys really, got into a fist fight, not an unusual occurrence. The boys lived together along with a bunch of other young men. The loser in the fight, one Calvin Glover, was teased badly because the winner, Barry Winchell, was gay. Something snapped inside young Glover, and two days later he took his revenge, beating Winchell to death with a baseball bat while he slept in their barracks. The incident occurred at Fort Campbell, Kentucky, and the two young men were privates in the United States Army.

As one would expect, the action was universally condemned. As one might also expect, people took very different lessons from it. For opponents of gays in the military, the incident demonstrated in extreme form the danger to unit cohesion and spirit that the presence of gays in the military presented. For proponents, it delivered a much different message, revealing the importance of strong leadership, which, proponents argued, was sadly lacking at Fort Campbell, resulting in an atmosphere that tolerated, perhaps even encouraged, a strong antigay message.

Until recently, open service of gays in the military was unthinkable. Since the Second World War, the army had issued a myriad of regulations intended to cover homosexual conduct. While the details evolved over time, the message was always the same: the presence of gays in the military is unacceptable and requires their prompt separation from the service. The army's discharge policy was occasionally challenged, but only when highly unusual circumstances made forced separation extremely unfair. Sergeant Perry Watkins, for example, succeeded in getting his forced separation overturned but only because he had been completely open about his homosexuality when he had been drafted into the army in 1967 and had thereafter served with distinction for sixteen years, all the time being open about his gayness. Under those circumstances, the army was deemed equitably estopped from discharging him.

Other than gay marriage, there was no issue involving gay rights that aroused more emotion than the right of gays to serve in the military. Yet the issue was sometimes misperceived. The issue was not whether gays in fact served in the military—they did—but whether they could be open about it. We have already discussed how President Clinton was unable to convince Congress at the start of his presidency to allow gays and lesbians to serve openly, with "Don't Ask, Don't Tell" (hereafter DADT) being enacted instead.

The issue of gays in the military was well aired before DADT was enacted. The Senate Armed Services Committee conducted hearings on four separate occasions totaling nine days; the Military Forces and Preparedness

Subcommittee of the House Armed Services Committee also conducted hearings on the issue. Virtually every aspect of the issue was discussed through testimony and prepared statements. Law professors considered questions of constitutionality; military personnel questioned how DADT would be applied, including the duty of soldiers to report information casting suspicion on a fellow soldier's orientation; the blurred boundary between status and conduct was discussed; the impact of gays on morale and on unit cohesion was closely examined. Both sides made important points. Supporters of DADT pointed out that although it was true that gays had served with distinction, they had done so largely while keeping their orientation secret. Proponents of open acceptance of homosexuality emphasized the negative impact of hiding one's orientation on job performance and suggested that greater openness might actually benefit unit cohesion.

Looming over the hearings was the most basic question of all: What would be the practical impact of any change in policy on the military's effectiveness as a fighting force? And here gay stereotyping of the worst kind reared its ugly head. It was a hard lesson. As Urvashi Vaid wrote, "When soldiers began talking about showers and foxholes, whatever mainstream legitimacy we had assumed, whatever straight acceptance we thought we had earned, vanished without a trace" (1995, 178).

While many of the opponents of gays in the military did not get the outright ban they had sought, they did block the one thing they had feared most: open acceptance of gays in one of America's most revered institutions. Supporters of acceptance, on the other hand, were angry given the high hopes engendered by Clinton's campaign commitments. The gay and lesbian community had a different name for Don't Ask, Don't Tell—Lie and Hide.

In September 1993 DADT was codified into law; the final vote was 92–7 in favor in the Senate and 268–162 in the House. Thirty-three senators had voted for a failed amendment that would have provided for open acceptance. Senator Paul Wellstone of Minnesota, one of the seven to vote against the final bill, captured the liberals' disappointment when he said, "We are today about to codify a policy based on fear and based on prejudice. It is a policy that does not look forward, it looks backward" (Embser Herbert 2007, 20). Wellstone was right. The net result of DADT was that gays were supposed to remain in the closet. The most important achievement of the gay rights movement—the willingness to acknowledge one's identity and fight for one's rights against stigmas and stereotypes—had no place in that policy. Yet, it was not always a question of prejudice. Thoughtful people like Colin Powell expressed a fundamental belief that open acceptance of gays was incompatible with the realities of military life and combat. Resistance in the military, particularly at the leadership levels, was a key factor in the failure of Clinton's initiative, but it wasn't the only factor. Clinton had made gays in the military one of the first issues he addressed as president. To the public, it may have seemed a case of undue emphasis on a controversial issue not at the center of national concerns. The reaction of the military and the public took even gay rights lobbyists by surprise.

Under DADT, homosexual conduct included admitting one was gay or acting in a way that would reveal one was gay. This was of immense importance because it meant that the military didn't need to show that the accused had actually engaged in homosexual activity. In effect, status had become conflated with conduct.

At the beginning, there was at least the hope that DADT would allow gays to serve honorably with a minimum of harassment. It did not work out that way, in part because once there was any evidence that an individual was gay, the burden shifted to the accused to show that he or she was not gay. As a result, the number of gays being dismissed actually began to exceed pre-DADT levels. In 1997, almost 1,000 service personnel were dismissed for being gay. The figure rose to more than 1,225 in 2001. The numbers declined sharply as the manpower needs of the military increased with the onset of the Iraq War but still averaged roughly 625 a year from 2003 forward. Altogether, roughly 13,000 service personnel were dismissed under DADT. With the military no longer screening for homosexuality, it seems that those service personnel opposed to serving with gays would sometimes take it upon themselves to root out homosexuals from the service. The kind of evidence deemed sufficiently "credible" to begin an investigation differed from base to base and from unit commander to unit commander. Leadership is extraordinarily important in a hierarchical society like the military, and a base command or unit commander could easily create an atmosphere in which personnel were encouraged to come forward with the "credible evidence" needed to begin an investigation.

To appreciate the extent to which DADT departed from basic constitutional principles, one must understand that the Supreme Court in a number of cases has made clear that status alone is not a basis for penalizing a person, so, for example, narcotics addiction is not itself a crime; actual use must be shown (*Robinson v. California*). DADT, however, essentially involved discrimination on the basis of status. Discovery of evidence showing even "a propensity or intent to engage in homosexual acts" shifted the burden to the accused to deny such propensity or intent, even in the absence of any actual proof of such conduct. Although at least one circuit found that the simple statement "I am in fact gay" was not a sufficient basis for forced separation from the military (see *Meinhold v. United States Department of Defense*), it doesn't appear that any decision of any court actually impacted the manner in which the military administered DADT.

Under DADT, even accidental discoveries could produce the most obvious injustice. Mike Almy was a major in the U.S. Air Force for thirteen years. He came from a family with a rich history of military service. In his March 18, 2010, testimony before the Senate Armed Services Committee, he recalled, "When I was growing up, I didn't really know what civilians were. I just knew I would always follow in my father's footsteps and become a military officer" (Almy 2010, 8). Among other things, he was once named the top officer of his base out of a group of about thousand and was one of six officers from the entire air force selected to attend Professional Military Education at Quantico Marine Corps Base, Virginia. He deployed to the Middle East four times, and in Iraq he led a team of almost two hundred men and women whose mission was to operate the systems that controlled the air space over Iraq.

While Almy was in Iraq, air force policy restricted access to all private e-mails, so personnel were authorized to use work e-mails for personal purposes. After Maj. Almy left Iraq, a routine search led to a discovery of e-mails, clearly labeled personal, that raised the suspicion that the major was gay. Then, Maj. Almy later testified, "the commander in Iraq, during the height of the insurgency, ordered a search of my personal e-mails solely to determine whether I had violated Don't, Ask Don't Tell and to gather whatever evidence could be used against me." The e-mails were duly forwarded to the commander at Almy's new base in Germany, who relieved Almy of his duties when Almy refused to discuss the e-mails with him. The commander assured him that it was no reflection on his performance as an officer. In Almy's words: "After that day I was in limbo for sixteen months," assigned to meaningless make-work tasks (2010, 9).

In the discharge proceedings, several former troops and squadron commanders wrote letters attesting to Almy's performance and urging the air force to retain him. Nevertheless, Almy was ultimately discharged. In his testimony he recalled, "As a final insult, on my last day of Active Duty, I was given a police escort from the base, as if I were a common criminal or a threat to national security. . . . I felt betrayed by my country and treated as a second class citizen" (2010, 9).

Almy had every right to be bitter. Almost his entire career had occurred while DADT was the operative regime, and Almy had not once violated the basic understanding, never disclosing any aspect of his private life. Nevertheless, he had been investigated through no fault of his own and discharged because of a personal trait that had absolutely no bearing on his performance. Multiply Almy's case by about 13,000 and it is not hard to see why DADT was a compromise in name only.

The fact that DADT was codified in federal law (section 654, Title 10, U.S. Code) was important because it meant that any change in policy would require congressional approval. President Clinton had originally wanted simply to end the ban on gays serving in the military through a policy directive. That goal was thwarted because the military opposed a policy of open acceptance and because Clinton knew that any policy directive from the Defense Department that did not have full support of the military would almost assuredly be overturned by Congress. The fact that Senator Sam Nunn of Georgia, chairman of the Senate Armed Services Committee, was adamantly opposed to lifting the ban meant that the one person in Congress with a powerful enough connection to the top military leadership to have helped secure an end to the policy was, instead, a major obstacle to its elimination.

Fifteen years after its enactment, with newly elected President Barack Obama and a Democratic Congress, DADT seemed in danger. President Obama, however, first had a financial crisis to deal with and then an economy in free fall. Add to that the pressure within the Democratic Party to enact health care and it is not surprising that repeal of DADT was not a priority. Though the time might not have been right during those first two years, things were much different than they had been in 1993. Public opinion had swung in favor of allowing gays to serve openly by a wide margin. Additionally, military insiders and knowledgeable observers knew that DADT had cost the services many valuable personnel at a time when the military had been significantly lowering its standards to attract recruits. The army had, for example, doubled the number of waivers between 2003 and 2006 for recruits with criminal backgrounds (Embser-Herbert 2007, 82). During the first ten years of DADT, the military lost fifty-four Arabic speakers and nine Farsi speakers as a result of the policy (Mucciaroni 2008, 175).

In his 2010 State of the Union address, President Obama again called for repeal of DADT. Nevertheless, opposition to repeal, led by Senator John McCain, seemed likely to carry the day when, in September 2010, the Democrats were unable to overturn the threat of a Republican filibuster. All was not lost, however. Earlier in 2010, Secretary of Defense Robert Gates had issued a memorandum directing a comprehensive review of what repeal of DADT would involve. The report, issued three weeks after the Republicans' stunning victory in the midterm congressional elections, supported the feasibility of repeal.

At first, it seemed that the report would be academic, given the Republican dominance in the newly elected House of Representatives which would convene in January 2011. There was, however, the lame duck session of Congress (November–December 2010) in which the Democrats would still be in control. When President Obama struck a deal with Republicans on taxation and unemployment benefits early in the lame duck session, there was an opportunity to focus on other matters during the brief remaining period of Democratic control. Once again the Senate took up the repeal issue, this time beating back an attempted filibuster with the votes of four Republicans (Senators Collins, Snowe, Brown, and Murkowski). Interestingly, of the four Republicans, three were women and the fourth, Scott Brown, was from Massachusetts, where same-sex marriage had been legal for six years and had lapsed into a virtual nonissue so widely was it accepted. After cloture, the Senate voted 65–31 (4 additional Republicans ended up supporting repeal) to end DADT once the president, secretary of defense, and the chairman of the Joint Chiefs of Staff could certify to Congress that repeal could be implemented in a manner not detrimental to military effectiveness.

The political silence following repeal was as telling as the vote itself. Notwithstanding Senator McCain's admonition that "if it isn't broke, don't fix it," coupled with his warning that repeal would probably harm "battle effectiveness," 77 percent of the public, according to an ABC News/*Washington Post* poll, supported allowing gays to openly serve in the military. That 77 percent included Senator McCain's own wife and daughter, who had expressed their support for the end of DADT.

Ten months later, in September 2011, DADT ended. It was a non-event. "Apart from some news accounts about joyful celebrations near various military bases, the event went off without newsworthy incident" (*Lesbian/Gay Law Notes*, October 11, 2012, 215). To the shock of many, the marines almost immediately began to seek out gay and lesbian recruits. In the lead up to formal repeal of DADT, several military leaders who had expressed reservations about repeal seemed pleasantly surprised by the reaction in the field. General James Amos, commandant of the Marine Corps, who had been the most outspoken of those expressing reservations about allowing gays to serve openly, testified to Congress after a field trip to Afghanistan, that "there hasn't been the recalcitrant pushback" nor "the anxiety of the forces in the field" that he had feared. One year after repeal of DADT it was clear that none of the dire warnings predicted had come to pass. Soldiers had not resigned; military effectiveness had not been compromised. The world, as Secretary of Defense Leon Panetta said, had "moved beyond it" (*New York Times*, September 20, 2012, A17). As many had predicted, open service had greatly improved the morale of gays serving in the military without harming anyone else.

As Senator Barry Goldwater, an air force reserve general who came to support open service long before its acceptance, said, "You don't have to be straight to shoot straight." You also don't have to be straight to bleed. The first solider to be wounded in the war in Iraq was Staff Sergeant Eric Alva, a gay marine, who lost a leg after stepping on a landmine.

Was DADT itself unconstitutional? The Supreme Court never ruled on that question and won't since the issue is now moot. While DADT was still in place, however, the Ninth Circuit Court of Appeals, in *Witt v. Department of Air Force*, held that Margaret Witt, an air force reservist officer, could not be discharged under DADT because *Lawrence v. Texas* recognized a fundamental right of privacy in the conduct of one's sexual relations that would be violated given the facts of the case. The court did not declare that DADT was unconstitutional on its face, just that it couldn't be constitutionally applied to Witt. The facts of the case are worth a brief recital because they also point to how DADT was hijacked, used to root out the very people it was intended to protect.

Margaret Witt joined the air force in 1987 and was commissioned a second lieutenant that year. She was promoted to first lieutenant in 1989 and to captain in 1991. In 1995 she transferred from active to reserve duty at McChord Air Force Base. In 1999 she was promoted to major. "By all accounts Major Witt was an outstanding Air Force officer" (*Witt*, 809). She was so highly thought of that she became a "poster child" for air force recruitment purposes, her face appearing prominently in air force promotional materials. In 1997, she began a long-term relationship with a same-sex partner. The couple lived in Spokane, Washington, 250 miles from McChord Air Force Base. Major Witt never disclosed her relationship to anyone, but in 2004 she was contacted by an air force investigative officer inquiring into her private relationships. She refused to answer any questions and ultimately received an honorable discharge because of her homosexuality.

Witt sued, contesting her discharge. When the case came to the Ninth Circuit, the court declared *Lawrence v. Texas* applicable to Margaret Will's case but remanded it back to the federal district court (Judge Ronald Leighton) to determine factually whether her honorable discharge violated her right of substantive due process under the Fifth Amendment. After considering all the facts, Judge Leighton concluded that the discharge did not significantly further any important governmental interest and that Witt was entitled to return to the air force. Aside from the case's constitutional interest, the facts clearly show the military violating, at a minimum, the spirit of its own policy, "asking" even when Major Witt had never told and had, in fact, been entirely discreet in her private behavior. The case was finally settled in May 2010 when the air force gave up its appeal of Judge Leighton's decision and agreed to remove Major Witt's discharge from the military record; she was allowed to retire with full benefits.

The military issue is over, at least for the time being; not so, however, for the many challenging issues that arise in the public school context, a subject to which we now turn.

# 9

## The Public School Struggle

Recall the isolation of the gay adolescent of the 1950s with whom I began this book. Obviously, such an adolescent living in 2013 is part of a much different world, yet bullying, as we already have seen, can still have devastating effects. A national survey conducted in 2011 by the Gay, Lesbian, and Straight Education Network (GLSEN) found that nearly two-thirds of the students questioned felt unsafe in their schools as a result of their sexual orientation and that more than eight in ten had been called names or threatened (xiv).

As we saw in *Dillon v. Frank*, inappropriate gender expression seems particularly difficult, even for adults, to handle. Debra Chasnoff, a San Francisco–based, Academy Award–winning lesbian documentary filmmaker focuses on the world of the public school student. In 2008, she made *Straightlaced—How Gender Got Us All Tied Up* and was struck by how crucial the issue of gender expression is for all students. Indeed, she sees a strong connection between the needs of straight high school boys to establish their maleness and the bullying of gay students who behave in stereotypically feminine ways. For these straight boys, bullying affirms their masculine identity. She points out that, in this important way, antigay prejudice affects all students, not just gays and lesbians. A major goal of her film, for which she interviewed numerous students, gay and straight, was "to create a platform for high school students to really reflect on how they are affected by the pressures to act or be in a certain way because they're male or female" (Chasnoff 2009). In working on the film, Chasnoff reflected that it was hard not to think back to her own high school experience, when "there were would have been no openly gay or lesbian or transgender students to be included in this film." Fortunately today, in contrast to twenty years ago, that is no longer the case, and the emergence of gay–straight alliance clubs is one of the reasons, for they provide precisely the kind of platform to discuss and explore feelings on a daily basis that Chasnoff sought to provide in her film for her interviewees.

## Gay–Straight Alliance Clubs

Twenty years ago, gay–straight alliance clubs were virtually nonexistent. Today there are more than 4,000 of them throughout the nation. A sanctioned club enjoys important advantages in many schools, including access to the public address system for announcements and the right to raise funds and distribute materials on school time, using school facilities. As with the tremendous growth of gay–straight alliance networks within large corporations, they represent a triumph of the gay rights movement. The number 4,000 may seem surprisingly high. Why didn't more school districts simply deny recognition of these clubs? GLSEN, a strong national umbrella organization aimed at promoting the introduction of gay–straight alliance clubs in public schools, provides part of the answer. An even bigger part, however, is simply that federal law prevents school districts from prohibiting such clubs. Ironically, the applicable federal legislation, the Equal Access Act, was actually sought by the religious right and signed into law by President Reagan in 1984.

The Equal Access Act applies to a public secondary school receiving federal funds and requires that schools allowing noncurriculum clubs not discriminate among them on the basis of the religious, political, philosophical, or other sort of speech at the group's meetings. The act's conservative sponsors wanted to assure that bible study groups and other student-led religious groups could use school facilities on the same basis as other student groups. The question immediately arose whether the act violated the Establishment Clause of the First Amendment, which prohibits Congress from making laws respecting the establishment of religion, by authorizing religious activities on public property. The Supreme Court in *Board of Education of Westside Community Schools v. Mergens* held that the act was constitutional because it met the requirements of the so-called Lemon test enunciated in a previous Supreme Court case, which includes a requirement that the act be for a secular purpose. The act's secular purpose, as determined by the Court, was to prevent discrimination against student speech.

The act has led most school boards to acquiesce in the creation of gay–straight alliance clubs, although recent law review articles detect an increase in litigation, particularly in more conservative parts of the country, in attempting to resist the alliances (see Woods 2010). The term *noncurriculum group* has been interpreted broadly by the federal judiciary to include even such activities as prom organizing and cheerleading, so that if a school wants cheerleaders or a prom, it must also allow a gay–straight alliance club. The American Civil

Liberties Union has played a major role in bringing that point home time and again to recalcitrant school boards. Between 2009 and 2013, for example, four different school boards in Pennsylvania (Waynesboro, Hermitage, Brownsville, and Chambersburg) were forced to reconsider their initial opposition to the gay–straight alliance clubs after the demands of the Equal Access Act were made known to them.

School boards trying to thwart the creation of alliance clubs on various pretexts have generally failed when their position was challenged in federal court, a major exception being a case involving the recognition of a gay–straight alliance club in Lubbock, Texas. The facts of that case were unusual in that the club made clear that it intended to discuss safe sex at its meetings, notwithstanding the school's stated policy of encouraging total abstinence. Even more damaging, the club had a link on its website to another site containing obscene material. The Court also emphasized that there were students as young as twelve years old in the school (*Caudillo v. Lubbock Independent School District*).

Nevertheless, the Equal Access Act does provide that schools do not need to permit noncurricular clubs that threaten the maintenance of order and discipline on school premises or that jeopardize the well-being of students. These were potentially broad exceptions to the requirement for equal access that school boards could have successfully exploited had federal courts been more receptive to arguments invoking them. It wasn't as if some school boards didn't try and may still try in the future. Two lines of resistance have been to claim that gay–straight alliances are sex-based clubs and therefore inappropriate for students or that they threaten order and discipline because they render gay students themselves vulnerable to harassment. The sex-based club argument rests on the premise that discussions about sex will necessarily be the focus of the clubs. In fact, however, this premise is almost always wrong, their real purpose most often simply being to provide an accepting place for gay students and to promote tolerance and discourage bullying. As for the argument that the alliances create a potential danger of disruption, this amounts to invoking what is sometimes called, in a free speech context, a heckler's veto and has not proved a successful argument for religious conservatives attempting to block the clubs.

A critical question in future litigation may involve the degree to which federal courts will scrutinize school board justifications for prohibiting gay–straight alliance clubs. Woods (2010) expresses some fear that federal courts will begin to defer too readily to school board claims unless courts require a clear showing based on concrete evidence that the clubs will lead to substantial disruption, the so-called Tinker standard, from a student free-speech case in which the Supreme Court held that the First Amendment right of students could not be bridged simply on the basis of an undifferentiated fear or apprehension of disturbance.

The effect of gay–straight alliance groups is not easy to measure. Few would deny their generally positive impact in providing an important refuge and resource for gays and in promoting gay acceptance. Emergence from the closet automatically guarantees the disapproval of at least some portion of the community, even if one has understanding parents and friends. A gay–straight alliance group provides a refuge of safety and support. Roughly half the high schools in the country now have alliance clubs according to GLSEN's 2009 survey, although only one-tenth of middle schools do (Schwartz 2012, 178).

Even some pro-gay-rights advocates, however, worry that alliances may encourage students to place too much stress on their sexual identity as a defining characteristic of their personality. This fear was expressed most cogently by Ritich C. Savin-Williams of Cornell University, in *The New Gay Teenager* (2005). Savin-Williams believes that many academic studies emphasizing gay teenage depression and low self-esteem may be skewed for a number of reasons, including the possibility that self-identifying gay teens with these very problems may make up a disproportionate number of study participants. On the basis of his own work and analysis of the work of others, he believes that academic scholarship needs to "rise above such 'doom and gloom' caricature and present the larger context of teenagers' lives" (221). "The fact is," he concludes, "the lives of most same-sex-attracted teenagers are not exceptional either in their pathology or their resiliency. Rather, they are ordinary. Gay adolescents have the same developmental concerns, assets and liabilities as heterosexual adolescents" (223). Notwithstanding his reservations, Savin-Williams recognizes the current value of the alliance clubs, describing as priceless the visibility these clubs give to nonheterosexuality.

As important as gay–straight alliance clubs have been, however, nothing replaces in importance an accepting family environment. The law can do many things but mandating a loving family is not one of them. In a 2009 article in *Pediatrics* magazine, for example, the Family Acceptance Project, an important research group begun in 2002 by Caitlin Ryan at San Francisco State University, reported that families characterized by patterns of rejection had a dramatic effect on the health of their LGBT children, resulting, among other things, in an almost nine times higher attempted suicide rate than for such children coming from more accepting families (Ryan et al. 2009). The project's work has been influential in leading groups such as Parents, Families and Friends of Lesbians and Gays (PFLAG) to take a more assertive role in family activities. As it has become abundantly clear to the project that children coming from highly religious homes are especially vulnerable, the project has embarked on an effort to provide booklets aimed at particular faiths to encourage greater family acceptance of their LGBT children. In 2012, the project issued its first such effort aimed at the families of Mormon children.

## Curriculum Issues

Schools cannot mandate love any more than the law can, but what they teach can be enormously important both in how gays view themselves and how others view them. The battle over the teaching of evolution in public schools is the best-known curriculum struggle, but curriculum issues as they relate to homosexuality are not far behind, particularly in school districts where religious conservatives object to what they perceive as curriculum choices that undermine the view of morality they wish to inculcate in their own children. Two important Supreme Court cases from the 1920s (*Meyer v. Nebraska* and *Pierce v. Society of Sisters*) have long stood for the proposition that parents have a liberty interest under the Fourteenth Amendment's Due Process Clause in controlling the upbringing of their children. Religious conservatives have shaped constitutional objections to certain curriculum decisions around concerns for parental autonomy as well as objections rooted in the First Amendment's Free Speech and Free Exercise of Religion Clauses. The law is far from settled, and the Supreme Court has not yet taken a case that addresses the clash between the constitutional claims of religious conservatives and the proponents of gay rights in the curriculum context..

This is not just an issue that arises in high school or middle school. Indeed, one of the most interesting and controversial cases, with reverberations leading all the way to California's fight over Proposition 8, dealt with a curriculum issue in Massachusetts at early grade levels. It began in January 2005 when Jacob Parker, a kindergartner, brought home a picture book titled *Who's in a Family?* showing various family combinations, including one with two moms and one with two dads. The book said nothing about marriage. In March 2006, a second-grader, Joey Wirthlin, Jr., told his parents about a book, *King and King*, that his teacher had read aloud in class, involving a prince who kept rejecting princess candidates until he discovered true love with another prince. The book concluded with a wedding scene and showed the two princes kissing with a red heart imposed over their mouths. The Parkers and Wirthlins strongly objected to these books and argued in a suit brought in federal district court that the books amounted to an attempt at indoctrination that violated their and their children's right to the free exercise of religion guaranteed by the First Amendment and also their right as parents to direct the upbringing of their children. The parents did not seek to ban either book but did seek an injunction to require the schools, among other things, to allow their children an opportunity to opt out of presentations or class discussions whose intent was to "embrace, affirm or celebrate views of human sexuality, gender identity, and marriage constructs" (*Parker v. Hurley*, 94).

Both the trial court and then the First Circuit Court of Appeals rejected the parents' claims (*Parker v. Hurley*). The circuit court found no violation of the children's religious rights, emphasizing that there was no governmental compulsion for either child to either do or refrain from doing something that was contrary to their religious belief or practice. The court did recognize that the reading aloud of *King and King* in a compulsory class setting was closer to the kind of indoctrination that the Free Exercise Clause might prohibit, but the court emphasized that Joey had not been required to affirm his belief in gay marriage or take part in the class discussion. The court also found that parental autonomy had not been fatally undermined. "Exposure to the materials in dispute here," wrote the court, "will not automatically and irreversibly prevent the parents from raising Jacob and Joey in the religious belief that gay marriage is immoral" (*Parker*, 100). The court also noted that, under well-established case law, while parents have a constitutional right to choose between public and private schools, they do not have a constitutional right to direct how a public school should teach their child.

The court's decision may seem harsh. After all, the parents were simply asking that their children not be exposed to material that they found deeply objectionable. On the other hand, an opt-out provision grants parents de facto veto power over school curriculum, an authority that courts are wisely reluctant to provide as a matter of constitutional law. And parents who object to school policies have any number of political avenues for change, including appealing to the local school board and, if that fails, trying to replace board members.

This case became something of a cause célèbre among social conservatives and was used effectively in the campaign for Proposition 8. Rob and Robin Wirthlin became as well known in California through television spots as they were in their home state of Massachusetts, probably more so. The Family Research Council produced a thirty-minute video on the case, which was also used during the campaign. Opponents of Proposition 8 pointed out that same-sex marriage has nothing to do with childhood education, but they were missing the emotional resonance of the *Parker* case for those religious conservatives who feel besieged by a society that increasingly supports what they view as immoral relationships. *Parker v. Hurley*, arising in a state that allows gay marriages, bore witness to conservatives' deepest fears. Following the favorable district court decision, the superintendent of schools, Dr. Ash, offered concerned parents the opportunity to view the school's diversity curriculum in advance so that they would know what was being taught and would be able to talk about the topics covered with their child at home, an offer that was rejected.

At the junior high and high school levels, sex education can be a deeply divisive issue, as differing conceptions about the origins of gay sexuality intrude with particular force. For those who believe that homosexuality is a lifestyle one chooses and that recruits children into it, any treatment of homosexuality that implies acceptance seems a direct invitation to their own children to give it a try. The case law in this area is still at an early stage. To some extent, its emergence as an issue reflects the increasing influence and assertiveness of gay rights advocates.

As recently as the late nineties, an important study of sexual orientation issues in public schools found that sexual orientation was rarely mentioned in the classroom, and the few schools that did include sexual orientation as part of the curriculum generally provided an opt-out provision for objecting parents. As more and more schools have sought to address sexual orientation issues in their health education programs, Christian rights legal organizations have initiated numerous court challenges, including ones in Ann Arbor, Michigan, Minneapolis, Minnesota, and Fairfield, Connecticut (NeJaime 2009, 337).

For the moment, challenges to local school district curriculum decisions seem to be failing. Thus, the First Circuit has rejected a parental challenge to a mandatory AIDS education program for high school students (*Brown v. Hot, Sexy and Safer Productions*), and the Second Circuit to mandatory middle school health classes (*Leebaert v. Harrington*). A federal district court also dismissed a challenge to mandatory diversity programming aimed at reducing antigay harassment (*Morrison v. Board of Education of Boyd County*). It has been suggested, however, that Christian right legal organizations will continue to bring lawsuits challenging programs they regard as problematical not only because this is a key battlefield for the Christian right but also in the hope that a conservative Supreme Court will be convinced to take a case, which could result in an important shift in doctrine (NeJaime 2009, 349).

One final issue in the curriculum area is whether and how to teach gay history. The subject touches the same nerve endings for fundamentalists as do many other gay issues because of its potential for being seen as an endorsement of gayness itself. Black leaders such as Martin Luther King and martyrs such as Andrew Goodman, Michael Schwerner, and James Chaney are staples of today's history texts. Should there also be a place for Frank Kameny and Matthew Sheppard? The issue cannot be avoided because most every state sets curriculum standards. In 2011, California became the first state to legislate a gay history requirement. The law adds "lesbian, gay, bisexual and transgender Americans" (as well as Americans with disabilities) to the list of ethnic and cultural groups whose role and contributions to California and the United States must be included as part of the curriculum. Additionally, the law adds sexual orientation to the list of characteristics that instructional materials can not reflect "adversely" upon. This may seem a relatively noncontroversial item, but, conforming to the pattern seen so often, any implicit endorsement of gay sexuality seems to draw religious opposition. In the battle over the California law, for example, the Campaign for Children and Families asserted that if the bill were passed, "children will be enticed into political activism in support of everything" by gay groups and that "children would be required to act as homosexuals when they are role playing to practice vocabulary." Interestingly, the new law simply added religion as well to a list of characteristics that textbooks should not reflect adversely upon.

## Student Expression

Students learn from each other as well as from the formal curriculum, and what they can say to each other and how they express themselves about gay issues has become another important area of legal conflict.

In an effort to foster a more accepting attitude toward gay students and discourage harassment, many schools, particularly upper and middle schools, have adopted policies and established programs encouraging tolerance toward gay students. These efforts can take several forms. Sexual orientation is sometimes included in a school's antiharassment policies. Diversity programs also encourage tolerant attitudes toward gay students. Some schools go further and support a Day of Silence, a day observed to focus attention on antigay harassment and the need to combat it. These efforts sometimes are resented by and meet resistance from students from religious families who wish to present a dissenting point of view on homosexuality. This tension can raise interesting and sometimes difficult First Amendment free speech questions.

By way of background, the Supreme Court has made clear that the First Amendment is very much alive in the public schools. In 1969, in the leading case of *Tinker v. Des Moines School District* (393 U.S. 503), the Court held that students had a First Amendment right to wear black arm bands protesting the Vietnam War to class, as long as their protest did not cause substantial disruption or interfere with the rights of other students. While *Tinker* remains good law, the Court in a major subsequent case sustained disciplinary action taken by school officials against a student who had used suggestive language in a speech given at a school assembly (*Bethel School District 403 v. Fraser*). Much more recently, the Court also upheld the disciplining of a student who displayed a sign that the school feared undermined its antidrug policy (*Morse v. Frederick*).

The constitutional crosscurrents at play in these kinds of cases can prove difficult to navigate. Consider the situation that developed at Poway High School in California, where the school supported a Day of Silence designed to teach tolerance, particularly of those with a different sexual orientation. To protest this observance, one student wore, on the Day of Silence, a T-shirt with "I will not Accept What God has Condemned" written on the front and "Homosexuality is Shameful" on the back. When the boy refused a request by the school administration to take the T-shirt off or turn it inside out, he was sent to the principal's office for the rest of the day. The boy and his parents, however, refused to let the matter rest and subsequently brought suit in federal court.

The Ninth Circuit Court of Appeals in a 2–1 decision upheld the school's decision on the ground that it was within the school's rights to protect the feelings and self-esteem of its most vulnerable students. Interestingly, the court rejected any distinction between condemning homosexuality and condemning homosexuals: "Perhaps our dissenting colleague believes that one can condemn homosexuality without condemning homosexuals. If so, he is wrong. To say that homosexuality is shameful is to say, necessarily, that gays and lesbians are shameful" (*Harper v. Poway Unified School District*, 1181). In trying to limit the potential reach of its decision, the court asserted that impressionable high school students needed a level of protection unnecessary for college students, whose greater emotional strength and maturity, in the court's view, would allow them to handle an antigay message. It also went out of its way to distinguish the antigay message from messages on controversial political topics like the Iraq War, or even T-shirt slogans such as "Young Republicans Suck" or "Young Democrats Suck."

This case evoked a wide range of reactions. A strong argument in the school's favor begins with the conceded role that schools are to play in shaping good citizens. Certainly, respect and tolerance for all persons is consistent with that message, and celebrating those values with a Day of Silence is a decision well within a public school's discretionary authority. Arguably, in *Harper*, the message conveyed on the Christian student's T-shirt undermined the school's message of tolerance, just as the student's sign had undercut the school's drug policy in *Morse v. Frederick*, which was decided after *Harper*. In *Morse*, the school also defended its action on the ground that the mental health and sense of self-esteem of all the students in the school were its responsibility and that the school had a right to protect its gay students from messages it deemed damaging to them.

All of this sounds reasonable, and yet for those who believe in robust First Amendment protection, a protection that has benefited the gay rights movement, the decision is troubling. There was no indication that the T-shirt was going to cause any disruption in the school, a critical qualification to the broad right of free speech as enunciated in *Tinker*, or that it was interfering in any way with the rights of other students, other than the possible right to be free from exposure to such comments as appeared on the T-shirt. Moreover, the message was conveying a viewpoint on homosexuality that is clearly very much a part of the political debate over gay rights. The court also ignored that the student wore the T-shirt in protest of the school's decision to allow a Day of Silence and probably would have been understood as such by the school's gay students. Moreover, hurt feelings presumably can't justify all forms of censorship if the First Amendment is to retain any vitality in the public schools. After all, there may have been students in the *Tinker* classrooms with brothers or even fathers serving in Vietnam, for whom the suggestion that their loved ones were risking their lives in an ignoble cause would have been deeply troubling.

Were the T-shirt wearer's First Amendment rights in *Harper* abridged by the school district? Undoubtedly, they were. Was that abridgement within the zone of discretion that we grant to public school administrators in meeting their responsibilities? Perhaps. The message "Homosexuality is Shameful" and "I will not Accept What God Has Condemned" was the kind of message that could have made any gay student feel less than whole. In his excellent work on gay rights law in the school setting, Stuart Biegel focused on the word "Shameful" on Harper's T-shirt, arguing that, even if unintended, the word "comes across as particularly nefarious, defamatory, and personal—especially in a setting where young and impressionable people interact" (2010, 99). As a middle ground, Biegel suggests that a T-shirt reading "Homosexual relations are prohibited by the Bible," being a mere general statement reflecting a commonly held belief much less personal in nature, should pass constitutional muster (99).

There is much to recommend in Biegel's approach. Tone matters, and the way in which the message may be perceived is certainly a factor that the school could take into account. Nevertheless, it is important to uphold First Amendment principles even when they pinch. If a generalized fear of disruption should not be a basis for denying First Amendment rights of students, perhaps a generalized fear of negative feeling based on a perception that a message is too personal should also be applied with caution, particularly when it prevents a student from expressing a view that was obviously extremely important to him. Biegel's sensitivity to tone seems to me to be on the right track but gives school boards relatively little guidance on how to strike the right balance in close cases.

Interestingly, in a subsequent case, a different circuit court (the Seventh) did require the issuance of an injunction against a high school that had sought to prevent a student from wearing a T-shirt with the message "Be Happy, Not Gay." Richard Posner, a noted scholar and highly respected conservative judge, wrote: "'Be Happy, Not Gay' is only tepidly negative: 'derogatory' or 'demeaning' seems too strong a characterization" *(Nuxoll v. Indian Prairie School District No. 204).* These fine lines are extremely subjective. After all, "Be Happy, Not Gay" can be viewed as just as harmful psychologically to a young gay or lesbian because it implies that (*a*) gays cannot be happy; (*b*) being gay is a choice; and (*c*) it is simply wrong to be a gay person.

Gay students as well as religiously conservative students have First Amendment rights. As gay students become more confident in themselves, some are understandably unwilling to settle for less than full equality. In high school that means going to the prom with the date of one's choice, even a same-sex date. Constance McMillen, a high school senior in Fulton, Mississippi, located in a sparsely settled rural county, wanted to take her girlfriend to the 2010 school prom, and when the school refused to allow it, she sued and won—sort of. In a thirteen-page decision, U.S. District Judge Glen Davidson agreed with Constance that her First Amendment speech rights had been violated by the school's decision to cancel the prom rather than let her wear a tuxedo (females were required to wear dresses) and attend the prom with her girlfriend. According to established precedents, the key in determining whether conduct has sufficiently communicative elements to bring it within First Amendment protection is whether the conduct is intended to convey a particularized message that would be understood as such by those who viewed it. Judge Davidson ruled that Constance had met that burden since her dress and choice of a date were clearly trying to send a message that, as a gay person, she had as much right to her identity as any straight person.

At the same time, however, Judge Davidson denied Constance's request that the school be required to hold the prom. As was widely done in many southern communities to avoid interracial school dances, parents sponsored a private prom to which, the court noted, all juniors and seniors, including Constance, had been invited, although she would not have been allowed to wear a tuxedo or bring her same-sex date. Judge Davidson's refusal to require the school to hold the prom flowed from his conclusion that "requiring Defendants [the school district] to step back into a sponsorship role at this date would only confuse and confound the community on the issue" and would also "defeat the purpose and efforts" of those parents who had worked to host the private prom. These are, however, from a constitutional standpoint, very tenuous reasons.

Was Judge Davidson correct in permitting the school's cancellation of its prom? His justifications from a doctrinal standpoint are tenuous. His concern with negating the efforts of the parents hosting the substitute prom bears no constitutional weight, for there is simply no basis for denying a person's constitutional rights on the ground that it may mean that private persons have wasted their time. Nor did he explain how the community would be "confused" and "confounded" by a simple order that the school be required to hold a prom that it had always held. The court's other rationale—that "it cannot go into the business of planning and overseeing a prom" hosted by the school district— also seems misplaced, since it assumed that the district would not plan the prom in good faith had an order to hold the prom been issued. The court also ignored the fact that allowing the district to cancel the prom undermined the very message Constance wanted to convey—that she, as a gay person, had a right to attend a public school function on equal terms with her heterosexual class- mates. Attendance at a private prom without her same-sex date hardly allowed her to convey that message. Had Judge Davidson ordered the prom, students would have had to choose which prom to attend, generating the very discussion Constance wished to trigger. Nevertheless, one senses here a good judge want- ing to do the right thing by the constitution without going too far in requiring the school district to make what he regarded as an empty gesture (see *McMillen v. Itawamba County School District*).

Constance's efforts were not all in vain, for her case established a further precedent (there was some earlier case law already in her favor in another cir- cuit) that attendance at a prom was a form of protected speech. Moreover, a few months later the school district settled her claim for money damages for the sum of $35,000 plus reasonable attorney's fees. That was not all. The gay com- munity certainly recognized the importance of her courage. Not only did the *New York Times* come to her defense (not necessarily a favor in her native Missis- sippi), but her stance led to appearances on several national television shows, including the *Ellen DeGeneres Show*, the award of a $30,000 college scholarship, and a place of honor as one of the three grand marshals in New York's annual Pride Parade for 2010.

## Conversion Therapy

In the fall of 2010, a rash of student suicides received national attention and reminded everyone of just how isolated and vulnerable gay students can feel. Joel Burns, a councilman in Fort Worth, Texas, read about the September 2010 suicides and decided it was time to come out of the closet. In an emotional thirteen-minute speech that received more than two million hits on YouTube, Burns, at times tearfully, tried to explain how difficult his own school years had been and how often he had craved the kind of support that would have allowed him to view his sexuality more positively.

Given the importance of self-acceptance, it is not surprising that one of the areas that concern gay rights advocates the most is the attempt of some parents to change their child's sexual orientation through various forms of "conversion therapy." Since the late 1990s, religious groups and other organizations have invested considerable resources in encouraging such interventions. In response, a number of professional organizations, including the American Academy of Pediatrics and the American Psychological Association, helped develop a pamphlet titled *Just the Facts about Sexual Orientation and Youth*. The pamphlet emphasized the severe stresses that gay youth face and concluded that the promotion of reparative therapy and transformational ministry "is likely to exacerbate the risk of harassment, harm and fear." The American Psychiatric Association has issued a statement describing the potential risks of reparative or transformational therapy as "great, including depression, anxiety and self-destructive behavior."

There is no question that many young men and women forced into conversion therapy by their parents have felt themselves badly damaged by the process. Does the damage rise to a level of abuse warranting legislative action, and if so, can restrictions on conversion therapy be constitutionally imposed? In 2012, the state of California became the first state in the nation to deal with this issue when it passed a law, signed by Governor Jerry Brown, which stated that therapists and counselors who use "sexual orientation change efforts" on clients under the age of eighteen are guilty of unprofessional conduct and subject to discipline by state licensing boards.

In 2012 Alan Chambers, the leader of Exodus International, long a force in the reparative therapy community, rocked that world when, at Exodus's annual meeting, he declared his belief that reparative therapy was not effective and gave many gay Christians false hope. Most disturbingly to many Christian conservatives, he went on to say that he believed that a gay person could engage in homosexual behavior and still gain admission to heaven. Chambers believes that all sex outside marriage is sinful, but, he said, "we've been asking people with same-sex attractions to overcome something in a way that we don't ask anyone else" (Eckholm 2012). Chambers admits to strong feelings of same-sex attraction but has been married for many years, "with a love and devotion much deeper than anything I experienced in gay life." Chambers's statement had an immediate negative financial impact on Exodus International: contributions dried up, and affiliated ministers and churches severed their ties with the organization. In June 2013, the organization announced that it would disband. Other Christian groups almost immediately began to fill the void created by the departure of Exodus International from the field, including the Restored Hope Network.

I mentioned earlier the critical importance of acceptance of a gay child by his or her heterosexual parents. That is, of course, not an issue when a child (whether gay or heterosexual) is being raised by one or two gay parents. For that child, however, recognition of the legitimacy and social acceptability of his or her family can be a matter of great importance.

# 10

## The Gay Family

In 1950s America, gays and lesbians were an unwelcome reality, but a gay family was simply inconceivable. Today, however, there are tens of thousands of gay parents raising children in the United States. Census data suggest that there are approximately 130,000 gay couples in the United States raising children under the age of eighteen. Most of them seem to be doing a good job. Studies confirm this fact, and even litigants opposing gay rights don't contest it. In one important Florida case discussed in this chapter, both sides stipulated that gays can be fine parents. A study based on 2000 census data reported that one in three lesbian women and one in six gay men in the United States are raising children—from previous marriages, surrogacy, or adoption (Russett 2012, 13).

The legal system becomes involved with family law issues when a gay couple or individual seeks to adopt or when issues of custody arise as part of the dissolution of a relationship in which a gay person (or two gay persons in the case of a same-sex relationship) is involved. I examine each situation separately.

One important point needs underscoring at the outset. While we may think of gay adoption and the concept of the gay family as expressing the conservative nature of the equality movement, the fact is that nothing brings gay individuals more out of the closet than raising a child. In that sense, it represents a real victory for the liberationist impulse that followed Stonewall, which demanded, above all, that gays be out and proud. As Carlos Ball concludes in his account of five key legal cases involving gay parenting, "It is likely that the path to parenthood for most of these individuals [litigants in the cases Ball describes] would have been considerably easier if they had chosen to stay in the closet. But to remain in the closet is to hide an important part of who one is; to lead a closeted life is, to some extent, to live a lie. And it goes without saying that good and effective parenting cannot be based on dishonesty" (Ball 2012, 209).

## Adoption

No development of the past twenty years has brought the gay community into continuing contact with establishment institutions more than the dramatic increase in the number of gay couples adopting children. About 19 percent of the approximately 650,000 same-sex couples in the United States reported raising an adopted child in 2009, compared to 8 percent in 2000 (Tavernise 2011). The number of such children totals at least 65,000. This equates to roughly 4 percent of all adopted children in the United States. An additional 14,100 foster children are estimated to be living with lesbian or gay parents, constituting 3 percent of the total number of foster children in the United States. Roughly 500,000 children are in the foster care systems in the United States, of whom it is estimated that 129,000 cannot return to their original families and are legally free for adoption.

Adopting a child, as any adopting parent can tell you, is a much more rigorous process than getting married. Two people can decide for themselves if they want to marry, and no one can stop them no matter how unsuitable they may be for each other. Not so with adoption. Prospective adopting parents must prove their suitability, and adoption itself is a formal legal process ultimately requiring court approval. In one sense, adoption is an even bigger commitment than marriage, for marriages can end in divorce but adoption is forever.

Since the adoption process is governed by state law, there are effectively fifty different adoption frameworks throughout the country, each with its own policies and processes. There is, however, a national policy to encourage adoption as embodied in the Adoption and Safe Families Act of 1997, which was intended to increase the number of foster-care children placed in permanent homes. In April 2011 the Obama administration sent to national child welfare agencies a memo underscoring that placement of a child in a gay or lesbian household puts the child at no greater risk than placement with a heterosexual family. The rapidly changing attitudes toward adoption by gays are particularly remarkable when one recalls that just a few decades ago Anita Bryant tried to rally support for her antigay views with the slogan "Save Our Children."

This is not to say that gay adoption is not contested or controversial. As one scholar has noted, it will continue to be so "[as] long as homosexuality is not fully accepted into the social fabric of the country" (Russett 2012, 16). Religious groups (primarily evangelicals, the Mormon and Catholic churches, and Orthodox Jewry) who fear any endorsement of gay relationships continue to oppose gay adoption. Unlike its position on employment discrimination laws, for example, the Vatican emphatically rejects the idea of a gay family. A 2003 document authored by Pope Benedict XVI when he was head of the Vatican's

Congregation for the Doctrine of the Faith called same-sex unions "gravely immoral" and asserted that allowing same-sex couples to adopt "would actually mean doing violence to these children" (2003, para. 7). Nevertheless, gay adoption registers a much lower decibel level on the political noise scale than do other social issues, such as abortion or same-sex marriage, which is just fine with advocates of gay adoption

Gays seek to adopt for the same reasons heterosexuals do: they want to create a family, or they want to give a child with whom they already have a relationship the security that comes with adoption. Family creation occurs where neither parent has a previous relationship with the adopted child; these are generally called stranger adoptions. Relationship recognition is involved in what are often called second-parent adoptions. Different legal issues arise for each form, and I treat them separately.

### Stranger Adoptions

In her brief but excellent account of the history of adoption, Cynthia Russett describes how adoption and a permanent home have become the preferred alternative for raising dependent children, slowly replacing orphanages in the first half of the twentieth century. She also describes how, before the 1920s, a single woman (sometimes in a community of women, sometimes with a single female partner in what was euphemistically called a Boston Marriage) was regarded by placement agencies as a suitable parent. This receptiveness changed, however, as "new studies of sexuality brought homosexuality out into the open, and female partnerships, once completely respectable, came under hostile scrutiny" (Russett 2012, 10). A new emphasis on marriage and romance also affected the acceptability of single women as prospective parents, leaving single women "on the margins, branded as odd and deviant" (10).

While gays are now generally free to adopt, it does not mean that they are treated equally in the adoption process. An important recent nationwide survey of adoption agencies, for example, undertaken by the Evan B. Donaldson Adoption Institute, found that agencies focusing on special needs children were the most likely to accept and even seek out gay applicants, whereas agencies focusing on healthy domestic infants and toddlers (where the number of prospective parents exceeds the supply of potential adoptees) were the least likely to effectuate placements with gays and lesbians. David Brodzinsky, in his report on this study, suggests that the relatively sparse number of domestic infant adoptions by gays reflects that many infant-oriented agencies are religious in nature and have very conservative beliefs about gays and lesbians (Brodzinsky and Pertman 2012, 78). Additionally, 26 percent of all agencies that accept applications to adopt from gays and lesbians reported receiving requests from natural parents that their infant not be placed with gays or lesbians (78).

Roughly 60 percent of the adoptions in this country are now of children in the foster care system (25 percent are from overseas and the other 15 percent are infants and toddlers born domestically) (Pertman and Howard 2012, 28). And while there is an oversupply of parents wanting to adopt domestic infants, there is an undersupply of parents willing to adopt children in the foster care system. Most foster care adoptions are handled through public child welfare agencies, which are much more open than many private agencies to gay adoption. As Adam Pertman and Jeanne Howard note, "the greatest prospects of becoming adoptive parents" for gays "is through the foster care system: Although this reality clearly reflects an ongoing social bias, one of its consequences is that a significant and growing number of gays and lesbians look to the child welfare system to become parents" (2012, 30).

Two states—Utah and Mississippi—currently have statutory restrictions that prevent unmarried couples—heterosexual or homosexual—from adopting. Florida and Arkansas did have statutes with prohibitions (Florida's also prohibited gay individuals from adopting), but both of those statutes were declared unconstitutional by their state judiciaries. Those decisions are worth exploring as examples of the growing unwillingness of courts to allow legislation based on outdated stereotypes.

The Florida prohibition was directed solely at gays and lesbians and applied to both individuals and couples. It was enacted in 1977 at the height of the attacks on gays in Florida by Anita Bryant and her Save Our Children Crusade and clearly reflected a deep animus against gays. When the bill was passed, its sponsor addressed the gay community directly: "We're really tired of you. We wish you'd go back into the closet. . . . homosexuals are surfacing to such an extent that they're beginning to aggravate the ordinary folks, who have a few rights of their own" (Eskridge 2008, 353). Obviously, one of those rights, according to Senator Curtis Peterson, was the right of heterosexuals to pretend that gays did not exist, at least for adoption purposes. The Florida story is particularly interesting because it shows how a state constitution can be interpreted to provide a stronger measure of protection for gay rights than its federal counterpart.

The story begins in the year 2000 when the Florida adoption statute was challenged in federal court, under the United States Constitution, as a violation, among other things, of the Fourteenth Amendment's Equal Protection Clause. This suit failed when the U.S. Court of Appeals for the Eleventh Circuit held that adoption under Florida law was not a fundamental right, homosexuals were not a suspect class, and the statute was not irrational since the Florida legislature could reasonably determine that heterosexual couples provide a preferred environment for children over same-sex couples (*Lofton v. Secretary of the Dept. of Children and Family Services*). The court also found that allowing a single heterosexual person but not a homosexual to adopt was not irrational since a single heterosexual could create the optimal environment in the future by marrying.

In 2004, however, a new case was brought claiming that the statutory prohibition violated Florida's own state constitution. This was an issue for the state courts to determine. The facts were compelling. A gay man had served for four years as a loving foster parent to two young children who had been badly abused by their natural parents, and he wanted to adopt them. Florida's Department of Children made clear that they would have happily approved his application but for the Florida prohibition: not a surprise given that the plaintiff and his partner had actually been presented by the department with its first Outstanding Foster Parenting Award (Tulin 2005–2006, 1622–1623). After rejection of his application, the man, known as F.G., sued. His suit did not raise an issue of a fundamental right, nor did he claim that homosexuals were a suspect class under Florida's version of the Equal Protection Clause. He simply alleged that the law was irrational.

After a nonjury trial lasting four days and involving numerous expert witnesses, mostly on behalf of the plaintiff, the trial court judge held that the statute lacked a rational basis. A different decision was hard to imagine once the Florida Department of Children and Families conceded, as it did in a stipulated set of facts, that homosexuals and heterosexuals make equally good parents. The adoption statute was truly irrational: it allowed even ex-felons and drug abusers to adopt; homosexuals were the only group categorically excluded. On September 22, 2010, Florida's Third District Court of Appeal, in a three-judge opinion, unanimously upheld the trial court's decision, and shortly thereafter Governor Charlie Crist announced his decision not to appeal.

The Arkansas statute was of much more recent vintage. In 2008, 57 percent of Arkansas voters chose to prohibit all unmarried couples (gay or straight) from adopting or even providing foster care for minors. Not surprisingly, the Arkansas Family Council and the Focus on the Family Action group had worked closely with Christian religious groups on behalf of the ballot initiative, known as Act I. Although Act I did not discriminate between same-sex and opposite-sex couples, its proponents made clear in the campaign that it was aimed at gay couples, arguing that some law was needed to stop gay adoption, which was part of the "homosexual agenda." Opponents of Act I included Arkansas Advocates for Children and Families, the Interfaith Council, the Arkansas Association of Social Workers, the Arkansas chapter of the American Society of Pediatrics, the Arkansas Psychological Association, and the American Civil Liberties Union. In April 2010, Pulaski County circuit court judge Chris Piazza ruled

Act I unconstitutional, finding essentially that it harmed children by reducing the number of potential families that could provide foster care or could create a permanent home through adoption and served no state interest.

On April 7, 2011, the Arkansas Supreme Court upheld the trial court ruling, agreeing that the statute was a violation of fundamental privacy rights under the Arkansas Constitution (*Arkansas Dept. of Human Services v. Cole*). Interestingly, the court looked at the case less from the standpoint of the children than from the standpoint of unmarried heterosexuals, finding that by forcing unmarried persons to choose between a relationship with a sexual partner, on the one hand, and adopting or fostering children on the other, Act I unconstitutionally burdened a right to sexual intimacy. In the end, the Arkansas Supreme Court, like the Florida appellate court, simply rejected any categorical assumptions when it came to who can and cannot adopt. After reviewing Arkansas's adoption procedures, the court wrote: "We have no doubt that this individualized assessment process is a thorough and effective means to screen out unsuitable applicants" (*Arkansas Dept. of Human Services*, 442).

In the end, both the Florida and Arkansas courts were applying basic constitutional principles in the face of a public not quite ready to abandon prejudices that seem less and less consistent with a fair application of law. Earlier, we saw how, even in the fifties and sixties, the darkest hours of modern gay history, a commitment to freedom of expression allowed gays to reach each other through important gay publications. Now, in a much different era, we see the courts of two southern states relying on basic legal principles to void two statutes aimed at discriminating against the gay community. Prejudice still finds its way into state law, however, as evidenced by the recent passage in Arizona of a statute requiring that heterosexual couples be given priority over same-sex couples in the adoption process.

We should not leave this subject without discussing one important area of controversy involving adoption through faith-based agencies. The question arose most dramatically in 2006 when the Massachusetts Department of Social Services (implementing the state law prohibiting discrimination on the basis of sexual orientation) adopted a regulation making nondiscrimination against gays a condition for the licensing of private adoption agencies. Catholic Charities, an entity dedicated to social service, was such an agency and a major force in the Boston metropolitan area for adoption. Following adoption of the Massachusetts law and regulations, the Boston archdiocese eliminated its support for adoption services.

The issue arises whether faith-based agencies should receive some kind of tailored exemption that would allow them to continue their work without processing placement applications of gay individuals and couples. The state of

Connecticut has included such an exemption in its adoption scheme. It is not an easy issue. On the one hand, the practical impact of forcing faith-based agencies from the adoption field is to reduce the number of agencies that are participating in helping children find permanent homes, not a good outcome. Also, social ministry is at the heart of the teachings and practice of many churches. Not to allow any concessions to what is clearly a matter of religious conscience for these groups, even if one dissents strongly from those beliefs, does prevent faith-based agencies from working in an area in which they have done good work. Such an exemption, however, does on some level validate a point of view rooted in deep prejudice and erroneous assumptions; moreover, there is an oversupply of parents wanting to adopt domestic infants and toddlers. Given that circumstance, the withdrawal of Catholic agencies, at least for this group, does not really undermine the likelihood of these children finding a permanent home.

Were the Catholic Church's constitutional rights in Massachusetts violated by forcing it not to discriminate against gays in order to pursue its adoption ministry? Probably not, and ironically, the key case was authored by none other than Justice Antonin Scalia. In 1990 in *Employment Division v. Smith*, the U.S. Supreme Court, reversing earlier decisions, held that the First Amendment's guarantee of freedom of religious worship was not violated by a neutral law of general applicability, even if it adversely impacted genuine religious practices. Prior to that case, the rule had been that such a neutral law could be applied in a way that impacted religious practice only if the state had a compelling interest in such application. In effect, in *Smith* the Court was making it much less necessary, as a constitutional matter, for government to accommodate religious practices in enacting and implementing general laws. While the subject is certainly open to debate, a law prohibiting discrimination on the basis of sexual orientation, like laws prohibiting discrimination on the basis of race and sex, is a neutral law of general applicability and therefore not one requiring accommodation to allow Catholic Charities to continue its adoption services.

Could the Massachusetts Department of Social Services have provided an exemption for faith-based organizations without violating the part of the First Amendment that prohibits enactment of laws respecting an establishment of religion? Again, this is an area where reasonable people can disagree, but the answer seems to be that it could. Title VII of the Civil Rights Law of 1964, for example, prohibits employers from discriminating on the basis of religious belief but contains an exemption for religious organizations. The exemption was unanimously upheld by the Supreme Court in a case in which the Mormon Church was allowed to fire the long-standing employee of a gymnasium that the Church had taken over simply because he was not Mormon (*Corporation of Presiding Bishop of Church of Jesus Christ of Latter Day Saints v. Amos*).

## Second-Parent Adoptions

Second-parent adoptions generally occur where a biological parent is in a committed relationship with a nonbiological parent and the two wish for the nonbiological parent to adopt. In many states, second-parent adoptions have proved legally troublesome even for heterosexual couples. The reason is that the language of many state adoption laws, written prior to the advent of artificial insemination and surrogate pregnancy, simply did not anticipate or cover the many possible permutations of the modern family. Even more troubling, some statutes require both biological parents to give up their parental rights as a condition of the adoption. Rigidly interpreted, this requirement makes no sense where one biological parent is still very much involved in the child's life and the goal is simply to make the nonbiological parent equal in status to the biological parent in the eyes of the law. Some states get around the problem by allowing step-parent adoptions, but usually the step parent must be married to the biological parent, obviously an option not available to same-sex couples in states that do not allow gay marriage or provide for civil unions.

Second-parent adoptions usually are in the best interest of the child. Psychologically (as well as legally) it means that children are in a permanent relationship with both of their caregivers. From a legal standpoint, there are many advantages for both the child and adopting parent. From the child's standpoint it means that, if the biological parent dies or becomes disabled, the other parent retains full legal responsibility for the child. From the adopting parent's standpoint it means protection from others claiming guardianship of the child. Adoption also provides protection for the nonbiological parent–child relationship in the event of a breakup of the couple; it also provides protection for the child under state inheritance laws and allows the adopting parent to put the child under his or her employer's health insurance policy. Finally, it also assures that the child can legally rely on the adopting parent for support.

Courts that tend to construe statutes strictly in accordance with their literal language generally will not allow second-parent adoptions if the statute seems to prohibit them. In 2010, for example, the North Carolina Supreme Court overruled jurisdictions in its state that had granted second-parent adoptions, holding that North Carolina statutory law clearly precluded them (*Boseman v. Jarrell*). For a much different and, in my opinion, more sensible view, there is *In the Matter of Jacob* in which the New York Court of Appeals (New York's highest court) held that, strictly enforced, the statute would lead to an absurd outcome which would nullify the advantage sought by the proposed adoption: the creation of a legal family unit identical to the actual family set up. The court refused to allow such a result and approved the adoption of Jacob by the nonbiological parent without requiring any waiver of parental rights by the biological parent.

In summary, the adoption story, in terms of gay rights, is largely a positive one. Progress, as we have seen in Arkansas and Florida, can come from state judiciaries increasingly uncomfortable with negative stereotypes. In his best-selling book about the Supreme Court, *The Nine*, Jeffrey Toobin relates how Justice O'Connor was in the habit of giving newly born children of all her clerks a T-shirt that said "grand clerk." When a gay clerk of hers adopted a baby, he too received one, another gesture that speaks volumes about the new realities of gay life (Toobin 2007, 187). At the end of the day, to deny gays the right to form families is simply to deny to many children the social recognition their families deserve. Opponents of gay adoption have every right to their views, but, as Jon Meacham recently wrote, "nothing should properly create more humility than discussions about detecting the will of God" (2012).

Of course the availability of adoption by gays does not necessarily mean that it will be implemented in a fair and uniform way. Sometimes, aggrieved applicants need to turn to the courts for help. Linda Kaufman, a Virginia resident, was deeply angered when the Virginia Department of Social Services refused to consent to her adoption of a second foster child, even though a licensed social welfare agency in the District of Columbia had extensively evaluated Kaufman and her life partner and had recommended adoption, and even though Kaufman had nine years earlier adopted a foster child, an adoption that, by all accounts, had proven very successful. Kaufman sued, and the department finally settled the case; not only was her application for adoption accepted but the department agreed to create new guidelines to assure that her experience would not be repeated. The Kaufman case is a good reminder that the best laws in the world mean little unless they are properly administered.

## Custody

Day-to-day implementation of adoption and foster care policies is done through social service organizations, charities, for-profit and nonprofit adoption agencies, and governmental entities. While courts might need to put their ultimate imprimatur on an adoption, the adoption process is generally handled by agencies outside the judicial process. Not so with issues of custody and visitation rights. Here the courts, usually family courts, are the front lines and ultimate decision-makers. Custody and visitation rights, unlike adoption, involve not the creation of families but how to deal with their dissolution.

Family law rules have historically been a matter for each state to determine for itself, within constitutional limits, and therefore reflect the mores and beliefs of individual state jurisdictions. Even within a state, a family court judge in Madison, Wisconsin, for example, might take a very different view of a case than a judge in some rural Wisconsin county. These differences matter because issues of custody and visitation rights leave a great deal of discretion in the hands of the individual trial judge, as a practical matter insulating their determinations from appeal.

In custody fights and arguments over visitation, family court judges are called upon to make the most difficult of decisions. They do so from a distinct disadvantage—they are, after all, trained in the law, not psychology or medicine or sociology. They do, however, have one advantage: they at least know what they are supposed to do—make a decision in the best interests of the child. To do that they often have to evaluate detailed psychiatric reports and test results; they must sometimes choose between conflicting versions of events; often they must make their own best guesses of character based on witness demeanor; they must consider the emotional needs and wants of the children themselves and sometimes evaluate their testimony; and, in the end, they must imagine the world of the children whose fates rest in their hands.

Nothing in the family law judge's job changes just because a gay individual or same-sex couple is involved. The judge's job is still to consider and evaluate all the evidence and make a decision in the best interests of the child. For this reason, all the arguments put forth by conservatives in opposition to the idea of gay parenthood, the most important being that children do best when they have both male and female role models, simply become irrelevant in the context of any specific case, as do the claims on the other side that gay parents can make equally good parents as heterosexual parents. Each case must be decided on its own facts.

There is no question, however, that stereotyping can detract from that individualized consideration. In her comprehensive study of Lambda's litigation history, Ellen Andersen pointed out how the prevailing concept of lesbian parents in the 1970s—that they were irresponsible, unpredictable, and potentially more abusive than heterosexuals—meant that lesbians and gay men "rarely initiated custody cases" but only fought when their existing custody or visitation rights were threatened. It also meant that Lambda "was hesitant to step into cases it was likely to lose, especially since their fact specificity made them more expensive than other kinds of cases to prepare" (Andersen 2006, 34).

Judicial attitudes toward the idea of gay parenthood had begun to change favorably in the eighties and nineties. Theodore Stein, for example, reported in 1996 that less than one-third of U.S. jurisdictions presumed that parental homosexuality was harmful to children (Andersen 2006, 54). Today, of course, the overwhelming evidence is that gay individuals and couples make just as good parents as heterosexual couples. The American Psychological Association, the American Academy of Child and Adolescent Psychiatry, the American Academy of Family Physicians, the American Academy of Pediatrics, the American Psychoanalytic Association, the National Association of Social Workers, and the American Medical Association all endorse this view. More and more, courts are abandoning presumptions against gay parenting, at least in principle. Some scholars worry that prejudice against gays still creeps into many decisions, and they are probably correct. Given the wide discretion of trial judges in these matters, however, only time and a growing acceptance of gay sexuality in society are likely to eliminate this difficulty.

There are no magic wands in family law. Nondiscriminatory treatment in custody cases, as in every area of family law, is very much a state-by-state battle. State appellate courts can be particularly helpful when they correct trial courts that have engaged in inappropriate stereotyping. The Georgia Supreme Court in *Mongerson v. Mongerson* and the Kentucky Court of Appeals in *Maxwell v. Maxwell* performed precisely this function when they overturned trial court orders. The trial court outcome in Georgia was based on the assumption that any contact between a child and gay friends of a gay parent was inherently harmful, and that in Kentucky assumed that a mother in a lesbian relationship could not provide a satisfactory home for her child (and thus the court had awarded custody to the father).

State high courts are not always allies in the fight against discrimination. In 1998, for example, in *Pulliam v. Smith*, the North Carolina Supreme Court took custody away from a gay father, Fred Smith, who had been raising his two sons for years. Remarkably, the court reversed the decision of the lower appellate court, which had found that the boys had been doing just fine in both school and at home. The Supreme Court used activities that defined the father as a homosexual against him. These acts, according to the court, included "regular commission of sexual acts in the home by unmarried people" (*Pulliam*, 904). In other words, Smith was not celibate; the fact that he was unmarried was hardly his own fault in North Carolina, which does not allow gay marriage.

The court's decision is particularly interesting because it shows how even a panel of distinguished judges can have a particularly hard time affirming gay rights when confronted with issues involving gay sexuality. It is clear in *Pulliam* that the North Carolina Supreme Court simply could not accept that homosexual activity (Smith was in a committed gay relationship) could occur in a normal home without damaging the children in it. Unfortunately, as one commentator noted, "the effect of *Pulliam* has been widespread in North Carolina. . . . *Pulliam* has likely discouraged many homosexual parents from raising children in a committed long-term relationship because it forces homosexual parents to choose between their children and their life partner" (Huffman 2008–2009, 258–259).

Custody cases come in an almost unlimited variety of factual situations. One particularly difficult area, now becoming more common, is how to handle dissolution of gay relationships where a nonbiological, nonadoptive parent wishes to continue involvement in the life of the child she has helped raise. Increasingly, state high courts have turned to the common law doctrine of in loco parentis to justify allowing such a parent his or her day in court to continue visitation rights or even share custody. In September 2011, the Nebraska Supreme Court in *Latham v. Schwerdtfeger* became the latest to adopt the doctrine. The court explained that "a person standing in loco parentis to a child is one who has put himself or herself in the position of a lawful parent by assuming the obligations incident to the parental relationship without going through the formalities necessary to a legal adoption, and the rights, duties, and liabilities of such person are the same as those of the lawful parent" (*Latham*, 128).

The loco parentis doctrine makes sense in the context of same-sex relationships. The criteria for ultimate determination of custodial arrangements will still be what is in the best interests of the child. The adoption of the doctrine simply prevents an artificial barrier from standing in the way of the broadest consideration of what the best interests of the child might require in any given case. (For an excellent discussion of the Nebraska case, see *Lesbian/Gay Law Notes*, September 2011, 171–172.)

## Relationship Recognition

Gay families are not just about parenting and children. Childless gay couples are also a family, but until the New York Court of Appeals decision in 1989 in *Braschi v. Stahl Associates*, the law seemed oblivious to that possibility. In *Braschi*, New York's highest court allowed the surviving partner of an AIDS victim to remain in the couple's Manhattan apartment under a New York rent control regulation that prevented a landlord from evicting either the surviving spouse of the deceased tenant or some other member of the deceased tenant's family who had been living with the tenant. The story of the lawsuit is one of the five recounted in Ball's *From the Closet to the Courtroom* (2010). As the focus of the gay rights movement has turned to marriage and civil unions, the importance of *Braschi* has dimmed. Yet recognizing that a gay couple could create a household and a relationship that was entitled to the same dignity under the rent control regulation as a heterosexual couple was truly a pathbreaking decision.

Since *Braschi* addressed a very specific state regulation, as opposed to raising an issue of constitutional dimension, its direct legal impact was somewhat limited. Nevertheless, as Ball shows, "the importance of *Braschi* lies not so much in the way future courts relied on its holding and reasoning . . . but rather in the fact that the highest court in New York adopted the movement's position on what constitutes a family. In doing so, it provided considerable legitimacy to the movement's claim that LGBT people were as capable of forming loving and lasting familial ties as straight people" (2010, 55). The recognition of gay couple relationships (whether childless or not) remains one of the key battlefields of the gay rights movement, for such relationships still enjoy little legal protection outside of the seventeen states that currently allow gay marriage and a second much smaller group that provides varying degrees of recognition of same-sex relationships.

Absence of recognition can have devastating personal consequences. In February 2007, two Washington state residents—Lisa Pond, thirty-nine-years-old, and her partner Janet Langbehn—were on vacation in Florida celebrating their anniversary when Pond collapsed as a result of an aneurism while playing basketball. She was rushed to a hospital in an ambulance and died eighteen hours later. During almost all that time, the nurses on duty barred Langbehn from visiting her. One of the nurses allegedly told Langbehn that Florida is an antigay state, as if that were sufficient explanation for keeping her from her loved one. The case became so widely known that when President Obama, in April 2010, ordered the Department of Health and Human Services to draft regulations for all hospitals receiving federal Medicare and Medicaid patients to give gay partners the same visitation and health proxy rights enjoyed by other immediate family members, his first phone call was to Janet Langbehn. Langbehn deserved the call for she had become a persuasive advocate for expanded visitation rights after her own mistreatment, an advocacy that led to a further conversation with President Obama when she was awarded the Presidential Citizens Medal in October 2011.

In the preceding chapters I have described the many ways in which the equality movement has moved forward in the past two decades and the controversies it has engendered. A remarkable change in public attitudes has been charted and the ways this change has been manifested in judicial opinions described. Few in the LGBT community quarrel with this progress, and all recognize the degree to which life is both less stressful and richer in possibility than it was even two decades ago. Yet there are important critics of the equality movement within the LGBT community, which we survey in the next chapter.

# 11

## The Movement's Critics

Critics of the modern gay rights movement fall into two broad, overlapping categories: those who worry that the equality movement has marginalized the ideal of a vibrant, inwardly focused gay community; and those who worry that the movement has moved forward in a noninclusive way, failing to include gay people of color, the gay poor, and the more marginalized of gay persons in either the agenda-setting process or the actual implementation of strategic goals. Many in this latter group also worry that the broad progressive agenda of the early seventies has been lost.

### The Cultural Dissent

Some see great irony in the way the gay rights movement has evolved. Take this statement: "Most gay liberationists of the 1960s and 1970s had no interest in imitating or assimilating into heterosexual norms. Those who first broke down the tightly secured door of the closet, deliberately spilling its contents all over the floor, never imagined they might be clearing the way for a new culture of domesticity" (Stacey and Davenport 2002, 357). While few in the movement have publicly opposed the gains the equality movement has sought, they do deeply regret some of its effects, including the need for the gay rights movement to present itself in as nonthreatening a way as possible. Stephen Engel reflected this concern when in 2002 he asserted that the explosive growth of media representation of gays and lesbians in film and popular television "is often one-sided and exclusionary, focusing on the members of the gay and lesbian community who do not pose a substantial threat to the prevailing middle-class hetero-normative gender dynamic," at the expense of all those in the LGBT community who do not fit "the middle-class, white and usually male paradigm" (Engel 2002, 400).

In Patrick Moore's view the whole idea of a gay community, rooted in common sexual desire, has fallen victim to the equality agenda. "The new view of gay life," Moore writes disapprovingly, "depends upon the belief that uncontrolled sex, particularly gay sex, is inherently wrong and must be either punished or hidden from view for the greater good of society" (2004, 186). He senses a gay youth in trouble, "full of shame that comes with no sense of identity," which leaves them "to play out that shame in isolation without knowing that there ever was a different world," a world in which, in Moore's view, "shame was transformed into a cherished gay identity; now shame is simply a risk" (182). Moore sees great value in the whole atmosphere of the late seventies, which was permeated by a sense of collective gay identity rooted in the openness and sexual freedom of that era.

In 1990, a small group of gays, mostly young, previously active in ACT UP, came together in anger, anger at a heterosexual society that had ignored the AIDS holocaust and a gay reformist movement that simply did not speak to their needs or concerns. The result of their initial meetings was the formation of Queer Nation. Queer Nation, and the many chapters in various cities which it inspired, did not last long. It had no concrete goals and seemed to value anarchy above all else. As Urvashi Vaid has written, "Queer Nation was a short-lived political organizing strategy whose chief legacy was the popularization of the word *queer* and the related idea that we are, as the word implies, not normal" (1995, 204).

Yet Queer Nation was important. What distinguished Queer Nation from ACT UP was its desire to be as in your face as possible about the very thing that made liberal supporters of gay rights least comfortable: sex. Queer Nation's light may have shined but briefly but its in-your-face attitude of "We're here, We're queer, Get used to it" has endured as a basic posture of many, one with roots going back to the very first leaflet distributed by the Gay Liberation Front with its headline "Do you think homosexuals are revolting? You bet your sweet ass we are."

In the forward to his 2002 book *The Attack Queers*, Richard Goldstein drew a distinction between gays and queers that also marks a political boundary: "By queer, I mean the whole gestalt, including sluts, punks, s/m dykes, trannies, sissies, sailors on leave and Anne Heche. By gay, I generally mean out and proud homosexuals" (2002, xiv–xv). Goldstein's book describes two entirely different worlds, one in which distinctions of economics and class are clearly drawn: "Oppression may not weigh heavily on boys who brunch, but it haunts the queer poor, who must navigate a social service system that refuses to recognize their existence. Homophobia may not be a clear and present danger in elite universities, but it's a recurring nightmare in the average American high school. And even in gay friendly circles, those who don't fit the gender mold suffer under a system best described by a variation of the old motto about race: If you're gay, it's okay; if you're queer disappear" (3).

Goldstein's book was an attack on what he called the gay right, represented by, among others, Bruce Bawer, who in 1993 had written a controversial work titled *A Place at the Table*. That book denounced a queer ethos that, in his view, excluded the vast majority of gays and encouraged gay youth to see their sexual orientation as the only important thing about themselves. This was a fight with the gloves off.

For Bawer, the queer subculture "welcomes you but on its own terms; it accepts you but it exacts a price. . . . Subculture-oriented gays visit schools to talk to young people about 'gay life' by which they mean gay life as it is understood by the subculture" (1993, 38). Not to be outflanked, Goldstein found in Bawer's politics the same intolerance that Bawer had found in him. Goldstein wrote, speaking of what he called the gay right: "Theirs is a single, morally correct way to be gay. No caucus of vegan leather men could approach this uniformity." Imagining a march called by the gay right, he wrote, "The sea of white faces would be a less louche version of the crowd on Fire Island during its pre-AIDS heyday. . . . And the ethos would be a wholesome version of the classic gay clone code: No freaks, femmes or feminists who aren't funny need apply. Rigidity is a common reaction to anxiety. . . . They deeply fear difference, including their own. No wonder they don't feel queer" (2002, 13–14).

The anger here is deep-seated and is certainly partly about sexuality. Goldstein accused the gay right of deeply fearing their own difference, a not very subtle way of claiming that its adherents were still in denial about their identity, that they had not fully come out and therefore had not fully accepted themselves. Those are fighting words which Bawer returned in full measure when he accused the queer subculture of a stiflingly narrow definition of what it means to be gay, one that effectively seeks to negate every other aspect of one's humanity and potential.

Interestingly, this debate shades over into an even more fundamental one: whether gays are in fact a people. Certainly, that is the view of the gay anthropologist Stephen O. Murray, who in his 1996 book *American Gay* decried the fact that "not since German-speaking Jewish professionals in the late nineteenth and early twentieth centuries tried to convince themselves that they were assimilated has there been a people with a set of intellectuals so bent on denying the existence of their own people, attacking attempts to discover tradition, and deriding any affirmations of identity and pride in the identity" (1996, 36–37).

It is no accident that Murray cited early twentieth-century German Jewish intellectuals to make his argument, for what better way to point out the dangers inherent in the denial of one's true identity than in citing the group that paid the highest price for its failure to recognize how that identity was perceived by others. I do not mean to suggest that Murray is equating late twentieth-century America with Nazi Germany, but he does equate assimilation with what he calls "neo-closetry," rooted in the delusion that "if only we avoid calling attention to our difference, hatred of us will go away—and those of us who aren't obvious are fully accepted" (37).

Perhaps the strongest attack on the gay rights movement has come from Shannon Gilreath in his book *Equality: The End of State Supremacy*. He writes: "Many times I have heard from Gays a variant of 'I'm gay but my sexuality doesn't define me.' It's a natural reaction that comes from living in a straight supremacist system that has systemically devalued and scorned Gay sexuality. Hope in this system comes from a cultivated ability to blend into the Heteroarchy, diminishing any qualities that might make one stand out, sexually speaking . . . it is a deadly posture, conditioning the survival of 'straight-acting gays' on the destruction of Gay-Identified Gays" (2012, 21).

There is no question that the equality movement, in both legal and political manifestations, has emphasized minimizing ways in which gays may be different. Shane Phelan, for example, has recognized that "some of us respond to our exclusion by trying to demonstrate our normality; much of the gay and lesbian rights movement takes this approach. Others reject dominant norms and adopt a position of pride in being outside that I think often neglects to see the ways in which we continue to participate in the dominant culture" (2001,13). Echoing Phelan, Michael Bronski has observed: "This major distinction—between claiming an outsider status and demanding acceptance as part of the 'normal' majority—has remained in various forms, the defining division of the LGBT movement" (2011, 181).

In her 1995 book *Virtual Equality*, Urvashi Vaid laid out an extended argument for a reconfigured gay rights movement, one that would not necessarily abandon specific legal equality goals but would insist on achieving those goals not by minimizing the idea of a separate gay identity but by celebrating it. Much more recently, in *How to Be Gay*, Donald Halperin, a professor at the University of Michigan, although agreeing that the gay rights movement has "been perfectly right to worry that any attention to our mental or emotional peculiarities would simply reconfirm ancient prejudices about our psychological abnormality," also worries that this "gambit" may have been rather "*too* successful," effectively closing off "the entire topic of gay subjectivity to respectable inquiry, making it impossible for us to inquire into ourselves or to explore in any systematic or meaningful way our unique sensibilities and cultures—beyond matters of sexuality" (2012, 71).

Halperin makes a key distinction between gay identity and what he calls gay subjectivity. For him, gay identity is a kind of convenient falsehood, a Potemkin village created to allow a political dialogue to go forward on favorable terms, but, unfortunately an artificial construction that hides the many ways in which gays are different in their sensibilities, ways that cannot be easily expressed or enumerated but are very real, indeed the essence of what gay culture is all about, a culture that arises not from politics or community but from the simple fact that gays, in his view, are different in important ways. Even for someone outside the gay community, Halperin strikes an important chord, recognizing that there are aspects of identity and a sense of belongingness that are almost beyond description. Reading Halperin, one is reminded of the statement of Conrad's narrator in *Under Western Eyes*, "Words, as is well known, are the great foe of reality."

Halperin's sense of a gay subjectivity resonates with the views of a much earlier gay writer, Jim Kepner. "Our commonalities," Kepner stated in the remarkable 1997 speech quoted earlier, "lie deeper [than a shared persecution] but I can't define them. I can only give suggestions." He then went on to discuss how "growing up with a feeling of being outsiders is an important element" and, unlike other minorities, "our estrangement goes deep and starts very early, often in our own family," leading to the need for self-understanding. Then, he stated, "this gives us some potential advantages, though many gays fail to develop that potential: an ability for empathy with others; an ability for nonlinear thinking; a tendency to relate to others on an 'I–Thou.' . . . and an ability to see around the corners erected by the straight world" (Kepner 2010, 110).

Generosity of spirit and nonlinear thinking weren't the only aspects of gay subjectivity that interested Kepner. Much earlier he had written: "Homosexuals are natural rebels. . . . Most become inured to breaking the rules. They must reject what they learned as children and still hear repeated about them. But when people break rules knowingly and are not sorry, they usually are forced to judge the rule irrelevant or wrong, to put their own judgment above the rules which represent society's judgment, and become rebels" (1998, 14).

The idea of a unique gay perspective can be affirming in important ways. One gay student never forgot when a legendary University of Texas English professor (female and straight) referred to his gayness as a gift. "It was the first time," he recalled, that anyone had said being gay could be an advantage, "and I don't think it's too much to say that her words changed how I looked at my life" (Schwartz 2012, 114). Ann Matter, a gay student at Oberlin College in the late sixties, recalls how a collective sense of humor brought her and her gay friends through that turbulent period: "We, the queer students really, we saw ourselves as having a sense of humor about life, of not being so deathly serious, of being more ironic. You know we had all the Noel Coward periphrastic ways of referring to ourselves. . . . We made fun of the kind of secrecy of it. And we weren't all that secret. . . . It's like the whole Berlin thing: we are the musical people, we are the vegetarians, we are the friends of Dorothy . . . we live in our own world . . . and we don't have to be like I Love Lucy" (Matter 2004).

This sense of difference has played out with particular force on the issue of same-sex marriage. As early as 1989, Paula Ettelbrick, in a famous 1989 article for *Out/Look* magazine titled "Since When Is Marriage a Path to Liberation?" staked out a position questioning the value of "emphasizing our sameness to married heterosexuals" in order to gain the right to marry. Indeed, for her the idea of marriage itself "rips away the very heart and soul of what I believe it is to be a lesbian in this world" and "is antithetical to my liberation as a lesbian and as a woman because it mainstreams my life and voice: I do not want to be known as 'Mrs. Attached-To-Somebody-Else.' Nor do I want to give to the State the power to regulate my primary relationship" (Ettelbrick 1997, 757–758).

Implicit in Ettelbrick's critique of marriage is a questioning of the value of monogamy, an issue that has also been intensely debated in the gay community. In the late nineties, Christopher Bram captured the emotional resonance of this issue when he wrote: "Is promiscuity soul-killing? Or is it the keystone of gay identity? Monogamy or soullessness? Sexual freedom or surrendering to mainstream hypocrisy? Such an extreme either/or . . . resembles the all-or-nothing approach that alcoholics must use with booze. There has to be a looser, more flexible way to think about sex" (2009, 107). As Bram pointed out in another work, gay history has always worked to encourage that flexibility: "since gay couples needed to invent their own rules anyway, they often chose rules that were more flexible and realistic than those handed down by centuries of heterosexual marriage. They were never a part of a tradition where the husband had all the legal rights and the wife had none" (2012, 109).

Interestingly, politically gay rights has always depended on a strong sense of gay identity, since without it neither the fight against discrimination nor the ideal of a separate gay community can hardly go forward. One strand of dissident thought, however—what is often called queer theory—stands in opposition to, or at least outside, this dependence on a fixed gay identity, or any gender-specific identity for that matter. Queer theory might best be viewed as an academic project aimed at questioning virtually every generally accepted notion of sex, sexuality, and culture by deconstructing their most fundamental premises, the fixedness of gender and the use of gender as an organizing principle of politics and culture. To an outside observer, queer theory, viewed most positively, is neither queer nor a theory but rather an impulse to look at things in a way that values formality and rigorous logic less than a willingness to trust one's own set of impressions and insights. Michael Warner, an important figure in queer theory, captured this idea when he recently praised queer theory for creating "a kind of social space" that has allowed "Queer People of various kinds, both inside and outside academe" to "continue to find their way to it, and find each other through it," in the process "keep[ing] alive a political imagination of sexuality that is otherwise closed down by the dominant direction of gay and lesbian politics" (2012, 8).

Of course one need not be a queer theorist to be concerned with the consequences of overclassifying experience. Martin Duberman, for example, also has wondered whether the whole emphasis on identity (sexual and otherwise) "isn't at bottom a strategy for de-limiting our options as human beings" (2009, 23). At the same time, he recognizes that the emphasis on identity may be necessary in forming a political movement. In a similar vein, Jeffrey Weeks has remarked on the difficulty every person can experience in thinking about identity: "Identities are not neutral. Behind the quest for identity are different and often conflicting values. . . . By saying who we are, we are also striving to express what we are, what we believe, and what we desire. The problem is that these beliefs, needs and desires are often patently in conflict, not only between different communities but within individuals themselves" (1991, 185).

The voices described so far comprise a cultural critique of the gay rights movement. A second strand of criticism worries that the movement has needlessly cut itself off from its roots in a broad social justice agenda. These critics look outward in a way that cultural critics do not.

## The Progressive Dissent

On the last Sunday of April 2000, a fourth gay rights march took place in Washington, D.C., a weekend marked not by demonstrations or acts of civil disobedience but by a huge "Equality Rocks" concert at RFK stadium. In attendance was the wife of the vice president of the United States. One young man attending his first march wondered, "Where was the energy? Where was the anger?" With all the booths promoting various gay rights publications and organizations, the event "seemed to boil down to hanging out on the Mall on a beautiful spring day" (Engel 2001, xvii).

Stonewall seemed very long ago. A revolution that in 1969 had been ignited by the most marginalized segment of the gay community now informally organized its national march around the theme "Faith and Family." There was even a family area with activities for kids and information about where one could rent baby strollers. The conservative theme was not surprising in that two main-stream organizations, the Metropolitan Community Church and the Human Rights Campaign, had taken the lead in preparing for the march, an effort that drew considerable resentment from some, who perceived the organizations as imposing an agenda for the march "from the 'top down,'" in contrast to the more disorganized but genuinely grassroots organizing for the previous marches (Smith and Haider-Markel 2002, 51).

This loss of an antipoverty, antiracist agenda is deeply troubling for some gay activists. In the May 2012 issue of the *American Prospect*, Urvashi Vaid relates how "a major gay rights broker told me that when his state legalized marriage equality, that state's gay-rights agenda would be done" (2012b, 38). For Vaid, the broker's statement reflected a complete ignorance of the plight of key parts of the gay community, including racial and ethnic minorities, the poor, and the homeless. Interestingly, Paula Ettelbrick voiced the same concern in her 1989 article on marriage, discussed earlier, when she argued that those who most wanted the right to marry were already the most privileged members of the community, not the working class, the poor, and people of color. For them, she worried, "if the laws change tomorrow and lesbians and gay men were allowed to marry, where would we find the incentive to continue the progressive move-ment we have started that is pushing for societal and legal recognition of all kinds of family relationships" (1997, 760).

For Vaid, the decoupling of the gay rights movement from a broader progres-sive movement is not only bad tactically but ethically wrong because it places the movement in an alliance with conservative voices whose views she rejects. In a speech in 2011, she argued: "Identity assertion is important. . . . But forming and celebrating queer identity is not and never was the progressive queer move-ment's destination. That destination instead was the space to live openly LGBT lives *in a transformed, wider world.* Identity assertion is a means to a greater end, namely the creation of a self-determined life, and through that life, the creation of *a more socially just and inclusive society for all*" (2012a, 17; my emphasis).

For Vaid, the gay rights movement should be about transformation, not just access, since only then will meaningful improvement occur in the lives of all gay people, not just the race-privileged, class-privileged, education-privileged group that, in her view, dominates mainstream gay rights organizations. Her 2012 book offers a sustained critique of the equality movement's failure to address the needs of large swaths of LGBT people: people of color, homeless youth, the poor, transgender persons. She applauds the successes of the equal access movement but argues that "an innovative LGBT movement must move beyond seeking the reform of laws to maximizing the life chances, freedom, and self-determination of all LGBT people" (2012a, xi).

Vaid sets a course that involves two basic ideas. First, she wants to make the LGBT movement more inclusive, more participatory, more transparent, more democratic. She criticizes the influence of major donors to mainstream gay rights organizations and sees the lack of democratic accountability as a major defect in the organizational structure of the movement. In words that recall the spirit of the liberationist groups of the early seventies, she states: "The individual member to any LGBT organization has no voice in electing its board, no formal role to play in the setting of organizational platforms, priorities and policy agendas. . . . As a result, the positions the national movement takes are not and cannot be said to be representative of the views of members of those organizations, much less of the diverse and far larger community that is not part of the formally organized LGBT infrastructure" (2012a, 26).

Vaid cites an interesting 2007–2008 study conducted by the Human Rights Campaign to show just how deep the separation is between, for example, the agenda of the mainstream movement and matters of importance to LGBT people of color (Vaid 2012a, 53–54). The survey found that the three major issues for people of color were health care, jobs, and equality for all people, none of which is part of a mainstream gay agenda, which generally ignores nongay issues. The study also found that persons of color ranked same-sex marriage and the right to serve in the military behind most other concerns when asked specifically about gay issues.

This leads directly to Vaid's second basic point: that a revitalized gay rights movement must embrace a larger social justice agenda, one that addresses issues of poverty, health care, and wealth inequality and focuses on the distorting effect of privilege on the life chances of everyday people. Vaid is not alone in her emphasis on the need for a deeper engagement with nongay issues. Another important gay rights leader, Virginia Apuzzo, for example, worries that a single-minded focus on marriage has come at the expense of the creation of a larger agenda: "Safety, security, a job, a good job—that doesn't have glass or cellophane or lavender ceilings, the kinds of social justice issues that involve coalition building with non-gay partners and an understanding of how to institutionalize progress" (2004, 90).

This progressive critique has strong roots in what I have referred to as the freedom period of the gay rights movement. When Harvey Milk addressed the 1978 Gay Freedom Day Parade in what became known as the Hope Speech, he talked about hope for everyone, and the issues he addressed—South Africa, racism, intolerance, violence—affected everyone, not just gays. At the end of his speech, he said: "Without hope, not only gays, but the blacks, the seniors, the handicapped, the us'es, the us'es will give up" (Shilts 1982, 363).

I believe that this progressive critique has considerable merit. The gay rights movement has been about creating a society in which gay persons have the widest range of choices for their own personal fulfillment. Certainly, a necessary part of that effort has been to fight for legal equality, since discrimination clearly narrows one's choices as well as marking one as in some way inferior. But the gay rights movement will have failed if it simply achieves equality in the midst of a society marred by poverty, deep economic inequality, and inadequate education and health care. The good society is as much a gay as well a heterosexual issue. It is in this larger goal that the gay rights movement naturally links up with broader progressive movements, because the pursuit of happiness for gays, as for everyone, depends on a society in which people have access to health care, jobs, a livable environment, and an ability to support themselves and their family, among other things.

Notwithstanding these broad critiques, virtually no one in the gay community actively opposes the quest for same-sex marriage, the ultimate prize in the relationship recognition category and the subject to which I now turn. Before I begin, however, let me note that same-sex marriage is itself an uncomfortable term, for same-sex marriage is no different than heterosexual marriage in the states that allow it. Though for convenience I use the term, the issue is the right of same-sex couples to marry, not the creation of some special form of marriage.

# PART THREE

# The Right to Marry

On June 26, 2013, the last day of the Supreme Court's 2012–2013 term, nine solemn justices filed into the Supreme Court's chambers to announce their decisions in two much anticipated cases involving same-sex marriage: *Hollingsworth v. Perry* and the *United States v. Windsor*. A short time later, six exuberant people emerged from the building's shadowed entrance onto the sun-drenched marbled steps below, arms raised in triumph, smiles bright enough to light a city. They were the two gay couples and two members of their legal team who had filed suit to invalidate California's heterosexuals-only marriage law. Two and a half years earlier, they had won an impressively broad decision from the federal district court in San Francisco, whose reasoning, if it had been adopted by the Supreme Court, would have required every state in the union to allow gay couples to marry. The Supreme Court did not, however, adopt Judge Walker's district court decision, nor did it affirm the narrower ruling of the Ninth Circuit Court of Appeals.

In fact, the Supreme Court never addressed the question of same-sex marriage in *Hollingsworth*. Rather, it dismissed the appeal on a technical ground that had nothing to do with the substance of the constitutional argument over same-sex marriage. So why were the plaintiffs so happy? Because the net result of the Supreme Court's decision was to allow the district court decision requiring same-sex marriage to stand. The plaintiffs would now be able to marry in California, which had been their goal all along. The opponents of gay marriage, however, could also exhale, for the technical nature of the Supreme Court's decision did not affect in any way the vast majority of states that had statutes or constitutional amendments expressly reserving marriage for heterosexual couples.

The opponents of same-sex marriage, however, had no consolation in the second decision announced by the Court that morning in the *Windsor* case. And this was a real advance for gay rights, the subject of banner headlines through-out the country, although no exuberant young plaintiffs emerged in celebra-tion, for the plaintiff in this case was an eighty-five-year-old woman named Edith Windsor, who had been legally married as far as the state of New York was concerned but not so in the eyes of the federal government because of the provision in the Defense of Marriage Act (the No Recognition provision) that recognized only heterosexual marriages for all federal law purposes. Among the many consequences of the No Recognition provision was that Windsor had to pay more than $400,000 in estate tax for the property she had inherited from her deceased spouse, Thea Spyer. Windsor would not have had to pay this tax but for the No Recognition provision because, as the legal spouse of the deceased, she would have been entitled to what is called the marital deduction for federal estate tax purposes. In a 5–4 decision, the Court struck down the No Recognition provision.

Marriage itself is both an event and a life process. In twenty-first-century America, marriage begins with a wedding and ends with either death or divorce. It wasn't always that way. Common law marriages, which were an important part of frontier life, did not begin with an event, and their legal existence was based not on a license but on the community's understanding and acceptance of a couple's relationship. The desire for a public understanding of their rela-tionship and the joy that comes with publicly proclaiming it in the currency of today's culture are what drive the same-sex marriage movement. They are what distinguish marriages from civil unions.

Catholicism and Protestantism do not look at marriage in the same way. Luther believed strongly in the existence of two kingdoms, the heavenly and the earthly. Marriage in the Protestant view belonged to the earthly kingdom, and responsibility for it therefore rested with the state. The Catholic view was, and still is, much different. Marriage is a sacrament in Catholicism but not in Protestantism, which is why divorce is prohibited in the Catholic Church but not among Protestant groups. Despite these differences, many conservative evangelical sects and the Catholic Church share a strong opposition to same-sex marriage, even as more liberal Protestant sects and the general public move toward acceptance.

Same-sex marriage is now legal in seventeen states and the District of Columbia. It is, however, explicitly prohibited in almost every other state either by state statute or constitutional amendment. How is it possible for such differ-ent policies respecting marriage to exist among the various states side by side? Aren't we one nation? The answer lies in the fact that our constitutional system is one of dual sovereignties, and historically, marriage has been a matter for states to decide.

This has been of critical importance because each state also has its own constitution, which contains its own guaranty of individual rights. In other words, residents of each state have constitutional protections emanating from the state constitution as well as from the United States Constitution. Since many state constitutions have provisions that guarantee, in one form or another, equal protection of the laws and/or forbid discrimination on the basis of gender, it was natural for gay rights activists, long before they dreamed of bringing a case to the United States Supreme Court, to first look to the state courts as a vehicle for achieving same-sex marriage in at least some jurisdictions.

Beginning in the late nineties, particularly after the Supreme Court's decision in *Romer v. Evans*, some gay rights lawyers felt the time was right to pursue constitutional challenges to the heterosexuals-only marriage laws. The ensuing state court battles, first in Vermont, then Massachusetts, later in Iowa and other states, produced favorable decisions and galvanized the same-sex marriage movement. The legal stakes in the fight for same-sex marriage could not be higher. In those states recognizing same-sex marriage (or civil unions), gay couples enter a new legal universe. State inheritance laws, for example, suddenly apply to them, as does the right to file a joint state tax return. Gays are no longer in danger of being denied the right to visit a dying partner, as has happened in the past. All of the legal areas regarding relationship recognition, including custody proceedings, get fought out on much different terrain. Same-sex marriage, however, is much more than a legal or constitutional issue. For gay rights advocates, it is the gold ring of acceptance; for its most fervent religious opponents, it is the Rubicon that must not be crossed.

The organization of this part III is straightforward. In chapter 12, I examine the state court battles in Hawaii, Vermont, Massachusetts, California, and Iowa and the political fallout that followed in each state. In chapter 13 I first look more closely at *United States v. Windsor*, scrutinizing the majority and dissenting opinions in that case and assessing their potential impact. I then examine more closely the *Hollingsworth* case and focus on whether the Equal Protection Clause of the U.S. Constitution indeed requires same-sex marriage, an issue the Supreme Court will likely confront again.

# 12

# The State Constitutional Battles

$A$s important as it may have been, June 26, 2013, is not the most important date in the same-sex marriage annals to this point. That spot should be reserved for November 6, 2012, when the voters of four states (Maine, Maryland, Washington, and Minnesota) in varying ways endorsed same-sex marriage. The election marked the first success gay rights forces had had at the polls after countless defeats when voters in state after state (including five that later voted for President Obama in both the 2008 and 2012 elections) voted against gay marriage. If you believe, along with Mr. Dooley, that the Supreme Court follows the election returns, then perhaps, if Election Day 2012 had gone differently, then June 26 might have as well. Instead, Maine became the first state in which the voters themselves authorized same-sex marriage; voters in Washington and Maryland ratified previous decisions of their respective legislatures authorizing gay marriage; and in Minnesota, voters rejected a proposed constitutional amendment that would have defined marriage as a heterosexuals-only institution, setting the stage for the Minnesota legislature's subsequent adoption of same-sex marriage in Minnesota.

In this chapter I focus on state high court decisions that have found a constitutional right to same-sex marriage. I should note, however, that in 2006 and 2007, high courts in New Jersey, New York, Maryland, Georgia, and Washington rejected gay marriage claims under their respective state constitutions. To cite just one decision, the New York Court of Appeals (New York's highest court) in 2006 held that heterosexuals-only marriage did not violate either the equal protection or due process guarantees of the New York Constitution. Among other things, the court found that the New York marriage statute was a facially neutral statute enacted without discriminatory intent (that is, it wasn't aimed specifically against gays); therefore, even if it did have a disparate impact on gay couples, the impact, applying established equal protection principles, did not constitute an equal protection violation. This was, and is, a line of reasoning not easily dismissed, particularly if the applicable standard is the rational basis test, that is, no heightened scrutiny (see *Hernandez v. Robles*). But let me begin at the beginning.

## Hawaii: The Bolt from the Blue

In 1993, the Hawaii Supreme Court, in *Baehr v. Lewin*, shocked the legal community when it held that the state's prohibition against gender discrimination might have the effect, if not justified by a sufficient state interest, of requiring that same-sex couples have the same right to marry as heterosexual couples. The court's decision rested on the simple proposition that when a man cannot marry a man but a woman can, a discrimination based on one's gender has occurred. The plaintiffs in *Baehr v. Lewin* were three same-sex couples who had sought and been refused marriage licenses. The prospects for success in the case were so low that the Lambda Legal Defense and Education Fund had refused to participate in the case and, in fact, worried that it was premature. A local attorney from the American Civil Liberties Union brought the case without the support of the national organization (Klarman 2013, 55). As subsequent events showed, Lambda's fears were not without foundation, although perhaps not for the reasons expressed. The Hawaii Supreme Court decision did not end with an order that gays be allowed to marry. Rather, the court remanded (returned) the case back to the trial court to hold a hearing to determine whether Hawaii had a "compelling interest" that would justify its heterosexuals-only marriage statute.

The lower court opinion, which the Hawaii Supreme Court reversed, had granted summary judgment to the state, meaning that the lower court had decided, *as a matter of law*, that the same-sex plaintiffs were not entitled to marriage licenses. When a court grants summary judgment, it has found that there is no state of facts on which one of the two sides in a case can prevail and therefore a trial to determine the facts is unnecessary. In such a case, the other side is said to prevail as a matter of law. What is a question of fact and what is a question of law is not always clear. Indeed, it would not have been beyond the pale for the Hawaii Supreme Court to have decided that, as a matter of law, the state had no compelling interest in excluding same-sex couples from marrying. The court, however, knew that this was a volatile issue, and this may have been one reason that the court referred the matter back to the lower court.

This suspicion is reinforced by the case's subsequent history. The lower court on remand decided that the state did not have a compelling interest in

preserving heterosexuals-only marriage. By the time of the lower court decision, however, forces were already under way to put the entire question of
same-sex marriage on the ballot. The Hawaii Supreme Court never took up the
case again, deferring any decision on the state's appeal from the lower court's
decision of no compelling state interest until after the voice of the Hawaiian
electorate was heard. In November 1998, the voters, by referendum, amended
the state's constitution to make marriage exclusively available to heterosexual
couples, effectively overturning the Hawaii Supreme Court's initial decision.
Almost 70 percent of the electorate had voted for the amendment. The lopsided nature of this vote was particularly shocking for those who believed that
Hawaii, with its great ethnic diversity and its prior history of sensitivity to gay
rights (it had been one of the first states to prohibit employment discrimination based on sexual orientation), would be a reasonable place to test public
sentiment on same-sex marriage.

The litigation in Hawaii did have one positive result for gays in Hawaii, for,
to get the referendum on same-sex marriage on the ballot, opponents of same-
sex marriage agreed to a legislative deal allowing two single adults access to
approximately 60 out of the 160 spousal rights available to heterosexual couples
under Hawaii law (Rosenberg 2008, 344). The deal may also explain the lopsided
nature of the 1998 vote against gay marriage since it allowed its opponents to
claim that Hawaii had already granted same-sex couples important legal rights.
Neither the attractive lesbian couple, Nina Baehr and Genora Dancel, the lead
plaintiffs in the Hawaii marriage litigation, nor anyone else ever got to marry in
Hawaii as a result of the high court's initial decision. The immediate impact, as
mentioned, was disastrous nationally, resulting in the federal Defense of Marriage Act, with more than twenty states also enacting laws or constitutional
amendments prohibiting same-sex marriage by the end of 1997. At about the
same time, California governor Pete Wilson (a man not without presidential
ambitions, who needed to improve his standing with party conservatives)
vetoed a modest domestic partnership law that would have provided, among
other things, hospital visitation rights to same-sex couples. Wilson claimed that
the law could pave the way to same-sex marriage (Klarman 2013, 58).

As bad as the immediate impact of the Hawaii decision may have been,
from the perspective of 2013, the view of Lambda's Evan Wolfson that the decision represented a "tectonic shift" in the legal fight for gay rights seems justified
(Moats 2004, 91). For the first time, it was possible to believe that sympathetic
state courts might have the tools to advance the cause of gay marriage. Indeed,
just making same-sex marriage a topic of real discussion elevated the issue to an
entirely new level. The battle was about to shift thousands of miles east to the
colder clime but warmer political atmosphere of New England.

## Vermont: A Huge Victory but Not Gay Marriage

The Hawaii Supreme Court's decision was not in any sense a vindication of the right of gay couples to legal equality but rather was based on a somewhat literal reading of the state constitution's prohibition against gender discrimination. The next important case, however, the Vermont Supreme Court's 1999 decision in *Baker v. Vermont*, met the issue head on. In the final sentence of the opinion, Chief Justice Jeffrey Amestoy wrote that gay Vermonters were seeking nothing more than "legal protection and security for their avowed commitment to an intimate and long lasting relationship," something that "is simply, when all is said and done, a recognition of our common humanity (*Baker*, 889).

The Vermont Supreme Court, however, did not declare Vermont's heterosexual marriage law unconstitutional, leaving it instead to the legislature to either amend the marriage law or provide for civil unions that would confer all the legal benefits of marriage on same-sex couples. Many gay rights supporters were upset by the decision, feeling that the court had eloquently established the case for gay marriage and then drawn back at the last minute. Pragmatically, the court's decision made civil union status the middle ground between gay marriage, on the one hand, and a possible constitutional amendment to completely overturn the Vermont Supreme Court's decision on the other. Yet the court's decision was still perceived as radical and unacceptable by social conservatives. Shortly after the decision, Robert Bork and columnist Cal Thomas attacked it, David Frum denounced domestic partnerships as an "alias" and dangerous step toward gay marriage, and in New Hampshire the influential *Manchester Union Leader* called the decision "Vermont's terrifying lurch toward lunacy" (Klarman 2013, 83).

Nevertheless, following the court's decision, the Vermont legislature, after vigorous debate, opted for civil union status. Conservative lawmakers had even opposed the civil unions route, preferring instead simply to ignore the Vermont Supreme Court decision. The debate was not without its humorous moments, as some conservative lawmakers placed little yellow plastic ducks on their legislative chamber desks to underscore their belief that civil union was no different than marriage (If it looks like a duck, walks like a duck, and quacks like a duck, then it is a duck) (Stacey and Davenport 2002, 355).

While some in the gay community were disappointed that the legislature did not provide for same-sex marriage, the more dangerous possibility was that the legislature would do nothing or opt for a constitutional amendment prohibiting even civil unions. For that reason, as soon as the vote was over, "everybody started hugging" and "it was like winning the World Series," recalled Holly Puterbaugh and Lois Farnham, plaintiffs (and longtime partners) in the Vermont lawsuit (Marcus 2002, 421). That autumn, the leading campaign issue in Vermont, ahead of the economy and health care among other issues, was the new civil unions law. Republicans made opposition to it and any recognition of same-sex relationships the focal point of their campaign to not only oust Governor Howard Dean, who had supported the civil union option, but to gain control of the state legislature.

They were partly successful, gaining control of the Vermont House of Representatives for the first time in fourteen years and just narrowly failing in their bid to defeat the governor. Dean's narrow victory, however, belies actual support for the measure in that Dean faced two opponents—a Republican, Ruth Dwyer, who had won the GOP primary by tapping into deep anger over any legal recognition of gay relationships, and Anthony Pollina, a former staffer for Vermont's only U.S. Representative, Bernie Sanders, who believed that Dean should have supported gay marriage, rather than the civil unions bill, after the Vermont Supreme Court's decision. Governor Dean had met Ralph Nader in the form of Anthony Pollina, but, unlike Vice President Al Gore, had lived to tell the tale.

Fast forward to April 2009. The state legislature, with the Democrats once again firmly in control, made Vermont the first state in the nation not under compulsion by a court order to legalize same-sex marriage. As promised, Republican governor Jim Douglas vetoed the bill. The original House vote on the bill had been 95–52, meaning that the bill was five votes short of the two-thirds margin needed to override a veto. The day after the veto, the Senate easily overrode it, and, to the shock of many, the House, with the support of six Republicans, overrode the veto as well: 100–49, without a vote to spare.

Vermont is certainly not your average U.S. state, boasting the nation's only socialist congressperson and a long history of going against the grain. (Vermont was, for example, the first state to outlaw slavery.) Nevertheless, the reversal of public opinion over little more than a decade is remarkable. Whereas in 1999, polling indicated that a majority of Vermonters opposed even civil unions, a July 2011 survey by Public Policy Polling, a highly respected polling firm primarily affiliated with the Democratic Party, found almost 80 percent of Vermont voters supported some form of legal recognition of same-sex couples, including 55 percent in favor of same-sex marriage. As important as the Vermont decision may have been, no high court had yet to hold that its constitution demanded that same-sex couples be allowed to marry. Then Massachusetts stepped up to the plate.

## Massachusetts: Victory without Qualification

*Lawrence v. Texas* was decided five months before the Supreme Judicial Court of Massachusetts (the state's highest court) legalized gay marriage in *Goodridge v. Department of Public Health*. The influence of *Lawrence* on the court was unmistakable. At the very outset of her opinion, Chief Justice Margaret Marshall discussed how the U.S. Supreme Court in *Lawrence* "affirmed that the core concept of common human dignity protected by the Fourteenth Amendment to the United States Constitution precludes government intrusion into the deeply personal realms of consensual adult expressions of intimacy and one's choice of an intimate partner" (*Goodridge*, 948). Justice Marshall asserted that the Massachusetts Constitution was, if anything, more protective of individual liberties than the federal constitution and held that the state had "failed to identify any constitutionally adequate reason for denying civil marriage to same-sex couples" (948). Notice here how the court itself, unlike the Supreme Court of Hawaii, determined the lack of an adequate state justification for prohibiting same-sex marriage, not remanding the case back to a lower court (961).

The court did not immediately order the issuance of gay marriage licenses. Instead, it stayed the entry of judgment for 180 days to give the legislature time to react to the court's opinion. As might be expected, the opponents of gay marriage did not halt their efforts to overturn the decision. The Senate majority leader interpreted the decision to require only civil union status and sought an advisory opinion from the Massachusetts Supreme Court confirming his view. The court promptly responded that if the institution of marriage was to be preserved at all in Massachusetts, it had to be available to gay couples on equal terms with heterosexual couples.

Following the court's advisory opinion, the legislature went into joint session to consider constitutional amendment proposals, and, after a passionate debate in which legislators on both sides spoke with great force and eloquence, the legislators voted 105–92 to propose a constitutional amendment that would have banned gay marriage but allowed for civil union status. Notwithstanding the legislature's recommendation and the subsequent efforts of Governor Mitt Romney to delay the effective date of the court's initial decision, on May 17, 2004, the 180-day stay period having expired, the state of Massachusetts began issuing marriage licenses to gay couples. Over 10,000 people gathered in Boston to celebrate the first marriages. Roughly 1,000 gay couples applied almost immediately for their licenses. Over the course of the first twelve months after the decision, approximately 6,000 gay couples would wed in the state (Rosenberg 2008, 349).

In November not a single legislator who had voted for gay marriage was defeated at the polls. This was an important development. The political sky had not fallen on the supporters of gay marriage, and the legislature in the next session promptly repudiated its proposed amendment (in Massachusetts, two successive sessions of the legislature must authorize a constitutional amendment for it to appear on the ballot) by a lopsided vote and after only a brief debate. Same-sex marriage had made it through to its first finish line. Four years later, the California Supreme Court would also interpret its constitution as requiring access to marriage for same-sex couples. This time, however, the political outcome would be much different.

## California: Victory, Then Defeat

In November 2000, California voters, following a nationwide trend, approved Proposition 22, which declared marriage to be a union of opposite-sex couples only. Just three years later, however, the California legislature enacted the Domestic Partner Rights and Responsibilities Act giving same-sex couples the same legal rights and responsibilities as opposite-sex couples. In essence, California had become a civil union state, just like Vermont, but of course California is not Vermont. For one thing, it has San Francisco.

In February 2004, San Francisco made international news when the county clerk, following a directive from the mayor, began issuing marriage licenses to same-sex couples. Images of same-sex couples lining up for their marriage licenses in San Francisco were beamed around the world. After a month, however, the attorney general of California stepped in and succeeded in getting an injunction to halt the marriages. His argument was that the city had exceeded its authority because the question of the constitutional right to marriage was a decision for the courts to make, not the mayor or county clerk. The stage was then set for the California Supreme Court to decide the issue, and in May 2008 the court in *In Re Marriage Cases* held that same-sex marriage was a fundamental right under California's constitution. Joy in the gay community was again short-lived, for in November 2008, California, through a ballot initiative known as Proposition 8, voted to amend the California Constitution to make marriage once again a heterosexuals-only institution. The Supreme Court of California subsequently upheld the constitutionality of Proposition 8, beginning the final chapter of the California saga.

The California Supreme Court's decision, though nullified by Proposition 8, is nevertheless important, for its opinion was the most thoroughly articulated argument that gay couples enjoy a fundamental right to marry. The court engaged in a two-step reasoning process. First, it reaffirmed what it felt it had previously decided in other contexts, namely, that the state constitution guaranteed "the substantive right of two adults who share a loving relationship to join together to establish an officially recognized family of their own" and then found that this right "does not depend upon the individual's sexual orientation"

(*In Re Marriage Cases*, 399, 400); therefore gay couples deserved the same access to marriage as heterosexuals.

The court seemed to look beyond the state constitution to the Declaration of Independence when it wrote: "The ability of an individual to join in a committed, long-term, officially recognized family relationship with the person of his or her choice is often of crucial significance to the individual's happiness and well-being. . . . [It] provides an individual with the ability to invest in and rely upon a loving relationship with another adult in a way that may be crucial to the individual's development as a person and achievement of his or her full potential" (*In Re Marriage Cases*, 424). Paradoxically, a case dealing with the right of a couple to marry had found its voice in thinking of that couple as two individuals.

## Iowa: Classic Equal Protection Analysis

Hawaii, Vermont, Massachusetts, and California are widely regarded as among the bluest states in America. Not so Iowa, a classic swing state, so it was particularly surprising when the Iowa Supreme Court found that the Iowa Constitution required that gays be allowed to marry. In contrast to California, the Iowa Supreme Court in *Varnum v. Brien* relied on traditional equal protection analysis to reach its conclusion in April 2009 that restricting marriage to heterosexuals violated Iowa's Equal Protection Clause.

In its analysis, the court asked and then answered three basic questions. First, the court asked, are same-sex couples similarly situated to heterosexual couples? The court answered yes, rejecting the assertion that same-sex couples cannot procreate naturally and are therefore not similarly situated to heterosexual couples. The court agreed that this was true as a statement of fact but irrelevant because the marriage laws were "designed to bring a sense of order to the legal relationships of committed couples and their families in myriad ways" (*Varnum*, 883–884), and same-sex couples are capable of forming the same kind of committed relationships and families as heterosexual couples. At the time of the litigation, there were an estimated 5,800 same-sex couples living in Iowa, with about one-third of them raising children.

Then, the court asked, does the heterosexuals-only marriage statute discriminate on the basis of sexual orientation? The court again answered yes, rejecting the argument that the marriage law did not discriminate on the basis of sexual orientation because it never mentioned sexual orientation but simply confined marriage to opposite-sex couples. Gays could still marry, the argument went, they just couldn't marry each other. The court had little difficulty disposing of this issue, finding that, although the marriage statute did not explicitly discriminate based on the sexual orientation, it clearly prevented same-sex marriages: "By purposefully placing civil marriage outside the reach of gay and lesbian individuals, the ban on same-sex civil marriages differentiates implicitly on the basis of sexual orientation" (*Varnum*, 885).

Finally, the court asked, is the discrimination on the basis of sexual orientation justified by a legitimate state interest and therefore consistent with the Equal Protection Clause? Here the court answered no, subjecting the law to intermediate scrutiny where the law must be substantially related to an important governmental interest to pass constitutional muster. In deciding that the prohibition against same-sex marriage required intermediate scrutiny, the court, applying traditional modes of analysis, found that (1) gays had suffered "a long and painful" history of discrimination; (2) gays were fully able to contribute to society; (3) being gay is highly resistant to change; and (4) the political power of gays, while it had helped gain them a measure of acceptance, was not so great as "to overcome the unfair and severe prejudice that history suggests produces discrimination based on sexual orientation" (*Varnum*, 895).

The only question then remaining was whether the law in fact survived intermediate scrutiny. The answer was no. From the court's vantage point, the government had not established an important governmental objective to which the law was substantially related. In so holding, the court found, among other things, that there was no governmental interest in maintaining the traditional view of marriage; that the ban on gay marriage was inconsistent with the best interests of children of gay and lesbian parents; and that the ban neither promoted procreation nor benefited the children of heterosexual couples, nor promoted stability in opposite-sex relationships.

*Varnum* was not a popular decision in Iowa, understandably since just a year before the decision a *Des Moines Register* poll found Iowans opposing gay marriage by 62 percent to 32 percent (Klarman 2013,127). In 2010, three of the judges who participated in what had been a unanimous opinion were defeated in their bid for another term. Since 2009, Republicans, who control the Iowa House, have repeatedly attempted to force a referendum on gay marriage, most recently in February 2013, all to no avail as the Democratic majority leader in the Senate, Michael Gronstal, has blocked consideration of any measure to put the issue on the ballot.

A February 2012 *Des Moines Register* poll suggests that Iowans are comfortable with the status quo though perhaps not in complete agreement with it; 56 percent of Iowa voters said they opposed a marriage referendum to 38 percent in favor, though a separate poll of Iowans showed that only 30 percent said they supported the *Varnum* decision, 36 percent opposed it, and 33 percent didn't care much either way. Of those who didn't care much, 75 percent opposed putting the amendment on the ballot. In another sign of the growing shift of public opinion toward gay rights, in the 2012 election, Justice David Wiggins retained his seat on the Iowa Supreme Court, notwithstanding his vote for same-sex marriage. Iowa reflects the extent of the partisan divide on same-sex marriage throughout the nation, with nearly two-thirds of Iowa Republicans in the 2012 *Des Moines Register* poll favoring a ban on same-sex marriage as opposed to only 15 percent of Democrats. Independents oppose a ban by 65 percent to 35 percent.

In each of their decisions upholding the right of gay couples to marry (or form civil unions in the case of Vermont), the high courts of Vermont, Massachusetts, California, and Iowa were interpreting different language and relied on somewhat different rationales. Ultimately, however, all reached the identical conclusion: the state could not regulate the institution of marriage in a way that excluded gay couples without violating a state constitutionally protected right. But what about the federal government? Does the U.S. Constitution's Equal Protection Clause (and its Due Process Clause) impose a similar limitation on Congress? That, of course, was precisely the issue that confronted the U.S. Supreme Court in *United States v. Windsor*, the case to which we now turn.

# 13

## The Supreme Court Confronts
## Same-Sex Marriage

On the morning that the decision in *United States v. Windsor* was announced in Washington, D.C., Edith Windsor awaited the outcome in the New York apartment of her attorney, Roberta Kaplan, who had argued the case before the Supreme Court. The case had attracted worldwide attention. Six months earlier, in an interview with the *Guardian*, Windsor expressed her optimism: "First of all, I'm the youngest in my family and justice matters a lot—the little one gets pushed around a lot. And I trust the Supreme Court. I trust the constitution—so I feel a certain confidence that we'll win" (Gabbatt 2013). Her confidence was justified but only by the margin of a single vote. As in many cases in which the Court's so-called liberal and conservative wings line up on opposite sides, the deciding vote was cast by Justice Anthony Kennedy. A few days after the *Windsor* decision was announced, the annual gay pride parade was held in New York City. At its head as one of the three grand marshals was Edith Windsor. As Constance McMillen, our Mississippi teenager, had found out just a few years earlier, in the world of gay rights, brave and persistent litigants can become heroes.

### *United States v. Windsor*

In her argument before the Supreme Court, Kaplan offered two distinct grounds for invalidating the No Recognition provision, which denied federal recognition of valid state same-sex marriages. The first emphasized that marriage has historically been a subject of state regulation and therefore the No Recognition provision improperly intruded on the right of the states to define the contour of its marriage laws. Given this tradition of state regulation, plaintiffs argued that the only possible motive for the No Recognition provision was to discourage states from allowing same-sex marriage, a motive rooted in the kind of animus that *Romer v. Evans* expressly forbids and that, in any event, was an affront to state sovereignty. The second ground was rooted in the basic concept of fundamental fairness implicit in the Due Process and Equal Protection Clauses of the Fourteenth Amendment. Here the argument centered not on state power but on the right of same-sex couples to enjoy access to such an important public institution as marriage unless there was some strong reason, rooted in public policy, for excluding them. Since, plaintiffs argued, there was none, the only possible justification for the No Recognition provision was to preserve the traditional view of marriage for its own sake, a justification that simply was insufficient under the constitution. Federalism and state sovereignty were the foundation of the first argument, the meaning of equality and the right to individual dignity the key to the second.

In response, the defenders of the No Recognition provision centered on the right of the federal government to have the same flexibility in shaping its legislation that the states enjoy. At oral argument, Paul Clement, the attorney defending the No Recognition provision, argued that "all DOMA does is take this term where it appears in Federal law and define it for purposes of Federal law" (*Windsor* argument transcript, 59). Clement pointed to the legitimate interest of Congress in having a uniform definition of marriage that would apply throughout the nation and tried to counter the portrayal of the No Recognition provision as a radical intrusion into the police power of the state by noting that it was passed at a time that the decision of the Hawaii Supreme Court raised the possibility that all states might be required to recognize same-sex marriage. Moreover, Clement noted, all the provisions of federal law to which the No Recognition provision applied "were passed with the traditional definition [of marriage] in mind" (Windsor argument transcript, 61). In other words, DOMA was not radical legislation but legislation preserving the status quo.

Clement's arguments were not insubstantial, and Justice Kennedy, writing for the majority, needed to address them. He acknowledged that heterosexual marriage "no doubt had been thought by most people as essential to the very definition of that term and its role and function throughout the history of civilization" (Opinion of the Court, 13). And he recognized that Congress had on occasion overridden state definitions of marriage, for example in legislating that a marriage entered into for the purpose of procuring an alien's admission into the United States as an immigrant would not qualify the alien for that status even if the marriage were valid for state law purposes.

Kennedy, however, found these points, valid as they might be, unpersuasive. In response, Kennedy seemed to adopt a combination of both the federalism and equal dignity arguments offered by the No Recognition provision's opponents in a way that relied on neither exclusively but whose combined weight he found controlling. In a key moment in the opinion, Kennedy begins by asserting that more than concerns for federalism are involved in the Court's decision: "The State's power in defining the marital relation is of central relevance in this case quite apart from principles of federalism." The reason becomes immediately clear, for Kennedy continues: "Here the State's [New York's] decision to give this class of persons the right to marry conferred upon them a dignity and status of immense import. When the State used its historic and essential authority to define the marital relation in this way, its role and its power in making the decision enhanced the recognition, dignity and protection of the class in their own community" (18). In this passage, Kennedy flirts with the notion, never fully articulated, that state power is worthy of particular solicitude when it is being exercised in furtherance of an individual right to dignity. Then comes the punch line. "DOMA, because of its reach and extent, departs from this history and tradition of reliance on state law to define marriage" (18–19). In this passage, Kennedy takes two separate principles (respect for state sovereignty and an individual right to equal dignity) and makes them complementary, uniting the idea of the "historic and essential authority" of the state to define marriage with marriage's key importance in conveying "a dignity and status of immense import." Depending on one's perspective, Kennedy was either acting in the best tradition of judicial creativity or was just winging it.

To the point that Congress had an interest in uniformity of definition, Kennedy offered two replies. First, he pointed to the interest of each state in a uniform definition of marriage within the state, something clearly at odds with the No Recognition provision. Second, he simply disagreed with the contention that uniformity had been the purpose of the legislation, asserting that the "essence" of the legislation, as amply demonstrated by its legislative history, was "interference with the equal dignity of same-sex marriages" (21). In the concluding passage of the opinion, Kennedy evokes the spirit of *Romer v. Evans* when he writes that "the principal purpose and the necessary effect of this law are to demean those persons who are in a lawful same-sex marriage."

Although Kennedy's rhetoric was not as soaring as that in *Lawrence*, it had its moments. It is precisely the kind of rhetoric anathema to Justice Antonin Scalia, whose dissent showed that ten years of gay rights progress since his vigorous dissent in *Lawrence v. Texas* had done nothing to soften his views or diminish his firepower. In a biting dissent, he accused the majority of undermining the power of the people, calling Kennedy's justifications "rootless and shifting" and essentially accusing the majority of demeaning those who oppose same-sex marriage by judging them "enemies of the human race." "I promise you this:" he writes toward the end of his dissent, "the only thing that will 'confine' the Court's holding is its sense of what it can get away with" (Scalia dissent, 22).

There were two other dissents in the case. Chief Justice John Roberts's brief dissent was aimed at only one thing: hemming in the *Windsor* majority by emphasizing the federalism aspect of the decision so that *Windsor* would actually be a favorable precedent for any future case in which the issue was whether the states could regulate marriage by excluding same-sex couples. Scalia and Roberts both are clearly part of the conservative majority, but one can't imagine two more different judicial temperaments. Justice Samuel Alito also offered a dissent which aimed at showing the inadequacies of the Kennedy opinion from the perspective of standard equal protection analysis.

The *Windsor* decision has already proved an important precedent with consequences none more profound than in New Jersey, where it has led directly to same-sex marriage. The New Jersey Supreme Court had decided before *Windsor* that gay couples were entitled under the New Jersey Constitution to all the legal benefits of marriage available to any other married couple, although not marriage itself. Now, however, as a result of *Windsor*, same-sex couples would have to be allowed to marry since marriage was the only way they could enjoy the same rights as heterosexual New Jersey couples to the federal benefits of marriage. (The *Windsor* decision did not open federal benefits to civil union couples.) On October 21, 2013, same-sex couples began marrying in New Jersey.

It is too early to judge the broader social consequences of the *Windsor* decision. It will certainly provide an added incentive for gay couples to marry in those states where it is legal and for gay couples in non-same-sex-marriage states to move to ones where they can marry, though they better like cold winters, for, with the exception of California and parts of Washington, that is what they will get. Larger questions aside, it didn't take long for the decision to begin to have profound consequences on individual lives.

Two days after the decision was announced, Lavi Soloway, a lawyer representing many same-sex couples, received a formal notice from the immigration authorities that his client, Traian Popov, a Bulgarian immigrant legally married to Julian Marsh, had been approved for a permanent resident visa. Soloway first thought that he must be reading the notice wrong. Then, when he realized its significance—that the immigrant spouse in a gay marriage now had the same right to a green card as an immigrant in a heterosexual marriage—he began to weep (Preston 2013). The rapid response to the Court's decision was possible because the United States Immigration and Citizenship Services was maintaining a list of couples for whom a permanent residency visa could be quickly approved in the event DOMA was struck down.

Popov and Marsh may also presage another effect of *Windsor*, for the couple, living now in Florida, intend to become same-sex marriage activists in that state. "We are first-class citizens in New York and in the eyes of the federal government, but second-class citizens in Florida," Marsh said. "We won't stand for that" (Preston 2013). Clearly, the *Windsor* decision has a gravitational pull whose political force only time will measure.

## Perry v. Schwarzenegger

Advocates of gay rights around the nation were stunned in 2008 when California, arguably the most permissive, freewheeling state in the nation, passed Proposition 8. Proposition 8, you may recall, reversed the decision of the California Supreme Court that had required gay persons be allowed to marry each other and restored the traditional view of marriage as between heterosexual couples only. The vote revealed 1.7 million persons who both voted for President Obama and against same-sex marriage. In 2008, President Obama was not a supporter of same-sex marriage.

The passage of Proposition 8 produced an unexpected marriage of its own. David Boies and Theodore Olson had been opposing counsel in *Bush v. Gore*. Olson is a lifelong Republican who lost his wife on 9/11 in the flight that crashed into the Pentagon. He had successfully represented candidate Bush in the Florida recount battle that culminated in the Supreme Court's decision in *Bush v. Gore*, and had achieved heroic status among conservatives as a result. Boies and Olson, who had become friends over the years, decided to team up in representing a lesbian couple, Kristin Perry and Sandra Stier, residing in Berkeley, California, and raising four children together, and Jeffrey Zarrillo and Paul Katami, a gay male couple living in Burbank, California. The goal of the suit was to claim same-sex marriage as a right guaranteed by the U.S. Constitution.

The trial took place over a two-week period in January 2010 before Judge Vaughn Walker, chief judge of the Federal District Court of San Francisco. Walker had been nominated to the bench by the first President Bush. The defendant in the case was Governor Arnold Schwarzenegger, since, as California's chief executive, it was his responsibility, along with the attorney general's, to defend the constitutionality of a state statute, in this case the law enacted by Proposition 8's passage.

Expert witnesses for the same-sex couples made a persuasive presentation. They testified, among other things, that marriage had a special communicative and symbolic significance that transcended the mere conveyance of legal benefits, that children raised by gay parents thrived but would still gain enormously by their parents receiving the right to marry, and that marriage itself as an institution had changed and evolved over the years so that recognition of the right to same-sex marriage would simply be one more shift in an ever-evolving institution.

The experts were cogent, but the most moving testimony came from the couples themselves, particularly the women. For Sandy Stier, marriage was about commitment: "making a public commitment to the world, to your partner . . . to our friends, our family, our society, our community, our parents." "We have," she added, "a loving, committed relationship. We are not business partners. We are not social partners. We are not glorified roommates" (trial transcript, 172–173). For Kristin Perry, it was about respect and clarification: "I'm a forty-five-year-old woman. I have been in love with a woman for 10 years and I don't have a word to tell anybody about it" (trial transcript, 154).

During his closing argument, Theodore Olson powerfully summarized plaintiffs' position: "What we're talking about here is allowing individuals who have the same impulses, the same drives, the same desires as all the rest of us, to have a relationship in harmony, stability and to form a family and neighborhood. . . . And, now, tell me how it helps the rest of the citizens of California to keep them out of the club" (trial transcript, 3099). Every case has its own specific context that can drive how the case is presented. Given California's comprehensive Domestic Partnership Law, the virtual equivalent in this instance of civil unions, it was critical for plaintiffs to establish the separate emotional, symbolic, and expressive value of being allowed to marry and call themselves married.

On August 4, 2010, Judge Walker issued a 137-page opinion, including 55 pages of factual findings, holding that Proposition 8 violated both the Equal Protection and Due Process Clauses of the Fourteenth Amendment. As a legal matter, Judge Walker found that there was no rational basis for the law, that Proposition 8 impermissibly discriminated on the basis of sexual orientation, and that marriage was a fundamental right and therefore a law restricting it to heterosexual couples was subject to strict scrutiny, a standard that Proposition 8 could not meet. Factually, he found that marriage is the "state recognition of a couple's choice to live with each other" (*Perry*, 961), that same-sex couples are "identical to opposite-sex couples" in their ability to form "successful marital unions" (967), and that the state had offered no legitimate interest to withhold the right from same-sex couples. He also found that gays were harmed in concrete ways by not being allowed to marry, including harm to their physical and psychological health. The victory for the plaintiffs could not have been more sweeping nor the opinion more favorable if it had been written by the plaintiffs themselves. The state of California decided not to appeal Judge Walker's opinion, but the official proponents of Proposition 8 were allowed to intervene to prosecute an appeal to the Ninth Circuit Court of Appeals, whose jurisdiction includes California.

## Hollingsworth v. Perry

On February 7, 2012, the Ninth Circuit Court of Appeals upheld Judge Walker's decision but on much narrower grounds. The court's decision pointedly failed to address whether same-sex marriage was a fundamental right or whether Proposition 8 was subject to heightened scrutiny for any other reason. Remarkably, relying substantially on *Romer*, the court simply held that because California already had given gay relationships all the legal benefits of marriage in its domestic partnership/civil union law, there was no legitimate reason for the passage of a law that treats similarly situated classes of people differently. In the eyes of two of the three judges hearing the appeal (there was a dissent), Proposition 8 had only one purpose: to strip same-sex couples of the ability they previously possessed to obtain and use the designation of "marriage" to describe their relationships. Since its sole purpose was an impermissible one—to deny a right or benefit to a disfavored group—it failed to satisfy even the minimal rational basis test.

Since no other state had granted and then taken away same-sex marriage rights, the Ninth Circuit's reasoning did not affect the prohibition against gay marriage in the more than thirty states that expressly prohibited it and had never allowed it in the first place. The Ninth Circuit's affirmation of Judge Walker's decision was, of course, good news for gay marriage advocates, but reasoning is important, and the much more limited basis for the decision could not have helped but be disappointing. Most of the moving testimony by the gay plaintiffs themselves and their experts could arguably have been dispensed with, indeed the whole trial largely avoided, had the participants realized how much of the case would end up on the Ninth Circuit's cutting room floor. Nevertheless, a victory is still a victory, and the defenders of Proposition 8 were down to their last strike if they were to save it.

If I had predicted that *Hollingsworth v. Perry* would be decided by the Supreme Court by a vote of 5–4, it would have surprised no one, given the ideological division on the Court between four generally "liberal" justices, four generally "conservative" justices, and one swing (though more often conservative) vote in the person of Justice Kennedy. Had I then added, however, that the five-person majority would be composed of conservatives Chief Justice Roberts and Antonin Scalia, and liberals Ruth Bader Ginsburg, Elena Kagan, and Stephen Breyer, with Kennedy in dissent, you would have politely invited me to consider some form of group therapy. Yet that is precisely what happened, for the simple reason that the case turned on nothing to do with the substance of the case but rather on whether the proponents of Proposition 8 had had any standing to appeal Judge Walker's decision once the executive branch, the original defendant, decided not to appeal. The five justices in the majority said no.

Under Article III of the Constitution, the article dealing with the national judicial power, federal courts are only empowered to hear "Cases" and "Controversies." This has been interpreted by the Supreme Court to mean that no one can bring a suit in federal court unless they have personally suffered an actual injury that can be redressed by judicial action. If there were not some such limitation, the Court has reasoned, it could easily become an academic forum with the federal court system drowning in cases brought by persons who simply believe that an act is unconstitutional. Under the standing concept, the injury can't just be a general injury, so, for example, a taxpayer does not have standing to bring a lawsuit challenging a particular appropriation simply because he thinks that the appropriation an improper use of his taxes. On the other hand, Edith Windsor did have a particularized injury because the No Recognition provision she contested directly impacted her tax bill.

The substance of the argument over standing need not detain us; it is a subject ordinarily of interest only to constitutional scholars and litigators. There is, however, one aspect worth pondering. Usually, the standing question splits the Court ideologically, with the liberals generally favoring a generous view of what constitutes a satisfactory basis for standing and conservatives a less generous view. Indeed, in the *Windsor* case there was also an issue of standing, for it was a group of Republicans from the House of Representatives that had to take up the cudgels to defend DOMA after President Obama declined to do so. True to form, the four conservative justices in *Windsor* would have found that the House members did not have standing, but the liberal justices and Justice Kennedy did find requisite standing and then decided the case on the merits.

While no one can know for certain what was motivating the peculiar majority in *Hollingsworth*, one cannot help but feel that what really united the three liberal and two conservative justices in this case was a belief that this was not the time to decide such a socially divisive issue as whether all the states had to allow gay marriage. The liberal justices might have felt that the Court had chewed off enough social change for the country by the decision in *Windsor*. They must also have been aware of the negative perception if the Court had decided on the same day that Congress couldn't impose its vision of marriage on the states but the Supreme Court could.

Whether the constitution requires that every state that provides for marriage must allow gay marriage is not an easy one. It is one, however, that the Court will likely face in the future. It is the final subject to which we now turn in this chapter, the subject that the Supreme Court effectively avoided in *Hollingsworth*.

## Strong Arguments on Both Sides

In *Windsor*, Justice Kennedy had written that the No Recognition provision in DOMA was unconstitutional as "a deprivation of the liberty of the person protected by the Fifth Amendment of the Constitution." The clause to which he was referring was the provision in the Fifth Amendment to the U.S. Constitution that forbids the federal government from depriving any person of life, liberty, or property without due process. There is a comparable provision in the Fourteenth Amendment, which binds the states. While it appears that due process refers only to procedure, in fact the Due Process Clause has been held to have a substantive component called substantive due process. Substantive due process was first used by conservative justices in the early part of the twentiety century to invalidate minimum wage and maximum hour laws, among many others, under the theory that these kinds of laws violated the liberty of parties to enter into their own agreements. That notion of substantive due process was later rejected by the Supreme Court in the mid-1930s; in the 1960s, however, substantive due process got a second life when it became associated with a constitutional right of privacy.

In his dissent in *Windsor*, Justice Scalia ridiculed the notion that substantive due process could require same-sex marriage because, in his view, the liberty interest in due process could only apply to ideals deeply rooted in our history and tradition. Same-sex marriage itself certainly doesn't meet that description. In his closing argument, however, in the district court case in *Perry v. Schwarzenegger*, Ted Olson, one of the counsel for the same-sex couple plaintiffs, argued that even though marriage was a civil institution, it was ridiculous to believe that it was intended to be for the benefit of the state or that it would be constitutional for the state to deny individuals the right to marry. So one response to Justice Scalia could be that, even if same-sex marriage is new, marriage itself is certainly deeply rooted in our tradition and therefore denying gay couples access to that institution has to be based on something more than a traditional moral view that it can only be for a man and a woman because it has always been that way. This is in part what Kennedy was getting at in his *Windsor* opinion.

Justice Scalia, however, argued that government does have the authority to forbid practices that offend society's sense of morality. Just as he is comfortable with a more robust presence for Judeo-Christian religiosity in the public square, so is he comfortable with society legislating the sense of morality underlying that religiosity, including opposition to homosexuality. This was the basis for Scalia's passionate dissent in *Lawrence v. Texas*, in which he made clear that in his view society had every right to single out homosexual sodomy for condemnation.

So one difference in the Court's next debate on same-sex marriage will be between a belief on the part of justices like Kennedy that denying gay couples access to marriage has not been shown to have any legitimate basis and those like Scalia who believe that depriving gay couples of the right to marry needs no legitimate basis beyond reflecting society's sense of right and wrong. Even, however, if one believes that the states are on thin constitutional ground in denying gay couples access to marriage, there may be strong reasons to proceed with caution. One of them involves something called the countermajoritarian difficulty, the belief that United States Supreme Court justices should be extremely cautious in voiding governmental acts on constitutional grounds since justices are unelected, therefore unconnected to the political process, and therefore acting undemocratically when they declare something unconstitutional.

This perspective is supposed to be applicable with particular force when the Court is asked to decide questions for which there is no clear answer in the constitutional text and for which the democratic process is itself engaged in a major debate on the merits of the practice in question; both of these factors seem applicable to the same-sex marriage question. The strength of the countermajoritarian concern is not the moral strength of 51 percent over 49 percent but the fact that majorities are created through citizen engagement and debate in the political arena, where we are supposed to settle most of our differences. It is also the arena in which meaningful compromises and even consensus can emerge from long and difficult arguments.

Some have questioned the basic premise of the countermajoritarian argument, pointing out, among other things, that U.S. Supreme Court justices are nominated by an elected president and confirmed by an elected Senate and therefore hardly unconnected to the political process. Others have observed that on certain issues, particularly where questions of individual rights are concerned, judges might actually represent the ideals of democracy better than legislative majorities or individual voters because they better embody the concept of disinterestedness, an essential requirement for a decision-maker approaching questions of moral value (see, for example, Eisgruber 2001, 46–78).

Those counseling caution would also point out that there is a profound difference between a question of national interest—same-sex marriage is certainly such an issue—and an issue that must be decided nationally. Right now, same-sex marriage is still an issue for each state to decide for itself. The traditional right of states to regulate marriage was certainly an important element of the *Windsor* decision. If same-sex marriage were to be declared a federal constitutional right—meaning that states could no longer deny access of gay couples to the institution of marriage—that limitation on state action could only be overturned by either the Supreme Court reversing itself at a later date or by a federal constitutional amendment, a very long and difficult process ultimately requiring approval by three-quarters of the states.

This does not mean that a broad decision favoring gay marriage would be wrong, but requiring acceptance of gay marriage in Mississippi or Utah, where popular opinion is overwhelmingly against it, certainly raises legitimate issues of democracy and federalism. Any decision striking down gay marriage prohibitions would have to do so in the face of the facts that defining the contours of marriage has been the prerogative of the states, and that same-sex marriage is a political issue about which the nation is deeply divided, that there are some regions of the country vociferously opposed to same-sex marriage, and that there are real educational and democratic benefits for the issue of gay marriage to continue to be worked through on a state-by-state basis, which would be lost if the Court simply imposed a national constitutional rule.

These factors might be a particular concern to someone like Justice Ginsburg, who had serious misgivings about the scope of *Roe v. Wade* at the time it was decided. Gratified as she was by the decision, she worried publicly that the decision had been too sweeping and had prevented the states from experimenting with different approaches and solutions to the issue. Her statements had been strong enough that some important reservations had been expressed by key figures in the women's movement when President Clinton first nominated her for the Court. Liberal justices and gay rights advocates in general might well ask themselves, why set off a storm on same-sex marriage that would inevitably place the Court at the center of the controversy and might actually set back the gay rights movement if the backlash was severe enough, particularly when time itself would seem to assure the ultimate acceptance of same-sex marriage in much of the nation through the political process, given its wide support among young people.

There may be another factor to consider. *Brown v. Board of Education* ending racial segregation in public schools was a unanimous Supreme Court decision. Chief Justice Earl Warren had worked hard to achieve that result. Any dissent, he reasoned, would make it much easier to justify resistance to the Court's decision. Any decision requiring same-sex marriage in all fifty states, however, would likely be achieved by a 5–4 vote, with passionate dissents from conservative justices, giving much ammunition to those states or local governments looking for an excuse to resist or undermine the Court's ruling.

It is true, as one historian for the plaintiffs in *Perry v. Schwarzenegger* had testified, that marriage is a secular institution that has undergone a number of transformations since the country was founded, including an end to the legal inferiority of wives to their husbands. Judge Walker relied on this testimony in his opinion, noting how "marriage was thus transformed from a male dominated institution into an institution recognizing men and women as equals. Yet individuals retained the right to marry; the right did not become different simply because the institution of marriage became compatible with gender equality" (*Perry*, 992–993). Judge Walker's point may be correct historically, but he seemed to ignore that the transformation of marriage from a male-dominated institution occurred over time, and that it occurred through wide-ranging debates in the political processes amidst a growing consensus on the part of society that gender inequality was not an essential element of marriage. The legal changes accompanying that transformation were made by the states voluntarily and not imposed by the national judiciary.

A federal district court judge and a Supreme Court justice have different responsibilities. Judge Walker's decision was based on his view of what the constitution requires, but only Supreme Court justices decide constitutional matters for the entire country. Federalism, democracy, institutional credibility, potential consequences—these all are important concerns of the Supreme Court in ways that simply don't exist for lower courts. Judge Walker was interpreting a constitution but the Supreme Court, in addition to interpreting the U.S. Constitution, is responsible for the constitutional system as a whole. At present, the public, in growing numbers, supports gay marriage but still believes that the issue should be left for the states to decide for themselves, at least for now. That latter view may well have been shared by the peculiar majority in *Hollingsworth*, which decided for better or for worse (no pun intended), to kick the can down the road.

# Conclusion

Social change can happen quickly, even for the most deeply embedded institutions. In *The Honor Code: How Moral Revolutions Happen*, Kwame Appiah (2010) describes how dueling in England and foot binding in China each disappeared within a generation when these long-standing practices became widely condemned and a source of embarrassment and shame. Appiah's work leads one to ask whether the revolutionary changes in the status of gays might also reflect a growing understanding in the heterosexual community of the human cost that prejudice has exacted and the cost to society of throwing competent people out of the military and pretending that gays and lesbians cannot form enduring relationships or be good parents.

In any event, there has been an extraordinary change in attitudes. The 2013 Pew survey discussed in earlier chapters showed that within less than a decade, one in five Americans had changed their view of whether it would be a big deal if their child was gay. This is an extraordinary shift, more marked in some regions of the country than others. Indeed, for better or worse, when it comes to gay rights we seem be living in a blue- and red-state America. It seems that even Republicans in blue states are much more supportive of gay rights than their brethren in other states. In 2012, for example, many voting districts in Maine that Republican presidential candidate Mitt Romney carried also voted for same-sex marriage (*Lesbian/Gay Law Notes*, December 2012, 1). Certainly the fact alluded to earlier that no state that voted for Mitt Romney has a law prohibiting discrimination on the basis of sexual orientation—in contrast to twenty-one of the states that supported Barack Obama—is no accident, nor is it any accident that it is in many of the reddest states that fundamentalist influence is strongest.

We have also seen the depth of the resistance to gay rights among some socially conservative groups. We have seen, among other things, that they not only oppose same-sex marriage but any recognition that would enable a gay employee to provide health coverage for his or her partner, not only open military service but any protection against employment discrimination, not only sex education but any teaching of gay history.

Yet it is important not to demonize gay rights opponents, for as we saw in our brief description of Arlene Stein's work on Timbertown, the source of anti-gay-rights feeling can be rooted in complex feelings reflecting family upbringing, community pressures toward conformity, and psychological and economic insecurity. One long-term positive outcome of open military service may well be the opportunity it presents for young persons from deeply religious backgrounds to encounter, work with, and sometimes take orders from openly gay men and women. That opportunity imposes a real responsibility on young gay service men and women, but if red states are ever to shift to the blue end of the spectrum on gay rights, the military would be a good place to begin.

The complex manner in which the personal and the public spheres overlap has always been a distinguishing feature of gay life. The few protestors brave enough to come out in the pre-Stonewall era first had to come to terms with their own sexuality. Barbara Gittings, for example, speaking in 1971, felt that lesbian women in the Daughters of Bilitis first had "to get over the really severe feelings of inadequacy about being gay that most of our people had" before the liberation movement could develop (Tobin and Wicker 1972, 212).

We have seen how the fifties and sixties were a time of both repression and recognition. Those two phenomena were not unrelated in that gays needed to depend on each other to share information and form informal networks to survive and maintain some semblance of a social life. These bonds were being forged largely underground, though a few brave souls such as Frank Kameny and Barbara Gittings began to protest publicly for gay rights. Stonewall and the subsequent organizing that culminated in what in essence was the first gay pride march helped ignite what we now call the gay rights movement. Those first years after Stonewall represented, in the words of Abraham Lincoln, "a new burst of freedom," a freedom that was often rooted in a journey of self-discovery that linked the personal and the political.

Just how the personal and political have wrapped around each other was movingly revealed by the responses of older men interviewed for the Twin Cities GLBT Oral History Project. When the men were given the choice of using pseudonyms or their real names, an overwhelming majority chose to use their real names, not only using but proudly announcing them "as if they were consciously and purposefully inscribing themselves into the archive." When asked why they were using their true names, many recalled how they had "struggled for years to be out to themselves and the world, so it meant a lot to them to go on the record" (Twin Cities GLBT Oral History Project 2010, 10). That simply saying one's real name can take on such richly symbolic meaning reminds us of both the depth of isolation of older generations and the distance traveled during their adult lives.

When political and legal struggles become inseparable from a person's sense of self-worth, those struggles take on a significance and urgency that go far beyond the ordinary public battles. That initial struggle, I have argued, is best seen in the seventies as a struggle for freedom: freedom to meet without fear, freedom to explore one's sexuality without being labeled a criminal, freedom to be openly oneself. That struggle continued in the eighties but was greatly complicated by the onset of the AIDS crisis, a holocaust that forced the gay community to engage with straight society in a way that helped make integration into that society a central goal of the gay rights movement starting in the early nineties.

That goal of integration was far from being realized when Bill Clinton was elected president in 1992. At that time, gays, as a recognized group, still had almost no visible presence in our corporations or schools, nor did their relationships enjoy legal protection. Same-sex marriage was not even on the radar screen of gay rights groups. Hate crime legislation still did not include crimes motivated by antigay bias. A majority of Americans still believed that homosexuality was morally wrong, and the Supreme Court had made no secret that it shared that viewpoint when it upheld laws that made acts of gay intimacy a crime. A Democratic Congress and Democratic president would be unable to make good on the promise of open service in the military or to pass a federal law prohibiting employment discrimination on the basis of sexual orientation.

The lesson that Urvashi Vaid and others drew from their experience in the first years of the Clinton administration was that access did not guarantee success, that there was a huge difference between having a conversation and wielding real power. "All the access in the world," said Vaid, "has not strengthened our ability to pass pro-gay legislation or to hold the President to his campaign promises" (1995, 129). So it is not surprising that in 1994, even before the passage of DOMA, Michael Nava (a lawyer) and Robert Dawidoff (a professor of history) could assert that "homosexuality disqualifies an American for citizenship. Whatever rights someone may enjoy on account of other identities, attributes, accomplishments and positions cannot ensure either the free exercise of individual liberty or equal protection of the laws if that person is known to be lesbian or gay" (1994, 1). Given this assessment, it is hardly surprising that Vaid could also write in 1995, twenty-five years after Stonewall: "The vast majority of our people remain closeted, still unwilling to acknowledge their sexual orientation" (1995, 1). Political progress had been made, she agreed, but "we have in many ways created a communal closet: It is roomier in here, more comfortable than the closets we lived in during the 1950's, but the ghetto ultimately proves to be as restrictive as the individual closet" (33).

Today, of course, that world of the early 1990s has changed dramatically. Hate-motivated violence has joined other forms of bias worthy of special condemnation; gay marriage is now legal in seventeen states; gay employee networks are a vibrant part of the corporate world and gay–straight alliance groups an important presence in half the high schools across the country; gays can serve openly in the military; twenty-one states (as opposed to two at the start of the nineties) now afford protection against discrimination in employment; and the culture war aimed at exploiting prejudice against gays is no longer a Republican priority, and indeed some within the party are looking to end its reflexive antigay bias. Gays are no longer presumptive felons; their private sexual life now enjoys the same federal constitutional protection as that of heterosexuals.

In 1983, a young law student named Evan Wolfson, a gay activist and leading proponent of same-sex marriage for three decades, wanted to write a third-year paper in law school about the issue. He did it but recently recalled that "a lot of the professors, even the liberals wouldn't even work with me on it. It was considered too weird and peripheral to take seriously" (Toobin 2012). What was too strange to take notice of thirty years ago, even in an academic environment, is today not only legal in seventeen states but something that, after *United States v. Windsor*, must now be not only noticed but accepted by the federal government.

It is a fair and important question to ask whether this new world is here forever. The answer, I believe, is yes, mainly for two reasons. One is the generational divide. Young people, across the spectrum of race and class, support gay rights in ever-increasing numbers. That trend seems only to be accelerating as gayness becomes an accepted part of our popular culture. The second reason, perhaps even more telling, has to do with the gay community itself, not public attitudes: there is now in place an organizational infrastructure pervading all aspects of gay life that will see gay people through temporary reversals of public opinion or political setbacks. As recently as 1991, Lillian Faderman reported that older lesbians, many of them professionals, were fearful of talking about themselves, because "they have little faith that the progress that has come about through the gay liberation movement is here to stay" (Faderman 1991, 157). That kind of fear no longer seems justified, and it is a major achievement of the gay rights movement and the gay community.

A gay teenager or young adult of today enjoys four key advantages compared to his or her counterpart of a half century ago: (1) a set of legal and constitutional rights that were simply nonexistent fifty years ago; (2) an organizational infrastructure, particularly in the school environment, ready to provide protection, comfort, and support; (3) a popular culture that both recognizes and affirms a person's identity as gay; and (4) career opportunities in all sorts of fields (including politics, the ministry, and the military) that increasingly need not be pursued at the price of a demeaning secrecy. These changes evoke wonder bordering on incredulity for an older generation of gay men. John D'Emilio, recalling in 2002 his early years, wrote: "I couldn't go to the local gay youth group to meet my peers or go to a Saturday night gay dance on a college campus. There were no big street festivals or parades . . . where I might hang out, strike up a conversation, and make some friends. I couldn't consult the gay yellow pages, or the listings in my local gay newspaper, or a recreational group—of runners, bowlers or bridge players—where I would meet men to have fun and find myself a date" (2002, 200). D'Emilio then contrasted that memory with life for a young gay man in 2002, "At the level of social life and daily experience, it is not too much to say that, for millions of gay men and lesbians, the changes of the past three decades have been nothing short of revolutionary. . . . Instead of being weighed down by a terrible loneliness that the enforced secrecy and invisibility of a homophobic society had imposed, gays and lesbians have created vibrant communities with robust institutions" (39).

If a gay teenager of the 1950s awoke, like Rip Van Winkle, in 2013, he would find a shocking new world, one in which an open lesbian was elected as a U.S. senator and another as mayor of Houston, Texas; six openly gay people serve as members of the U.S. House of Representatives; the Speaker of the Rhode Island General Assembly (described by *Time* magazine in its December 5, 2011, issue as "perhaps the most powerful figure in state government") is openly gay; an openly gay poet delivers an extraordinary poem in celebration of America at a presidential inauguration; being gay and a Boy Scout are no longer mutually exclusive; an openly gay man plays soccer for a major league soccer team; Gay Days at Disneyland, an annual week-long celebration, attracts more than 150,000 visitors to the Orlando area and pours more than $100 million into the local economy; police departments (Los Angeles, for one) have gay advisory committees; a straight, professional hockey player, deservedly known as one of the roughest players in the National Hockey League, and the president of the United States support same-sex marriage; the secretary general of the United Nations declares that any attack on LGBT people "is an attack on the universal values of the United Nations"; and even the pope himself seems eager for a less judgmental church.

If our gay teenager wanted to see some physical manifestation of all these changes, he could visit Chicago's $20 million LGBTQ community center, opened in 2007, a center boasting a staff of sixty-five full- and part-time employees and made entirely of glass, a fitting symbol for a new era. If he visited other cities, our teenager could consult the mammoth guide to gay-friendly places in the United States published by Fodors, and if he had academic aspirations, he could bring along the Princeton Review Guide for college living for gays and lesbians.

Thirty-five years ago George Will called the repeal of the Dade County gay rights ordinance "eminently defensible" and compared gay rights to "the riptide that washes away old moorings" (Duberman 1991, 352). Another conservative, Michael Novak, could write: "Only a decadent society would grant them [gay people] equal status" (352). Today, these quotations reflect a point of view that a clear majority of Americans, and possibly even the authors themselves, no longer embrace.

What has been the role of the courts, a major focus of our examination, in bringing these changes about? Have they been a mere handmaiden of public opinion, affirming inevitable trends, or has the judiciary itself been a catalyst for change? It is not an easy question to answer.

To make an imperfect analogy, every judicial opinion can be thought of as creating its own gravitational field. Important decisions have greater mass than run-of-the-mill decisions and operate at a closer distance to some public issues than others. *Lawrence v. Texas* acted with greater gravitational force on the issue of same-sex marriage than it did on the subject of sodomy, which it actually addressed, because by the time of its issuance the sodomy issue was already at a great distance from the center of the gay rights debate. This circumstance suggests why simple cause and effect is not a fruitful way of thinking about the relation between judicial judgments and social change, for it ignores the complexity and simultaneity of the universe of which judicial decisions form a part.

I would argue that the judiciary has made its most important contribution to the gay rights movement when it has simply applied established principles, as, for example, the best interests of the child in family law, in a fair and unbiased manner. The overall record of the judiciary in the last twenty years has, in contrast to prior periods, been a creditable one. There was (and still is), for example, a sufficient amount of play in the Equal Access Act to have allowed a hostile judiciary to limit its protection for gay–straight alliance clubs, but that simply didn't happen. The Nabozny case was of great importance in encouraging school districts to take complaints about bullying more seriously, but the court wasn't creating new law in so doing but simply assuring that school districts did not escape a clear liability for treating a member of a disfavored group differently than they would have treated someone else, a clear equal protection violation. The courts have also, by and large, erred on the side of protecting gay students from hostile comments from their peers and in upholding the right of school districts to promote tolerance in the schools. While there are exceptions, the record of the judiciary in recent years, in custody and adoption cases, is also on the whole positive. Certainly, the refusal of the Arkansas and Florida courts to accept statutory distinctions rooted in prejudice has not been insignificant, and certainly state supreme court decisions on same-sex marriage helped push that issue to the top of the gay rights agenda.

There are important ways in which our constitutional structure has, in the end, contributed to the gay rights movement. We have seen that the Supreme Court's position in the constitutional hierarchy has led to three key decisions, within the last two decades, favorable to gay rights. As important, because power in our system is balanced between the federal government and the states, gay rights advocates have been able to concentrate their influence and resources in the communities and states most disposed toward gay rights claims. Our federal structure has allowed gay rights advocates to lobby blue state legislatures with success; there advocates are able to work on much more sympathetic terrain, and a number of the obstacles to passing federal legislation are not present within the states, including the hold of the evangelical movement on the national Republican Party and a U.S. Senate filibuster rule requiring sixty rather than a simple majority of fifty senators to support any legislation, an almost insurmountable obstacle even with a clear national consensus.

A second benefit flowing from our federal structure is that it appears that state judiciaries have been significantly more disposed to protecting gay rights than has the federal judiciary. In *Gay Rights and American Law*, Daniel Pinello statistically analyzed 468 state and federal appellate cases involving gay rights claims between 1981 and 2000 and found, among other things, that "state courts decided cases in favor of lesbian and gay rights more than twice as frequently as federal fora" (Pinello 2003, 110). Interestingly, he also found that "state courts interpreting state constitutions were far more receptive to lesbian and gay rights claims than either court system was in applying the federal Constitution" (110). Pinello's statement was made before either the *Lawrence* or DOMA decisions, but his findings, focusing as they did on lower courts, still are meaningful.

Nothing suggests more vividly the length of the road traveled and the way in which the judiciary can and, for the most part, has played an increasingly constructive role than a case arising in Minersville, Pennsylvania, a small town deep in the ailing anthracite coal region of western Pennsylvania, which had lost half its population between 1940 and 2000. On the evening of April 17, 1997, a young man, Marcus Wayman, was arrested with his companion as they were parked in a lot near a Minersville beer distributing business that had been the victim of several burglaries. The arresting officer suspected that the two young men were homosexual and about to engage in consensual sex, facts to which they both admitted. At headquarters, Officer Wilinsky threatened to tell Wayman's grandfather that Wayman was homosexual unless Wayman told his grandfather himself. As they were leaving the station Wayman confided to his friend that he was going to kill himself and made good on his threat a short time later. Wayman's mother sued the borough of Minersville as well as Wilinsky for violating, among other things, her son's right to privacy under the Fourteenth Amendment. Minersville claimed that no constitutional right had been violated, but the Third Circuit Court of Appeals disagreed, holding in *Sterling v. Borough of Minersville* that Wilinsky might have a cause of action under the federal, post–Civil War statute providing a right of damages for violations of constitutional rights occurring under color of state law. After the circuit court decision, Minersville settled the suit for $100,000. A nation that in the fifties would go to any lengths to discover and then disclose publicly a person's homosexuality, often with horrendous personal consequences, now protected the right of a teenage boy to keep that same secret from his family, with a municipality paying a six-figure settlement to avoid going to trial on an alleged violation of that right.

I have remarked on how the gay rights movement talks about sex as little as possible. That is, of course, understandable in a world in which heterosexual politicians themselves usually acknowledge their own sex drive only in the glare of television cameras after some unwanted revelation. This need not to talk about the very thing that originally made a gay rights movement necessary, a deep antipathy in the culture to same-sex relations, has helped contribute to a kind of neutering of the equality movement, encouraging gay leaders to talk about rights but not themselves.

When the artist Keith Haring first discovered the Paradise Garage, a gay disco, frequented by young men of color, many of them street kids, he later said, "I knew I never would be the same" (Cruz-Malave 2007, 81). As Arnaldo Cruz-Malave observed: "Some critics have likened this encounter with the Paradise Garage to Gaugin arriving in Tahiti. . . . Haring must have felt as if the subject of so many of his drawings and paintings, those utopian homoerotic chains of homeboys dancing had somehow come alive and was inviting him to participate" (81). Cruz-Malave adds that it was the disco's "particular racial, ethnic, social and sexual mix—from freestyling homeboys to vogueing drag queens, straight-identified banjee boys to recently 'out' gays, up and coming media celebrities to East Village underground experimental artists, and music industry insiders to homeless and thrown away kids" that explained Haring's intense reaction to the Garage, which became "his home away from home" (83).

The gay rights movement, as it has evolved, for better or worse, has had relatively little room for Haring's world in it, because gayness, for Haring, was a way of being that simply stood outside notions of equality. For him, gayness was very much about sex and also about being an outsider with a particular vision. He valued his gayness because he saw it as a different way of experiencing the world, something that, as an artist, was a rich source of inspiration. This viewpoint came naturally since, as with all committed artists and writers, the world was his to use, not to adapt to, and to be different in an important way was to experience a new version of truth.

An interviewer once mentioned to James Baldwin that he must have felt very handicapped indeed to be black, poor, and gay, to which Baldwin replied, on the contrary, "I felt I'd hit the jackpot" (Kaiser 1997, vii). It may seem strange to conclude a book that has focused on things like law, politics, and the constitution by discussing an artist like Haring. Obviously, celebrating homeboys and drag queens is hardly the message of choice for a gay rights movement lobbying state legislatures for gay marriage and antidiscrimination laws and Congress for the right to serve in the military and the repeal of DOMA. Nor is it the avenue for reducing homophobia in the general population. Nevertheless, an important part of gay history is lost if there is no place for artists like Haring, for he reminds one that the overriding goal of the gay rights movement, rising above all of the individual issues we have discussed, is simply for all gay persons to enjoy the kind of freedom and joy that Haring's work and his attitude toward life expressed.

It will take more than political victories, however, to achieve this goal, for no amount of political success can protect a young child from the inner stress that comes from being different. An inner sense of freedom and joy cannot be legislated; it is earned individual by individual through life experience, but how individuals, particularly young persons, see themselves can depend very much on how each is viewed by others and what resources are there to help through difficult times. That is why the organizational infrastructure we have discussed is so important and must be seen as equally important as the legal and political successes of the movement. In *Oddly Normal* (2012), John Schwartz's affecting memoir of his son's struggle with his gayness, a turning point occurs when Schwartz and his wife, desperate to help their son, learn of a gay community center in Manhattan where their son can finally feel accepted; their son even learns that he is not nearly as bad off as others who are completely rejected by their families. These personal victories, however, do not minimize law's importance. While social acceptance can't be mandated by law, it can be facilitated by the vindication of legal rights, which helps create an environment that makes social acceptance possible.

Perhaps, on one level, the achievements of the gay rights movement and the shifts in public opinion on gay rights issues do not require deep explanation. Most Americans value a sense of fairness and also believe deeply in the idea of freedom, even though we often (perhaps more often than not) fall far short of the mark in our actions. Unjustified discrimination unfairly limits a person's choices and thus violates ideals of both freedom and equity. As long as discrimination against gays could itself remain in the closet because gays themselves were not willing to come forward in sufficient numbers or with sufficient energy to contest it, discrimination, and even persecution, was easy. Once the battle was joined, however, it has become increasingly clear that the gay rights movement aligns itself much more closely with the basic view of how Americans like to imagine themselves than does its opponents.

Although it is useful to think of the gay rights movement as having two phases—the first being a fight for freedom from oppression, the second being a fight for full integration into society—it is important to recognize how, in the second phase, concepts of freedom and equality begin to overlap in a way they did not in the first phase, when gays were fighting for the right to celebrate themselves without fear and to be allowed some measure of dignity. The logo of the Human Rights Campaign is an equals sign, but the equality that gays have been fighting for in this second phase concerns all the freedoms that most people take for granted, including the freedom to marry. As that argument has taken hold, the tide of public opinion has shifted, and with it the terrain on which the battle has been fought.

It is still too early, however, to run a victory lap or hang up a Mission Accomplished sign. Much of the opposition to homosexuality comes from religious sources, and same-sex relations continue to be repugnant to many in the culture, so gays, like other minorities, will continue to draw hatred for the foreseeable future, even if gay rights loses its salience as a political issue. A grim reminder of where prejudice can lead occurred on the evening of May 17, 2013, when a young gay man was shot to death by a total stranger just a few blocks from the Stonewall Inn in what seems to have been a classic hate crime.

No prospect for federal protection against employment discrimination appears likely as long as Republicans control the House of Representatives, although Republican support for such legislation may be one way for the national party to show some concern for gay rights without alienating its social conservative base. (As this is being written, the U.S. Senate seems poised to pass the Employment Non-Discrimination Act, but it appears that Speaker Boehner will not allow the bill to come to the House floor for a vote.) A majority of states still have no laws protecting gays from employment or other forms of discrimination. Ironically, the very success of the gay rights movement has made this lack of protection more acute. Shannon Price Minter, a civil rights lawyer and legal director of the National Center for Lesbian Rights, observed in June 2013 that "as gay people are able to participate more in the normal activities and institutions of everyday life, their visibility in the workplace is more apparent, and they are a more visible target of employment discrimination. . . . We are seeing people run into problems because of that or be fired" (Bernard 2013). The mind-set that led an otherwise law-abiding and apparently normal Rutgers University student to secretly video his gay roommate in a romantic encounter and put it on the Internet, perhaps contributing to the roommate's suicide, has not disappeared.

The recent decision by the Boy Scouts of America to allow gay Scouts marks both the progress made and the distance yet to be traveled. The decision itself is particularly significant because it resulted from a referendum, ordered by the Boy Scouts' national board, and voted upon by the more than 1,400 delegates attending the Scouts' annual meeting. At the same time, the national board decided to maintain the Scouts' policy barring openly gay men from serving in leadership positions, meaning that a gay Eagle Scout still has no future with the organization once he turns eighteen. More than 70 percent of Scout troops are chartered by faith-based groups, so it will be fascinating to observe their response to the change in policy. The immediate reactions suggest a diversity of views, ranging from the statement of a Baptist minister that "we are not willing to compromise God's word" (his 2,300-member congregation cut its ties to its sponsored troop) to that of a Catholic bishop, located in Tennessee, that there is no inconsistency between the new Scout policy and Catholic teaching, "which upholds the dignity of each and every human being regardless of sexual orientation" (Smietana 2013).

Most gay persons simply want to live their lives on their own terms. "The stories of the men interviewed for this book," wrote Peter Robinson at the conclusion of his study of eighty Australian gay men, "were remarkable for the relatively conventional, even ordinary, lives they revealed. The two central relationships in their intimate lives . . . were the couple relationship and friendship" (Robinson 2008, 177). There is no reason to believe that this finding is not equally true of gays in the United States, a nation built around sociability.

Since sexual orientation inevitably affects the direction of one's social life, it is hard to imagine that gayness will not always be an important component of a gay person's identity. As one middle-aged subject in Peter Robinson's study declared, "I need to have other people around me who are the same" (2008, 141). Of course it is also partly a question of arithmetic. When 95 percent of those to whom a person might be attracted have no interest in the kind of relationship that person may want, it is pretty important to have separate institutions—be they social, cultural, professional, or ethnic—that help the person identify the other 5 percent.

My own belief is that gay and lesbian life will continue to evolve along a broad spectrum, with some persons deeply committed to the idea of a gay community and most comfortable in predominantly gay neighborhoods, and others fully integrated into predominantly straight environments and thinking of their sexual orientation as a simple fact about themselves not that much different from other physical facts about themselves. Ultimately, a world of genuine acceptance would be one in which gay persons could make as much or as little as they want of their gay identity, without fear of negative consequences, where gay men can hold hands in a downtown stroll and a lesbian couple can exchange a casual kiss outside familiar territory without endangering their safety or attracting stares. Even if we are fortunate enough as a country to reach that point, the gay and lesbian twenty-year-olds of that era and their straight counterparts should still know the history of the struggle that created such freedom and the many brave and creative people who made it possible.

# SUGGESTED READING

The body of works on the gay and lesbian experience is immense. No one can read them all. Here I highlight what I believe to be some of the best resources available. They span a broad range of topics and forms but have in common that they are uniformly well written and enjoyable to read. They will lay a firm foundation for anyone interested in the subject. Full bibliographic details on these works are found in the reference list following. For anyone wishing to keep current on legal matters relating to gay rights, the periodical *Lesbian/Gay Law Notes*, created and edited by Arthur Leonard of New York Law School, is an indispensable resource. I know of nothing like it in any other field of law.

## LAW

Andersen, Ellen Ann, *Out of the Closets and into the Courts*
Ball, Carlos A., *From the Closet to the Courtroom: Five LGBT Rights Lawsuits That Have Changed Our Nation*
———, *The Right to Be Parents*
Eskridge, William N., Jr., *Dishonorable Passions: Sodomy Laws in America, 1861–2003*
Klarman, Michael J., *From the Closet to the Altar: Courts, Backlash and the Struggle for Same-Sex Marriage*
Murdoch, Joyce, and Deb Price, *Courting Justice: Gay Men and Lesbians v. the Supreme Court*

## SPECIAL STUDIES

Biegel, Stuart, *The Right to Be Out: Sexual Orientation and Gender Identity in America's Public Schools*
Bram, Christopher, *Eminent Outlaws: The Gay Writers Who Changed America*
Canaday, Margot, *The Straight State: Sexuality and Citizenship in Twentieth-Century America*
Engel, Stephen M., *The Unfinished Revolution: Social Movement Theory and the Gay and Lesbian Movement*
Faderman, Lillian, *Odd Girls and Twilight Lovers*
Gallo, Marcia M., *Different Daughters: A History of the Daughters of Bilitis and the Rise of the Lesbian Rights Movement*
Johnson, David K., *The Lavender Scare: The Cold War Persecution of Gays and Lesbians in the Federal Government*
Stein, Arlene, *The Stranger Next Door*

## ESSAYS

Berube, Allan, *My Desire for History*
Bram, Christopher, *Mapping the Territory*
D'Emilio, John, *Making Trouble: Essays on Gay History, Politics, and the University*
——, *The World Turned*
Duberman, Martin Bauml, *The Martin Duberman Reader: The Essential Historical, Biographical and Autobiographical Writings*
Holleran, Andrew, *Chronicle of a Plague, Revisited*

## INTERVIEWS/CONVERSATIONS

Claxton, Mae Miller, ed., *Conversations with Dorothy Allison*
Gambone, Philip, *Travels in a Gay Nation: Portraits of LGBTQ Americans*
Marcus, Eric, *Making Gay History: The Half-Century Fight for Lesbian and Gay Equal Rights*
Tobin, Kay, and Randy Wicker, *The Gay Crusaders*
Twin Cities GLBT Oral History Project, *Queer Twin Cities*

## DISSENTING VOICES

Goldstein, Richard, *The Attack Queers*
Halperin, David M., *How To Be Gay*
Sonnie, Amy, *Revolutionary Voices*
Vaid, Urvashi, *Irresistible Revolution: Confronting Race, Class and the Assumptions of LGBT*

## NARRATIVE HISTORIES

Andriote, John-Manuel, *Victory Deferred: How AIDS Changed Gay Life in America*
Carter, David, *Stonewall: The Riots That Sparked the Gay Revolution*
Chauncey, George, *Why Marriage? The History Shaping Today's Debate over Gay Equality*
Clendinen, Dudley, and Adam Nagourney, *Out for Good*
Eisenbach, David, *Gay Power: An American Revolution*
Gould, Deborah, *Moving Politics*
Hirshman, Linda, *Victory: The Triumphant Gay Revolution*
Miller, Neil, *Out of the Past: Gay and Lesbian History from 1869 to the Present*
Stein, Marc, *Rethinking the Gay and Lesbian Movement*
Vaid, Urvashi, *Virtual Equality: The Mainstreaming of Gay and Lesbian Liberation*

## URBAN HISTORIES

Atkins, Gary, *Gay Seattle*
Faderman, Lillian, and Stuart Timmons, *Gay L.A.: A History of Sexual Outlaws, Power Politics, and Lipstick Lesbians*
Kaiser, Charles, *The Gay Metropolis: 1940–1996*
Stein, Marc, *City of Sisterly and Brotherly Loves: Lesbian and Gay Philadelphia, 1945–1972*

## BIOGRAPHY

Schiavi, Michael, *Celluloid Activist: The Life and Times of Vito Russo*
Shilts, Randy, *The Mayor of Castro Street: The Life and Times of Harvey Milk*

## MEMOIRS

Duberman, Martin Bauml, *Cures: A Gay Man's Odyssey*
Hoffman, Amy, *An Army of Ex-Lovers*
Merla, Patrick, ed., *Boys Like Us: Gay Writers Tell Their Coming Out Stories*
Schwartz, John, *Oddly Normal: One Family's Struggle to Help Their Teenage Son Come to Terms with His Sexuality*

# REFERENCES

Adam, Barry D. 1995. *The Rise of a Gay and Lesbian Movement*. Rev. ed. New York: Twaynee Publishers.

Almy, Michael D. 2010. Statement before the U.S. Senate Armed Services Committee Hearing to Receive Testimony Relating to the Don't Ask Don't Tell Policy. March 18.

Andersen, Ellen Ann. 2006. *Out of the Closets and into the Courts*. Ann Arbor: University of Michigan Press.

Andriote, John-Manuel. 1999. *Victory Deferred: How AIDS Changed Gay Life in America*. Chicago: University of Chicago Press.

Appiah, Kwame Anthony. 2010. *The Honor Code: How Moral Revolutions Happen*. New York: W.W. Norton.

Apuzzo, Virginia. 2004. Interviewed by Kelly Anderson for the Voices of Feminism Oral History Project. June 2 and 3.

Arana, Gabriel. 2012. "My So-Called Ex-Gay Life." *American Prospect*, May, 54.

Atkins, Gary. 2003. *Gay Seattle*. Seattle: University of Washington Press.

Baim, Tracy, ed. 2008. *Out and Proud in Chicago*. Chicago: Surrey Books.

Baird, Robert M., and Stuart E. Rosenbaum, eds. 2004. *Same Sex Marriage: The Moral and Legal Debate*. 2nd ed. Amherst, NY: Prometheus Books.

Ball, Carlos A. 2010. *From the Closet to the Courtroom: Five LGBT Rights Lawsuits That Have Changed Our Nation*. Boston: Beacon Press.

——, 2012. *The Right to Be Parents*. New York: New York University Press.

Bawer, Bruce. 1993. *A Place at the Table: The Gay Individual in American Society*. New York: Simon Schuster.

Berg, James J., and Chris Freeman, eds. 2000. *The Isherwood Century: Essays on the Life and Work of Christopher Isherwood*. Madison: University of Wisconsin Press.

Bernard, Tara Siegel. 2013. "Fired for Being Gay? Protections Are Piecemeal." *New York Times* June 1, B1, then B4.

Berube, Allan. 1983. "Marching to a Different Drummer: Lesbian and Gay GIs in World War II." In *Powers of Desire, the Politics of Sexuality*, ed. Ann Snitow, Christine Stansell, and Sharon Thompson, 88–99. New York: Monthly Review Press.

——. 1990. *Coming Out under Fire: The History of Gay Men and Women in World War II*. Chapel Hill: University of North Carolina Press.

——. 2011. *My Desire for History*. Chapel Hill: University of North Carolina Press.

Biddle, Donna. 2009. Interviewed by Linda Lenzke. University of Wisconsin–Madison Archives Oral History Program.

Biegel, Stuart. 2010. *The Right to Be Out: Sexual Orientation and Gender Identity in America's Public Schools*. Minneapolis: University of Minnesota Press.

Blasius, Mark, and Shane Phelan, eds. 1997. *We Are Everywhere: A Historical Sourcebook of Gay and Lesbian Politics.* New York: Routledge.

Boswell, John. 1989. "Revolutions, Universals and Sexual Categories." In *Hidden from History: Reclaiming the Gay and Lesbian Past*, ed. Martin Duberman, Martha Vicinus, and George Chauncey, 17–36. New York: Meridian.

Bosworth, Lewis. 2009. Interviewed by Scott Seyforth. March 20. University of Wisconsin–Madison Archives Oral History Program.

Bram, Christopher. 2009. *Mapping the Territory.* New York: Alyson Books.

———. 2012. *Eminent Outlaws: The Gay Writers Who Changed America.* New York: Twelve/Grand Central.

Branch, Taylor. 2009. *The Clinton Tapes: Wrestling History with the President.* New York: Simon and Schuster.

Brigham, John. 1996. *The Constitution of Interests.* New York: New York University Press.

Bright, Susie. 2000. "Interview: Come Out if You're Gay or Straight!" *Gay and Lesbian Review Worldwide* 7(1): 40–41.

Brodzinsky, David M., and Adam Pertman, eds. 2012. *Adoption by Lesbians and Gay Men: A New Dimension in Family Diversity.* Oxford: Oxford University Press.

Bronski, Michael. 2011. *Queer History of the United States.* Boston: Beacon Press.

Cain, Patricia. 1993. "Litigating for Lesbian and Gay Rights: A Legal History." *Virginia Law Review* 79: 1551–1641.

Canaday, Margot. 2009. *The Straight State: Sexuality and Citizenship in Twentieth-Century America.* Princeton: Princeton University Press.

Canning, Richard. 2011. "The Epidemic That Barely Was." *Gay and Lesbian Review Worldwide* 18: 25–27.

Carter, David. 2004. *Stonewall: The Riots That Sparked the Gay Revolution.* New York: St. Martin's Press.

Case, Mary Anne. 1993. "Couples and Coupling in the Public Sphere: A Comment on the Legal History of Litigating for Lesbian and Gay Rights." *Virginia Law Review* 79: 1643.

———. 2010a. "Couples and Coupling in the Public Sphere: A Comment on the Legal History of Litigating for Lesbian and Gay Rights." *Virginia Law Review* 79: 1643–1694.

———. 2010b. "A Lot to Ask: Review Essay of Martha Nussbaum's *From Disgust to Humanity: Sexual Orientation and the Law.*" *Columbia Journal of Gender and Law* 19: 89–124.

Chasnoff, Debra. 2009. Interview by Groucho. January 2. http://www.grouchoreviews.com/interviews/263.

Chauncey, George. 2004. *Why Marriage? The History Shaping Today's Debate over Gay Equality.* New York: Basic Books.

Claxton, Mae Miller, ed. 2012. *Conversations with Dorothy Allison.* Jackson: University Press of Mississippi.

Clendinen, Dudley, and Adam Nagourney. 1999. *Out for Good.* New York: Simon and Schuster.

Coates, Ta-Nehisi. 2011. "The Legacy of Malcolm X." *Atlantic,* May, 100–107.

Cohen, Micah. 2012. "Gay Vote Proved a Boon for Obama." *New York Times*, November 15, A20.

Cohen, Stephen L. 2007. *The Gay Liberation Youth Movement in New York: "An Army of Lovers Cannot Fail."* New York: Routledge.

Congregation for the Doctrine of the Faith. 1992. "Some Considerations concerning the Response to Legislative Proposals on the Non-Discrimination of Homosexual Persons." http://www.doctrinafidei.va/documents/.

———. 2003. "Considerations regarding Proposals to Give Legal Recognition to Unions between Homosexual Persons. http://www.vatican.va/roman_curia/congregations/cfaith/documents/.

Cory, Donald Webster. 1951. *The Homosexual in America: A Subjective Approach*. New York: Greenberg Press.

Cruz-Malave, Arnaldo. 2007. *Queer Latino Testimonio, Keith Haring, and Juanito Xtravaganza*. New York: Palgrave Macmillan.

Daley, James. 2010. *Great Speeches on Gay Rights*. Mineola, NY: Dover Publications.

D'Emilio, John. 1983. *Sexual Politics, Sexual Communities: The Making of a Homosexual Minority in the United States*. 2nd ed.. Chicago: University of Chicago Press.

———. 1992. *Making Trouble: Essays on Gay History, Politics, and the University*. New York: Routledge.

———. 2002. *The World Turned*. Durham, NC: Duke University Press.

———. 2008. "Gay Power!" In *Out and Proud in Chicago*, ed. Tracy Baum, 70–71. Chicago: Surrey Books.

D'Emilio, John, William B. Turner, and Urvashi Vaid, eds. 2000. *Creating Change: Sexuality, Public Policy, and Civil Rights*. New York: St. Martin's Press.

Devlin, Patrick. 1968. *The Enforcement of Morals*. Oxford: Oxford University Press.

Drescher, Jack, and Kenneth J. Zucker, eds. 2006. *Ex-Gay Research: Analyzing the Spitzer Study and Its Relation to Science, Religion, Politics, and Culture*. New York: Harrington Park Press.

Duberman, Martin Bauml. 1986. *About Time: Exploring the Gay Past*. New York: Gay Presses of New York.

———. 1991. *Cures: A Gay Man's Odyssey*. New York: Dutton.

———. 1993. *Stonewall*. New York: Dutton.

———. 2009. *Waiting to Land: A Mostly Political Memoir, 1985–2008*. New York: New Press.

———. 2013. *The Martin Duberman Reader: The Essential Historical, Biographical and Autobiographical Writings*. New York: New Press.

Dugan, Kimberly B. 2005. *The Struggle over Gay, Lesbian, and Bisexual Rights: Facing Off in Cincinnati*. New York: Routledge.

Eaklor, Vicki L. 2006. *Steve Endean: Bringing Lesbian and Gay Rights into the Mainstream: Twenty Years of Progress*. New York: Harrington Park Press.

———. 2008. *Queer America: A GLBT History of the 20th Century*. New York: New Press.

Eckholm, Eric. 2012. "Rift Forms in Movement as Belief in Gay 'Cure' Is Renounced." *New York Times*, July 6, A11.

Eisenbach, David. 2006. *Gay Power: An American Revolution*. New York: Carroll and Graf.

Eisgruber, Christopher. 2001. *Constitutional Self-Government*. Cambridge: Harvard University Press.

Embser-Herbert, Melissa Sheridan. 2007. *The U.S. Military's Don't Ask, Don't Tell Policy: A Reference Handbook*. Westport, CT: Praeger Security International.

Engel, Stephen M. 2001. *The Unfinished Revolution: Social Movement Theory and the Gay and Lesbian Movement*. Cambridge: Cambridge University Press.

———. 2002. "Making a Minority: Understanding the Formation of the Gay and Lesbian Movement in the United States." In *Handbook of Lesbian and Gay Studies*, ed. Diane Richardson and Steven Seidman, 377–402. London: Sage Publications.

Epstein, Joseph. 1970. "Homo/Hetero: The Struggle for Sexual Identity." *Harper's Magazine*, September, 37–51.

Epstein, Steven. 1999. "Gay and Lesbian Movements in the United States." In *The Global Emergence of Gay and Lesbian Politics*, ed. Barry D. Adam, Jan Willem Duyvendak, and Andre Krouwel, 30–90. Philadelphia: Temple University Press.

Eskridge, William N., Jr. 1996. "Privacy Jurisprudence and the Apartheid of the Closet, 1946–1961." *Florida State University Law Review* 24: 703–838.

———. 2008. *Dishonorable Passions: Sodomy Laws in America, 1861–2003.* New York: Viking.

Eskridge, William N., Jr., and Nan D. Hunter. 2011.*Sexuality, Gender, and the Law.* New York: Foundation Press.

Ettelbrick, Paula. 1997. "Since When Is Marriage a Path to Liberation?" In *We Are Everywhere,* ed. Mark Blasius and Shane Phelan. New York: Routledge. Originally published in *Outlook,* 1989.

Faderman, Lillian 1991. *Odd Girls and Twilight Lovers.* New York: Columbia University Press.

Faderman, Lillian, and Stuart Timmons. 2007. *Gay L.A.: A History of Sexual Outlaws, Power Politics, and Lipstick Lesbians.* New York: Basic Books.

Gallo, Marcia M. 2006. *Different Daughters: A History of the Daughters of Bilitis and the Rise of the Lesbian Rights Movement.* New York: Carroll and Graf.

Gambone, Philip. 2010. *Travels in a Gay Nation: Portraits of LGBTQ Americans.* Madison: University of Wisconsin Press.

Gabbatt, Adam. 2013. "Edith Windsor and Thea Spyer: 'A Love Affair That Just Kept On and On. *Guardian,* June 26; http://www.guardian.co.uk/world/2013/jun/26/.

Garnes, David. 2000. "A Single Man, Then and Now." In *The Isherwood Century: Essays on the Life and Work of Christopher Isherwood,* ed. James J. Berg and Chris Freeman, 196–201. Madison: University of Wisconsin Press.

Gartrell, Nanette, and H. Bos. 2010. "U.S. National Lesbian Family Study: Psychological Adjustment of 17 Year Old Adolescents." *Pediatrics* 126: 28–36.

Gates, Gary. 2012. "LGBT Identity: A Demographer's Perspective." *Loyola of Los Angeles Law Review* 45 (spring): 693–714.

Gay, Lesbian and Straight Education Network. 2011. "The 2011 National School Climate Survey." http://www.glsen.org.

Gilreath, Shannon. 2012. *Equality: The End of Straight Supremacy—Realizing Gay Liberation.* Cambridge: Cambridge University Press.

Goldstein, Richard. 2002. *The Attack Queers.* London: Verso.

Gould, Deborah B. 2009. *Moving Politics.* Chicago: University of Chicago Press.

Gurganus, Allan. 1996. "He's One Too." In *Boys Like Us,* ed. Patrick Merla, 43–72. New York: Avon Books.

Halperin, Donald. 2012. *How to Be Gay.* Cambridge: Harvard University Press.

Harden, Victoria. 2012. *AIDS at 30.* Washington, DC: Potomac Books.

Harper, Jorjet. 2008. "Literary Powerhouse: Valerie Taylor." In *Out and Proud in Chicago,* ed. Tracy Baim, 59. Chicago: Surrey Books.

Hart, H.L.A. 1969. *Law, Liberty and Morality.* Stanford: Stanford University Press.

Harvie, Kim Crawford. 2010. Interviewed by Philip Gambone. In *Travels in a Gay Nation: Portraits of LGBTQ Americans,* 148–155. Madison: University of Wisconsin Press.

Herdt, Gilbert, ed. 1992. *Gay Culture in America: Essays from the Field.* Boston: Beacon Press.

Hertz, Frederick, and Emily Doskow. 2012. *A Legal Guide for Lesbian and Gay Couples.* 16th ed. Berkeley, CA: Nolo.

Hirsch, H. N., ed. 2005. *The Future of Gay Rights in America.* New York: Routledge.

Hirshman, Linda. 2012. *Victory: The Triumphant Gay Revolution.* New York: Harper Collins.

Hoffman, Amy. 2007. *An Army of Ex-Lovers.* Amherst: University of Massachusetts Press.

Holleran, Andrew. 2008. *Chronicle of a Plague, Revisited.* New York: De Capo Press.

Huffman, M. Blake. 2008–2009. "Out of Step: Why *Pulliam v. Smith* Should be Overruled to Hold All North Carolina Parents—Gay and Straight—to the Same Custody Standard." *North Carolina Law Review* 87: 257–304.

Human Rights Campaign. 2002–2013. *Corporate Equality Index: Rating American Workplaces on Lesbian, Gay, Bisexual and Transgender Equality.* Human Rights Campaign Foundation; www.hrc.org/corporate-equality-index.

Inrig, Stephen. 2011. *North Carolina and the Problem of AIDS*. Chapel Hill: University of North Carolina Press.

Johnson, David K. 2004. *The Lavender Scare: The Cold War Persecution of Gays and Lesbians in the Federal Government*. Chicago: University of Chicago Press.

Kaiser, Charles. 1997. *The Gay Metropolis: 1940–1996*. Boston: Houghton Mifflin.

Katz, Jonathan Ned. 1992. *Gay American History: Lesbians and Gay Men in the U.S.A., A Documentary History*. Rev. ed. New York: Meridian.

Kayal, Philip M. 1993. *Bearing Witness: Gay Men's Health Crisis and the Politics of AIDS*. Boulder, CO: Westview Press.

Kenney, Moira Rachel. 2001. *Mapping Gay L.A.: The Intersection of Place and Politics*. Philadelphia: Temple University Press.

Kepner, Jim. 1998. *Rough News—Daring Views: 1950's Pioneer Gay Press Journalism*. New York: Haworth Press.

———. 2010. "Why Can't We All Get Together, and What Do We Have in Common." In *Great Speeches on Gay Rights*, ed. James Daley, 85–112. Mineola, NY: Dover Publications.

Kinsey, Alfred C. 1948. *Sexual Behavior in the Human Male*. Philadelphia: Saunders.

Klarman, Michael J. 2013. *From the Closet to the Altar: Courts, Backlash and the Struggle for Same-Sex Marriage*. Oxford: Oxford University Press.

Kohler, Will. 2013. "Watch CBS Reports 'The Homosexuals' Hosted by Mike Wallace (1967)—Rare Video Copy." http://www.back2stonewall.com/2013/01/gay-archives-1967.

Kramer, Larry. 1997. "1,112 and Counting." In *We Are Everywhere*, ed. Mark Blasius and Shane Phelan, 578–586. New York: Routledge. Originally published in *New York Native*, March 1983.

Lauritsen, John. 2009. "Radical Spirit and Vision." In *Smash the Church, Smash the State*, ed. Tommi Avicolli Mecca, 108–113. San Francisco: City Light Books.

Leonard, Arthur S., and Patricia A. Cain. 2009. *Sexuality Law*. 2nd ed. Durham, NC: Carolina Academic Press.

LeVay, Simon. 2011. *Gay, Straight and the Reason Why*. New York: Oxford University Press.

Levy, Ariel. 2013. "How Edith Windsor Learned She Won." http://www.newyorker.com/online/blogs/newsdeck/2013/06/.

Lund, Sean, and Cathy Renna. 2010. "An Analysis of the Media Response to the Spitzer Study." In *Ex-Gay Research: Analyzing the Spitzer Study and Its Relation to Science, Religion, Politics, and Culture*, ed. Jack Drescher and Kenneth J. Zucker, 277–290. New York: Harrington Park Press.

Marcus, Eric. 2002. *Making Gay History: The Half-Century Fight for Lesbian and Gay Equal Rights*. New York: Harper Collins.

Matter, Ann. 2004. Interviewed by Joey Plaster. August 25. Oberlin College LGBT Community History Project website; http://www.oberlinlgbt.org/content/Personal-Histories/The-1970s.

Meacham, Jon. 2012. "Commentary: Of God and Gays and Humility." *Time*, July 30, 16.

Mecca, Tommi, ed. 2009. *Smash the Church, Smash the State: The Early Years of Gay Liberation*. San Francisco: City Lights Books.

Merla, Patrick, ed. 1996. *Boys Like Us: Gay Writers Tell Their Coming Out Stories*. New York: Avon Books.

Miller, Jack. 2009. "Savannah and the Spirit of Stonewall in 1969." *Gay and Lesbian Review Worldwide* 16: 45.

Miller, Neil, 2006. *Out of the Past: Gay and Lesbian History from 1869 to the Present*. New York: Alyson Books.

Mixner, David. 2010. "LGBT History: The Decade of Lobotomies, Castration and Institutions." July 28. Live from Hells Kitchen blog; http://www.davidmixner.com/2010/07.

Mixner, David, and Dennis Bailey. 2000. *Brave Journeys: Profiles in Gay and Lesbian Courage.* New York: Bantam Books.

Moats, David. 2004. *Civil Wars: A Battle for Gay Marriage.* Orlando, FL: Harcourt.

Moore, Patrick. 2004. *Beyond Shame.* Boston: Beacon Press.

Mucciaroni, Gary. 2008. *Same Sex, Different Politics: Success and Failure in the Struggles over Gay Rights.* Chicago: University of Chicago Press.

Murdoch, Joyce, and Deb Price. 2002. *Courting Justice: Gay Men and Lesbians v. the Supreme Court.* New York: Basic Books.

Murphy, Kevin P. 2010. "Gay Was Good." In *Queer Twin Cities*, ed. Twin Cities GLBT Oral History Project, 305–318. Minneapolis: University of Minnesota Press.

Murray, Stephen O. 1996. *American Gay.* Chicago: University of Chicago Press.

Nava Michael, and Robert Dawidoff. 1994. *Created Equal: Why Gay Rights Matter to America.* New York: St. Martin's Press.

NeJaime, Douglas. 2009. "Inclusion, Accommodation, and Recognition: Accounting for Differences Based on Religion and Sexual Orientation." *Harvard Journal of Law and Gender* 32 (summer): 303–382.

Nussbaum, Martha C. 2010. *From Disgust to Humanity: Sexual Orientation and Constitutional Law.* Oxford: Oxford University Press.

O'Leary, Jean. 2000. "From Agitator to Insider: Fighting for Inclusion in the Democratic Party." In *Creating Change: Sexuality, Public Policy, and Civil Rights*, ed. John D'Emilio, William B. Turner, and Urvashi Vaid, 81–114. New York: St. Martin's Press.

Ormsbee, J. Todd. 2010. *The Meaning of Gay: Interaction, Publicity and Community among Homosexual Men in 1960s San Francisco.* Lanham, MD: Lexington Books.

Ortiz, Daniel R. 1993. "Creating Controversy: Essentialism and Constructivism and the Politics of Identity." *Virginia Law Review* 79: 1833–1857.

*Perry v. Schwarzenegger.* N.d. Trial transcript. American Foundation for Equal Rights website; www.afer.org/our-work/hearing/transcripts.

Pertman, Adam, and Jeanne Howard. 2012. "Emerging Diversity in Family Life: Adoption by Gay and Lesbian Parents." In *Adoption by Lesbians and Gay Men*, ed. David Brodzinsky and Adam Pertman, 20–35. Oxford: Oxford University Press.

Phelan, Shane. 2001. "On the Citizenship of Strangers: A Tim Miller Interview." *Gay and Lesbian Review Worldwide* 8: 12–13.

Pinello, Daniel R. 2003. *Gay Rights and American Law.* Cambridge: Cambridge University Press.

Pizer, Jennifer C., Brad Sears, Christy Mallory, and Nan D. Hunter. 2012. "Evidence of Persistent and Pervasive Workplace Discrimination against LGBT People: The Need for Federal Legislation Prohibiting Discrimination and Providing for Equal Employment Benefits." *Loyola of Los Angeles Law Review* 45: 715–780.

Poling, John. 2008. "Mattachine Midwest: Standing up for Gay Rights." In *Out and Proud in Chicago*, ed. Tracy Baim, 62–68. Chicago: Surrey Books.

Preston, Julia. 2013. "Green Card Is Approved for Gay Men in Florida." *New York Times*, July 1, A11.

Raeburn, Nicole C. 2004. *Changing Corporate America from Inside Out.* Minneapolis: University of Minnesota Press.

Rayside, David, and Clyde Wilcox, eds. 2011. *Faith, Politics and Sexual Diversity in Canada and the United States.* Vancouver: UBC Press.

Richardson, Diane, and Steven Seidman, eds. 2002. *Handbook of Lesbian and Gay Studies.* London: Sage Publications.

Robinson, Peter. 2008. *The Changing World of Gay Men.* New York: Palgrave Macmillan.

Rodriguez, Margot Kelley. 2000. "Introduction: We Are the Ones We Have Been Waiting For." In *Revolutionary Voices*, ed. Amy Sonnie, xxi–xxvi. Los Angeles: Alyson Books.

Rosenberg, Gerald N. 2008. *The Hollow Hope*. 2nd ed. Chicago: University of Chicago Press.

Russett, Cynthia. 2012. "American Adoption: A Brief History." In *Adoption by Lesbians and Gay Men*, ed. David Brodzinsky and Adam Pertman, 3–19. Oxford: Oxford University Press.

Ryan, Caitlin, David Huebner, Rafael M. Diaz, and Jorge Sanchez. 2009. "Family Rejection as a Predictor of Negative Health Outcomes in White and Latino Lesbian, Gay and Bisexual Young Adults." *Pediatrics* 128, no. 1: 346–352.

Savin-Williams, Ritich C. 2005. *The New Gay Teenager*. Cambridge: Harvard University Press.

Schiavi, Michael. 2011. *Celluloid Activist: The Life and Times of Vito Russo*. Madison: University of Wisconsin Press.

Schroder, Rick. 2008. *Finding the Enemy: Coming Out in Corporate America*. Dallas: Durban House.

Schwartz, John. 2012. *Oddly Normal: One Family's Struggle to Help Their Teenage Son Come to Terms with His Sexuality*. New York: Gotham Books.

Senak, Mark. 2003. *Every Trick in the Book*. New York: M. Evans.

Shames, Shaun L., Didi Kuo, and Katherine Levine. 2004. "Culture War." In *Faith, Politics and Sexual Diversity in Canada and the United States*, ed. David Rayside and Clyde Wilcox, 29–48. Vancouver: UBC Press.

Shilts, Randy. 1982. *The Mayor of Castro Street: The Life and Times of Harvey Milk*. New York: St. Martin's Press.

Simmons, Roy, and Damon DeMarco. 2006. *Out of Bounds*. New York: Carroll and Graf.

Smietana, Bob. 2013. "Churches Sever Scout Sponsorship." *U.S.A. Today*, May 31–June 2 (weekend ed.), A1.

Smith, Raymond A., and Donald P. Haider-Markel. 2002. *Gay and Lesbian Americans and Political Participation*. Santa Barbara, CA: ABC-Clio Inc.

Snitow, Ann, Christine Stansell, and Sharon Thompson, eds. 1983. *Powers of Desire: The Politics of Sexuality*. New York: Monthly Review Press.

Sonnie, Amy. 2000. *Revolutionary Voices*. New York: Alyson Publications.

Spitzer, Robert. 2006. "Can Some Gay Men and Lesbians Change Their Sexual Orientation, 200 Participants Reporting a Change from Homosexual to Heterosexual Orientation." In *Ex-Gay Research: Analyzing the Spitzer Study and Its Relation to Science, Religion, Politics, and Culture*, ed. Jack Drescher and Kenneth J. Zucker, 35–63. New York: Harrington Park Press. Originally published in *Archives of Sexual Behavior* 32(5): 403–417.

Sprigg, Peter. 2010. "The Top Ten Myths about Homosexuality." Washington, DC: Family Research Council; http://www.frc.org.

Stacey, Judith, and Elizabeth Davenport. 2002. "Queer Families Quack Back." In *Handbook of Gay and Lesbian Studies*, ed. Diana Richardson and Steven Seidman, 355–374. London: Sage Publications.

Stalstrom, Ollie, and Jussi Nissinen. 2006. "The Spitzer Study and the Finnish Parliament." In *Ex-Gay Research: Analyzing the Spitzer Study and Its Relation to Science, Religion, Politics, and Culture*, edited by Jack Drescher and Kenneth J. Zucker, 309–321. New York: Harrington Park Press.

Stein, Arlene. 2001. *The Stranger Next Door*. Boston: Beacon Press.

Stein, Marc. 2000. *City of Sisterly and Brotherly Loves: Lesbian and Gay Philadelphia, 1945–1972*. Chicago: University of Chicago Press.

———. 2012. *Rethinking the Gay and Lesbian Movement*. New York: Routledge.

Stewart-Winter, Timothy. 2009. "Essay: The Castro: Origins to the Age of Milk." *Gay and Lesbian Review Worldwide*, January–February, 12.

Sullivan, Andrew. 2005. "The End of Gay Culture." *New Republic*, October 24, 17.

Tarr, Hal. 2009. "A Consciousness Raised." In *Smash the Church, Smash the State*, ed. Tommi Avicolli Mecca, 22–30. San Francisco: City Lights Books.

Task Force of American Psychological Association on Appropriate Therapeutic Responses to Sexual Orientation. 2007. *Task Force Report* (available on American Psychological Association website).

Tavernise, Sabrina. 2011. "Adoptions Rise by Same-Sex Couples, Despite Legal Barriers." *New York Times,* June 14, sec. A, 11–12.

Terkel, Studs. 1995. "Coming of Age." New York: New Press.

Tobin, Kay, and Randy Wicker. 1972. *The Gay Crusaders.* New York: Coronet Communications.

Toobin, Jeffrey. 2007. *The Nine.* New York: Doubleday.

———. 2012. "Evolution." *New Yorker,* May 28, 26.

Tulin, Edward L. 2005–2006. "Where Everything Old Is New Again—Enduring Episodic Discrimination against Homosexual Persons." *Texas Law Review* 84: 1587–1632.

Turner, William B. 2002. "Mirror Images: Lesbian/Gay Civil Rights in the Carter and Reagan Administrations." In *Creating Change: Sexuality, Public Policy, and Civil Rights,* ed. John D'Emilio, William B. Turner, and Urvashi Vaid, 3–28. New York: St. Martin's Press.

Twin Cities GLBT Oral History Project. 2010. *Queer Twin Cities.* Minneapolis: University of Minnesota Press.

Vaid, Urvashi. 1995. *Virtual Equality: The Mainstreaming of Gay and Lesbian Liberation.* New York: Anchor Books Doubleday.

———. 2009. "What about LGBT Pride." Speech, Kalamazoo, MI Pride, June 13, 2009. Transcript available at http://urvashivaid.net/wp/?p=133.

———. 2012a. *Irresistible Revolution: Confronting Race, Class and the Assumptions of LGBT Politics.* New York: Magnus Books.

———. 2012b. "Still Ain't Satisfied: The Limits of Equality." *American Prospect,* May; www.prospect.org.

Warner, Michael. 2012. "Queer and Then?" *Chronicle of Higher Education,* January 1; http://chronicle.com/article/QueerThen-/130161.

Weeks, Jeffrey. 1991. *Against Nature: Essays on History, Sexuality and Identity.* London: Rivers Oram.

White, Edmund. 1988. "The Art of Fiction No. 105." Interviewed by Jordan Elgrably. http://www.theparisreview.org/interviews.

Whyte, William H., Jr. 1956. *The Organization Man.* New York: Simon and Schuster.

Williams, Walter L., and Yolanda Retter, eds. 2003. *Gay and Lesbian Rights in the United States: A Documentary History.* Westport, CT: Greenwood Press.

*Windsor* Argument Transcript. Available on official website of the U.S. Supreme Court, in "Oral Argument Transcripts."

Woods, Jordan Blair. 2010. "Gay–Straight Alliances and Sanctioning Pre-textual Discrimination under the Equal Access Act." *New York University Review of Law and Social Change* 34: 373–424.

Yeardon, James. 2009. Interviewed by "Questions from Audience at Campus Talk." April 5. University of Wisconsin–Madison Archives Oral History Program.

# CASES

Acanfora v. Board of Education of Montgomery County, 359 F. Supp. 843 (D.Md. 1973).
Acanfora v. Board of Education of Montgomery County, 491 F.2d 498 (4th Cir. 1974).
Adar v. Smith, 639 F.3d 146 (5th Cir.) (En banc) (2011).
Alaska Civil Liberties Union v. State of Alaska, 122 P.3d 781 (Ak. S. Ct. 2005).
Apilado v. North American Gay Amateur Athletic Alliance, 2011 WL 5563206 (W.D. Wash., Nov. 10, 2011).
Application of William J. Thom, 33 N.Y. 2d 609 (NY Ct. App. 1973).
Appling v. Doyle, 2013 Wi. App. 3 (Dec. 20, 2012).
Arkansas Dept. of Human Services v. Cole, 380 S.W. 3rd 429 (Ark. S. Ct. 2011).
Baehr v. Lewin, 852 P.2d 44 (Haw. S. Ct. 1993).
Baker v. Nelson, 191 N.W.2d 185 (Minn. 1971), appeal dismissed, 409 U.S. 810 (1972).
Baker v. Vermont, 744 A.2d 864 (Vt. 1999).
Bethel School District No. 403 v. Fraser, 478 U.S. 675 (1986).
Board of Education of Westside Community Schools v. Mergens, 496 U.S. 226 (1990).
Boseman v. Jarrell, 704 S.E. 2d 494 (N. Car. S. Ct. 2010).
Boutilier v. Immigration and Naturalization Service, 387 U.S. 118 (1967).
Bowers v. Hardwick, 478 U.S. 186 (1986).
Boy Scouts of America v. Dale, 530 U.S. 640 (2000).
Braschi v. Stahl Associates Co., 543 N.E.2d 49 (New York 1989).
Brown v. Board of Education, 347 U.S. 483 (1954).
Brown v. Hot, Sexy and Safer Productions, 68 F.3rd 525 (1st Cir. 1995).
Carolene Products case, 304 U.S. 144 (1938).
Caudillo v. Lubbock Independent School District, 311 F. Supp. 2d 550 (N.D. Texas 2004).
Christian Legal Society v. Martinez, 130 S. Ct. 2971 (2010).
City of Cleburne, Texas v. Cleburne Living Center, 473 U.S. 432 (1985).
City of New York v. New Saint Mark's Baths, 497 N.Y.S.2d 979 (1986).
Corporation of Presiding Bishop of Church of Jesus Christ of Latter Day Saints v. Amos, 483 U.S. 327 (1987).
Department of Children and Families v. In the Matter of the Adoption of X.X.G and N.R.G, 45 So. 3d 79 (Fla. App. 3d Dist. 2010).
Diaz v. Brewer, 656 F.3d 1008 (9th Cir. 2011).
Dillon v. Frank, 952 F.2d 403 (6th Cir. 1992).
Donaldson and Guggenheim v. State of Montana, DA 11–0451 2012 MT 288 (2012).
Employment Division v. Smith, 494 U.S. 872 (1990).
Finstuen v. Crutcher, 496 F.3d 1139 (10th Cir. 2007).
Gay Alliance of Students v. Matthews, 544 F.2d 162 (4th Cir. 1976).

Gay Law Students Association v. Pacific Telephone and Telegraph Company, 595 P.2d 592 (Cal. S. Ct. 1979).

Gay Lib. v. University of Missouri, 558 F.2d 848 (8th Cir. 1977) cert. denied, 434 U.S. 1080 (1978).

Gay Students Org. v. Bonner, 509 F.2d 652 (1st Cir. 1974).

Goodridge v. Department of Public Health, 798 NE.2d 941 (Mass. 2003).

Griswold v. Connecticut, 381 U.S. 479 (1965).

Grutter v. Bollinger, 539 U.S. 306 (2003).

Harden v. Zinnemann, 2003 Westlaw 21802250 (Cal. Ct. App. 2003).

Harper v. Poway Unified School District, 445 F.3d 1166 (9th Cir. 2005).

Hernandez v. Robles, 855 N.E.2d 1 (N.Y. 2006).

High Tech Gays v. Defense Industrial Security Clearance Office, 895 F.2d 563 (9th Cir. 1990).

Hollingsworth v. Perry, (Slip Opinion) vacating 671 F.3d 1052 (2012).

Hutchinson v. Cuyahoga County Board of Commissioners, 2011 WL 1563874 (N.D. Ohio).

Hurley v. Irish-American Gay, Lesbian and Bisexual Group of Boston, 515 U.S. 557 (1995).

In Re the Adoption of Evan, 583 N.Y.S.2d 997 (1992).

In Re the Matter of the Parentage of L.B., 122 P.3d 161 (Wash. 2005).

In Re Marriage Cases, 183 P.3d 384 (Cal. S. Ct. 2008).

In the Matter of Jacob, 86 N.Y.2d 651 (1995).

Jones v. Hallahan, 501 S.W. 2d 588 (Ky. Ct. App. 1973).

Korematsu v. United States, 323 U.S. 214 (1944).

Latham v. Schwerdtfeger, 282 Neb. 121 (Neb. S. Ct., August 26, 2011).

Lawrence v. Texas, 539 U.S. 558 (2003).

Leebaert v. Harrington, 332 F.3d 134 (2nd Cir. 2003).

Levy v. Louisiana, 391 U.S. 68 (1968).

Lewis v. Harris, 188 N.J. 415 (2006).

Lofton v. Secretary of the Dept. of Children and Family Services, 358 F.3d 804 (11th Cir. 2004).

Log Cabin Republicans v. United States of America, 658 F.3d 1162 (9th Cir. 2011).

Loving v. Virginia, 388 U.S. 1 (1967).

Manual Enterprises Inc. v. Day, 370 U.S. 478 (1962).

Matlovich v. Secretary of the Air Force, 591 F.2d 852 (D.C. Cir. 1978).

Maxwell v. Maxwell, 2012 5050588 (Ky. App., Oct. 19, 2012).

McConnell v. Andersen, 451 F.2d 193 (8th Cir. 1971).

McDonnell Douglas Corp. v. Green, 411 U.S. 792 (1973).

McGriff v. McGriff, 99 P.3d 111 (Idaho S. Ct. 2004).

McMillen v. Itawamba County School District (U.S.D.C., Nor. D. Miss., 2010.).

Meinhold v. United States Department of Defense, 34 F.3d 1469 (9th Cir. 1994).

Meyer v. Nebraska, 262 U.S. 390 (1923).

Mongerson v. Mongerson, 285 Ga. 554 (Ga. S. Ct. 2009).

Morrison v. Board of Education of Boyd County, 507 F.3d 494 (6th Cir. 2007).

Morse v. Frederick, 551 U.S. 393 (2007).

NAACP v. Alabama, 357 U.S. 449 (1958).

Nabozny v. Podlesny, 92 F.3d 446 C.A.7 (Wisc.) 1996.

National Pride at Work v. Governor of Michigan, 748 N.W.2d 524 (Mich. S. Ct 2008).

Norton v. Macy, 417 F.2d 1161 (D.C. Cir. 1969).

Nuxoll v. Indian Prairie School District No. 204, 523 F.3d 668 (2008).

ONE Inc. v. Olesen, 355 U.S. 371 (1958).

Padula v. Webster, 822 F.2d 97 (D.C. Cir. 1987).

Parker v. Hurley, 514 F.3d 87 (1st Cir. 2008).

Patterson v. Hudson Area Schools, 551 F.3d 438 (6th Cir. 2009).

Perry v. Schwarzenegger, 704 F. Supp. 2d 921 (N.D. Cal. 2010).

Pickering v. Board of Education, 391 U.S. 563 (1968).

Pierce v. Society of Sisters, 268 U.S. 510 (1925).

Price Waterhouse v. Hopkins, 490 U.S. 228 (1989).

Prowel v. Wise Business Forms, Inc., 579 F.3d 285 (2009).

Pulliam v. Smith, 501 S.E.2d 898 (1998).

Quiroz v. Neely, 291 F.2d 906 (5th Cir., 1961).

Robinson v. California, 370 U.S. 660 (1962).

Romer v. Evans, 517 U.S. 620 (1996).

Roth v. United States, 354 U.S. 476 (1957).

Rowland v. Mad River Local School District, 730 F.2d 444 (6th Cir. 1984), cert. denied, 470
    U.S. 1009 (1985).

Rumsfeld v. Forum for Academic and Institutional Rights, Inc., 547 U.S. 47 (2006).

Scarborough v. Morgan County Board of Education, 470 F.3d 250 (6th Cir. 2006).

Singer v. Hara, 522 P.2d 1187 (Wash. Ct. App. 1974).

Singer v. United States Civil Service Commission, 530 F.2d 247 (9th Cir. 1976).

Sterling v. Borough of Minersville, 232 F.3d 190 (3d Cir. 2000).

Stoumen v. Reilly, 234 P.2d 969 (Cal. S. Ct. 1951).

Stroder v. Commonwealth of Kentucky Cabinet for Health and Family Services, U.S. Dist.
    Ct., West Dist. Kentucky, Louisville Div., March 20, 2012.

Tinker v. Des Moines School District, 393 U.S. 503 (1969).

Turner v. Safley, 482 U.S. 78 (1987).

United States v. Carolene Products, 304 U.S. 144 (1938).

United States v. Windsor, 570 U.S. ____ (2013).

Vallegra v. Department of Alcoholic Beverage Control, 347 P.2d 909 (Cal. S. Ct. 1959).

Varnum v. Brien, 763 N.W.2d 862 (Iowa S. Ct. 2009).

Washington v. Glucksburg, 521 U.S. 702 (1997).

Weaver v. Nebo School District, 29 F. Supp. 2d 1279 (1998).

Witt v. Department of Air Force, 527 F.3d 806 (9th Cir. 2008).

Wisconsin v. Mitchell, 508 U.S. 476 (1993).

Zablocki v. Redhail, 134 U.S. 374 (1978).

# INDEX

# ABOUT THE AUTHOR

WALTER FRANK, former chief of commercial litigation for the Port Authority of New York and New Jersey, is the author of *Making Sense of the Constitution* (2012), designated an outstanding university press book by the American Library Association. He has also written several law review articles dealing with constitutional aspects of the electoral process. Frank currently serves as co-chair of the Law and Literature Committee of the New York County Lawyers Association.